# Additional Praise for *The Future of the Word*

"This is an impressively conceived and well-rese       ...udy of the intricate ways in which texts participate in the ...uture of God's promise—or fail to participate. The Future of the Word draws deeply from theology, literary and cultural theory and criticism, and contemporary events and pop culture to show how our world is shot through with the hope, including the productions of so-called secular authors. Perhaps the most exciting element of this study is its convincing account of the way literary works, and our acts of reading and interpreting them, should be envisioned as a participation in the unfolding of God's hope and promise for the entire creation. As such, the 'future of words' becomes a profoundly sacred and mindful activity, one in which we are all called to contribute as worthy 'scribes' trained in God's eschatological purposes. The sheer scope of the research is impressive; but even more impressive is the user-friendly prose in which the author conveys difficult theoretical and theological concepts—it is challenging yet highly readable, and overall is a bracing, elevating, and edifying reading experience."

**Harold K. Bush**
**Saint Louis University**

"In a period where many question the value of reading, studying, and writing about literature, Tiffany Eberle Kriner has written a timely book on the continuing value of both literature and reading. The fundamental question that Kriner's book poses for readers is not an instrumental question regarding what literature can do for us, nor is it an ideological question regarding what literature has done to us. Rather, for Kriner, the fundamental question is what we as readers can do for texts, our reading itself being a part of the ongoing redemption, resurrection, and reconciliation of the word."

**Peter Kerry Powers**
**Messiah College**

# The Future of the Word

# The Future of the Word

## Word

### An Eschatology of Reading

Tiffany Eberle Kriner

Fortress Press
*Minneapolis*

THE FUTURE OF THE WORD
An Eschatology of Reading

Copyright © 2014 Fortress Press. All rights reserved. Except for brief quotations
in critical articles or reviews, no part of this book may be reproduced in any
manner without prior written permission from the publisher. Visit
http://www.augsburgfortress.org/copyrights/ or write to Permissions, Augsburg
Fortress, Box 1209, Minneapolis, MN 55440.

Cover image: Photodisc / Thinkstock
Cover design: Laurie Ingram

author photo: Michael Hudson Photography

Library of Congress Cataloging-in-Publication Data
Print ISBN: 978-1-4514-7032-1
eBook ISBN: 978-1-4514-8765-7

The paper used in this publication meets the minimum requirements of
American National Standard for Information Sciences — Permanence of Paper
for Printed Library Materials, ANSI Z329.48-1984.

Manufactured in the U.S.A.

This book was produced using PressBooks.com, and PDF rendering was done by
PrinceXML.

*To the Word and the love of the Trinity.*

*"Beyond the desert of criticism, we wish to be called again."*
*—Paul Ricoeur, The Symbolism of Evil*

# Contents

# Preface

On January 21, 2013, Barack Obama opened his second term as President of the United States with an oath sworn on a stack of Bibles—the travel Bible of Rev. Dr. Martin Luther King Jr. and the personal Bible of Abraham Lincoln. News outlets discussed the symbolic meaning of the use, how it seemed to fuse the work of two monumental leaders in the movement for freedom—and to place President Obama as the heir to their legacy. The King family was delighted at Obama's gesture; they asked that the President and Chief Justice sign the Bible to commemorate its inaugural use. But Cornel West, philosopher at Union Theological Seminary, spoke of being deeply "upset" at Obama's decision. In his view, it was unmeet that Obama should so lightly "use [King's] prophetic fire as just a moment in a presidential pageantry." Rather, we should understand King's significance as linked to the history of the people for whose sake he died, but even more to the future for which he fought—a future without Jim Crow, without war crimes, and without poverty. West connected Martin Luther King Jr.'s message to the ongoing quest to eradicate injustice, enjoining the country and the president to "allow his prophetic voice to be heard," and warning them, "don't tame his prophetic fire." Instead of *using* the tradition, West said, we should let "the subversive power . . . be heard" to bring about the future for which King suffered and died.[1]

The differing ways of reading President Obama's symbolic use of the pair of Bibles are, at bottom, arguments about which larger story ought to frame his action. Is Obama's inauguration part of the history—and ongoing future—of government-sanctioned, official, and approved pursuit of freedom in America? Or is it part of a prophetic resistance and refusal that goes against established powers in its pursuit of freedom? The Bible as object has a basic function in an inauguration—a guarantee of good faith in the act of taking the oath of office. But, of course, no person taking the presidential oath is required to use the Bible in order to increase the solemnity of the swearing in. And there is presumably nothing that would force a President to tell the truth because of a hand on the Bible. Yet oath-takers swearing on the Bible treat it almost as a magical object—as if God will smite them if they do not act in good faith, like Huckleberry Finn, who lies with ease only *after* he notices that the book on which he swears "warn't nothing but a dictionary."[2] Apparently, the force of the biblical statement against swearing in Matt. 5:37, which enjoins people to simple truth-telling, letting their yes be yes and no be no, is comparatively weak at this level of pomp. Even so, the main issue in the use of the King Bible for the Obama inauguration oath is not the power in the book, but the power of the narrative within which the use takes place. Cornel West seeks a larger story as context for the using the Bible: the past that produced King and the future of his prophetic message. Obama's use, to West, is just that, a "moment in political calculation."[3] Barack Obama may have seen the act as one of more political aspiration than West gives him credit for, given that the oath on the Bibles was *inaugural* and therefore rather forward-looking, but the conflict of interpretation remains. Both West and Obama understood that a larger story was being advanced—not just remembered—as they considered the use of King's Bible; they disagreed about which larger story.

While this example of interpreting symbolic action refers to a different sort of reading, perhaps, than the kind where the Bible is *open*, it suggests that the use of a text may play into how a larger story unfolds. In this book, I suggest that not just the symbolic act of swearing on but also the actual reading and interpretation of texts participates in the unfolding of a larger story—the story of the future of Christ, the word of God. Texts have an eschatology, a part in God's purpose for the cosmos set in motion at creation. They, with all creation, move toward participation in what Stanley Grenz has called the eschatological "community of the new creation," the Trinity's expanding, creative love.[4] This book tells the story of how readers participate in the future of the word, the eschatology of texts.

## Eschatology, the Theology of Hope . . . for Texts?

It is by no means automatically clear that eschatology, the larger story of God's plan for the cosmos, bears that much on texts or our understanding of them. Broadly speaking, eschatology is the theology of Christian hope, of last things.[5] It is, however, more beginning than ending, more foundation than culmination, as scholars recognized anew early in the twentieth century, when Albert Schweitzer and Johannes Weiss rediscovered a less-understood part of Christ's message, *thoroughgoing eschatology*.[6] As the eschatological framework of the New Testament was recovered, eschatology was newly understood to orient theology—and Christianity—as a whole. Karl Barth famously wrote in his *Epistle to the Romans*, "If Christianity be not altogether *thoroughgoing eschatology*, there remains in it no relationship whatever with Christ" (emphasis added).[7] Jürgen

Moltmann has declared that eschatology is "the medium of Christian faith as such"[8] and Paul O'Callaghan that eschatology is "the definitive vantage point from which to contemplate the entirety of Christian revelation."[9] While the term's etymology links eschatology with the study of "last things," Stanley Grenz, among others, has argued that the term should refer to ultimate things rather than final ones.[10] Indeed, given the fact that the Bible, Old and New Testaments, are shot through with promise, eschatology, the study of last things, is as much the study of first things, or as G. C. Berkouwer wrote, the study of the promise of the First and Last, Christ himself.[11] As Trevor Hart has put it, Christian theology is "irreducibly eschatological."[12]

But how is eschatological hope related to texts? First, eschatology has to do with the purpose for the cosmos. Texts are a part of the created order, and they are part of God's purpose for the creation.[13] While texts, even the inspired texts of the biblical canon, might be considered secondary creations—that is, they are made by human agents—they are yet of interest in an eschatological discussion. Texts are part of the created order, and thus God will judge them.[14] Even from the limited point of view of personal eschatology, texts as human works (even the most chance-inflected works cannot escape the influence of human agency) will be judged as their makers are judged. But eschatology is an exploration of the purpose for which everything was made, or, of the *meaning* of all creation's story. Texts, having very much to do with both meaning and story, merit a special place in the discussion of that purpose.

For one text, eschatological importance may be assumed. God's word, Isa. 40:8 reminds us, will stand forever. It thus has a special eschatology. But of course, the "word of God" in Isa. 40:8 refers as much to the promises of God as any textual instantiation of the word of God. And in that passage particularly, the promise of God is actually that God himself will fulfill his promise by *coming* as the God of promise, judgment, and charity:

> See, the Lord God comes with might,
> and his arm rules for him;
> his reward is with him,
> and his recompense before him.
> He will feed his flock like a shepherd;
> he will gather the lambs in his arms,
> and carry them in his bosom,
> and gently lead the mother sheep. (Isa. 40:10-11)

For Christians, the promises of the Old Testament are the promises of Christ, and their assurances are of Christ's triumph in and over history.[15] As Jürgen Moltmann puts it, "In the gospel the Old Testament history of promise finds more than a fulfillment which does away with it; it finds its future. 'All the promises of God in him are yea, and in him Amen' (II Cor. 1.20). They have become an eschatological certainty in Christ, by being liberated and validated, made unconditional and universal."[16] Because the God of the covenant promises is the God who raises Christ, the eschatology of the Bible is, after all, the future of Christ the divine word, who is subject, enactor, guarantor, and liberator of the divine promise. The future of the word is the future of the incarnate God.

The bodily form of the incarnate God may seem to downplay the textual future that this book asserts. However, this book argues that, rather than foreclosing it, the future of the incarnate Christ founds the future of texts. For the divine word, Christ, is creator and savior; his future of creation and salvation crafts future becoming into all creation. John 1 declares, "All things *came into being* through him, and without him not one thing *came into being*" (1:3). That is, Christ, the word become flesh, is the agent of creation, and his crafting, as the abundant repetition of coming and becoming in John 1 seems to indicate, has brought things into becoming—has made them to become. Revelation 21:5 pictures the "one who was seated on the throne," Christ, saying, "See, I am making all things new." In Christ all things continue to become. He is making all things new, even in the new Jerusalem, which joins and transforms the earthly Jerusalem.

And Christ will have had to make things new for them to enter his kingdom in the first place. Revelation declares that the "first things" of death, mourning, and crying will have passed away as the "first earth" passes away (Rev. 21:1, 4), but that nonetheless, things will survive and go into the new Jerusalem: "[T]he kings of the earth will bring their glory into [the new Jerusalem]" and "people will bring into it the glory and the honor of the nations" (Rev. 21:24, 26). Revelation asserts that "nothing unclean will enter [the new Jerusalem], nor anyone who practices abomination or falsehood, but only those who are written in the Lamb's book of life" (Rev. 21:27). Since all of the earth is tainted by sin and decay, nothing and no one may enter the Lamb's book of life or the New Jerusalem without the Lamb redeeming and transforming it. Thus Christ's "See, I am making all things new" draws our attention to how God prepares things for the new Jerusalem that comes down to join the earthly city. Because of him, all manner of glory and culture may enter it, as he makes them new—even the words that are to be brought in with the glory of the nations.[17]

The second reason that eschatology concerns texts is that, linked as it is to the meaning of all creation, eschatology always has to do with human orderings of time, that is, with history. The theology of hope makes history historic, as Moltmann has written, since "[t]he promises of God disclose the horizons of history" and "events . . . experienced within the horizon of remembered and expected promises . . . are experienced as truly 'historic' events."[18] History is made of interpretations of time; and since eschatology has to do with the interpretation of time, it also is a story of time's meanings. Textual formations of all kinds—in their relationship to syntax, grammar, and the sentence—interpret and organize time. Since text, from the moment of its composition, is under temporal pressure and entails an interpretation of time, it is related structurally to eschatology.

Not only do both texts and eschatology organize and interpret time, they also share a common temporal shape: the not yet. Eschatology acknowledges and texts enact a gap of meaning that in the articulation of the past creates desire for and orientation toward the future. This mood of future-from-the-past is not just the linearity or sequence of some stories as they work toward endings or closure. Literary expression has a special—textual—claim to not-yet-ness. Literary texts are not closed—their meanings are deferred, shifting, negotiable, even at their ends. Even while limited by established boundaries of the physical/digital text or the interpretive community, their meanings are renegotiable in new settings and times. Even if seemingly designed for closure, any interpretable word is open. The nature of text is not yet.

The third link between eschatology and texts is their communal nature. The divine goal for all creation is community, or communion—the communion of the Trinity extended to the creation.[19] Conceiving eschatology as the theology of *hope* in particular—personal hope, even—also emphasizes its relational nature.[20] Gabriel Marcel asserts that the one who hopes is one who receives a gift: "[T]here can be no hope which does not constitute itself through a *we* and for a *we*. I would be very tempted to say that all hope is at bottom choral."[21] The communal dimension of eschatology parallels textual communality, for meaning is made communally in text. Private interpretations, in the strictest sense, do not exist: the text is not a text at all without, at least, an implied reader. The text may be the receipt of a gift from an author, a conversation of sorts between author and reader, a set of relations between implied authors and implied readers, but for there to be text, there must be encounter.[22] And beyond even the complex set of relations for one person and text (with all their attendant implied and imaginary roles), the larger reading community holds and reshapes a text's shifting meaning between them. Literature is poorly read without a community; we see our private poverty most clearly by contrast when we experience the vast riches of engaging with others in our reading.

## Wait, What Do We Mean by "Texts"?

Already in this book, the question should be raised of what is meant by the words "literature" and "texts," two terms that have been thrown around with what might seem an astonishing liberality. This is no accident. The definitions and delineations of these particular ideas, which we might expect at this point in an academic argument, are self-defeating in this particular case. For the definition of at least the term "literature," and most likely the term "text" as well, or even "writing" or "books," historically presupposes either a form or a function, both of which point to precisely that which I am trying to call into question. This book seeks to draw what has been referred to within the larger story—and to understand it within the temporal becoming that Christ gives all things. Thus the terms of the discussion will, at times, feel hazy. It would be fair to ask, as a colleague of mine did, whether the ideas in this book apply to all texts, used grocery lists and old car manuals as well as *The Iliad*. And it would be fair to wonder whether only written materials—or if also orature—have a place here. The argument here is intentionally inclusive, insofar as the inquiry aims at the future of the creation in the kingdom of God and seeks also a generative function in theology and literary studies.

## On the Structure of This Book

The argument of this book proceeds as follows. The introduction asks, "Why might an eschatology of text matter?" It looks into contemporary ideas about reading practices both popular and scholarly and finds within them an aspiring quality—an openness to plentitude or mystery that is profoundly—though limitedly—eschatological in shape. Using the work of Jacques Ellul on means and ends, and of Augustine on use and enjoyment, I suggest the resources of Christian eschatology—that is, the future of the word of God in the resurrected Christ—are an enrichment and clarification of these widespread aspirations. In the first chapter, "The Future of the Word," I argue that the future of Jesus Christ, the word of God, grants not only the creation at large, but also texts in particular, a purpose in God's eschatological kingdom as well as signifying-power toward that kingdom's ends.

The second chapter, "Reading for the Future of the Word," shows how an anthropology of creation and an anthropology of the new creation may ground the idea of reading for the future of the word as participation in the kingdom of God. In the chapter, I use the "scribe trained for the kingdom" in Jesus' parable as a scriptural base from which to explore a few of the many possibilities for reading for the future of the word, including preservation, utterance, translation, criticism, and call and response. This theological exploration funds a sense of possibility or hope for reading that leads into the first of several engagements with literary works, *scrivenings*, that intersperse the chapters. The first of these scrivenings is tentative, foregrounding not my own readings, per se, but literary works' readings of other literary works. I show how select literary texts—from light concept pieces such as *Pride and Prejudice and Zombies'* reading of *Pride and Prejudice* to bestsellers such as Haruki Murakami's *1Q84*, which rereads George Orwell's *1984*, to even 19th-century African American poet Frances Ellen Watkins Harper's interpretation of Charles Dickens's *Oliver Twist* in verse—offer ways of thinking through how texts might be futured-forth both in concert with and dissonant from standard or popularly predominant interpretations.

From here, the argument must hesitate to consider a potential challenge to readers' participation in the future of the word—ways that reading can not only till and keep the future of the text as Adam and Eve the garden of Eden, but could seek to inhibit the future of the text. Chapter 3 considers evil reading, a privative embrace of nothingness rather than eschatological becoming. In the chapter, I describe two possible threats to our participation in the future of the word: reading that seeks to freeze a text in interpretive certainty and reading that seeks to freeze a text in interpretive uncertainty. The first amounts to the insistence on a static, univocal meaning. The second amounts to a refusal to read, in which the multiplicity of meaning so overwhelms a reader that engagement with the text becomes impossible. Following this chapter, in a second attempt at scrivenings, I explore how two works of American literature, Henry James's *Daisy Miller: A Study* and Tony Kushner's *Angels in America*, pose similar questions and offer their own provisional and troubled anatomies and prognoses of evil reading.

The final theological chapter in the book considers how best, in reading for the future of the word, we might encounter the faults and fallenness of texts. Knowing that offenses must come, that readers cannot, even in an era of prejudgment, avoid them, this chapter offers a theology of reading what variously offends us as readers—that is, texts we consider obscene, or false, or ugly, or worthless. In chapter 4, I look to John the Baptist as a model of the dual requirement of prophetic judgment and prophetic forgiveness within the community of engagement with the word; I describe and argue for reconciliation with the text. In the scrivenings that follow this claim, I seek to reconcile with Francine Rivers's *Redeeming Love*, an inspirational evangelical romance novel that retells a version of the story of Hosea set in Gold Rush California.

The book ends not with the Four Horsemen of the eschatological apocalypse, but, as we are, still in the not yet. The conclusion closes out the argument in scrivenings that seek the creative plentitude of the Trinity's love even from within a text that seems to repudiate it: Vladimir Nabokov's infamous *Lolita*, the lyrical, enchanting apologia of a pedophile, a work that was tried for obscenity in 1955 and remains significantly troubling after more than fifty years in print. From the perspective of the Come-Lord-Jesus, *Maranatha* end of the Bible, the close of any book is always an openness, a futuring forth and a becoming of the word through the fellowship of the love of the Trinity. By ending in readings, I end in hope, in an open book and the future of the word.

### On Literature and Theology, On the Choice of Texts

The seeming-despair that has attended my own reading practice and that of a wider body of readers, both academic and popular, over the last several years, drove me to dig in this book at the theological warrant for reading. Alan Jacobs's book *A Theology of Reading: The Hermeneutics of Love* sketches out the lineaments of a charitable engagement with literary texts; his chapter, "Love and the Suspicious Spirit," rightly diagnoses the problem with a field tied so strongly to a hermeneutics of suspicion: "[T]he hopeless interpreter, in the lassitude of despair, can neither receive nor offer gifts: Having petrified the *personae* of human discourse and thereby transformed them into the *res* of commodified 'texts,' he or she has nothing left to love, and in the end lacks even the consolations of interpretation itself."[23] Thus for me, this book: eschatology, the theology of hope, became the way to investigate the assumptions and warrants on which a practice or life of reading charitably may proceed. Perhaps, then, this book is a prelude to the love Jacobs sets forth, though of course the confluence of the supernatural virtues of faith, hope, and love make it also something of a harmonic to his work.

When I reenter the library, however, buttressed by the eschatological assertion that readers, too, may be scribes trained for the kingdom, I find that literary texts do not line up behind theological affirmations as neatly as shelved codices behind the bookend. In fact, the reading of texts demonstrates that the tracing out of the future of a text is far messier—distinctly imperfect, nonlinear, and nonteleological—than the arguments I have forwarded might suggest. Thus the relationship of literary text to theological claim in this book is not precisely practice to theory, nor is it precisely illustration or application to claim. Readings seem to dance between the already and the not yet—not only from within the fraught process of meaning-making at the level of linguistic DNA, but also in the larger interactions between texts and contexts over time. We participate in the glorious future of the word under conditions vulnerable to sin and error, which lead to interpretive difficulties of many kinds.

Because my home, training, and inclination are not primarily in theology but in literature, the complicated interrelationship of any given text's past, present, and future remains *the* vital place, for me, out of which questions may proceed and in which moments of topmost glory reside. It did, however, seem necessary to make the theological claim to reach across disciplinary subdivisions. Instead of relying on examples from literary texts to illustrate the claim for an audience mired in the ins and outs of a complex argument, this work relies on theological assertions to offer shared vocabulary and starting points that expand in the ins and outs of the literary texts.

The literary works under discussion have been selected for their challenge and possibility in relation to the claim, rather than for their representativeness or canonical greatness. Because I am making an unapologetically enormous claim about meaning's repletion in Christ, it makes sense to choose works that operate outside out of a Christian framework; they will most readily illustrate the difficulties. None of the works under consideration here are explicitly apocalyptic or self-consciously eschatological under commonly held understandings of those terms. Aside from the biblical text, the only works mentioned here written from an expressly Christian perspective have been chosen for the ways their popular, accessible styles and generic commitments *risk* their literary futures rather than for their enduring greatness. It seemed necessary not simply to consider the future of the obviously long-lived texts from available traditions, but nineteenth-century popular verse or a pulpy Christian romance novel that one may or may not wish to be caught dead reading. In addition, I am intentionally dealing with works outside a great books tradition—recent works even, which may or may not stand long in the light of popular or scholarly approval. These raise for me the most pressing questions about the future of the word. One might not be surprised, perhaps, to think about *Paradise Lost* having some sort of place in the kingdom of God—perhaps as cultivating the future of the biblical text in some way. *Pride and Prejudice and Zombies* seems a bit more of a stretch; but, it is therefore more worth investigating for the possibilities, problem areas, and nuances involved in the cultivation of the future of the word in the kingdom of God.

Thus in the scrivenings sections of the book, I look into this ragtag assortment—first tentatively reading a few texts' readings of *other* texts, then reading texts *about* reading, and finally, trying to reconcile with a few literary texts of the past and present. The book makes its way from a beginning thick with theology to an ending thick with literature—reading in hope for the future of the word.

## Notes

1. Cornel West, "Cornel West Explains Why It Bothers Him That Obama Will Be Taking the Oath with MLK's Bible," n.p. YouTube, http://youtu.be/96d_CzrfxsM, accessed January 21, 2013.

2. Mark Twain, *Adventures of Huckleberry Finn*, ed. Thomas Cooley (New York: Norton, 1999), 187.

3. West, "Cornel West Explains Why It Bothers Him."

4. Stanley J. Grenz, *Theology for the Community of God* (Nashville: Broadman & Holman, 1994), 623.

5. The seventeenth-century term has become a container for any number of theological topics. Stanley Grenz has divided these into three subcategories: personal eschatology (having to do with issues surrounding death, resurrection, and the afterlife), corporate eschatology (having to do with time, history, and apocalypse), and cosmic eschatology (having to do with judgment, heaven, hell, and new creation). Eschatological debates have traversed these topics across the centuries, with particular vicissitudes of emphasis (e.g., the question concerning the rapture and those "left behind," say, or the timing of the second coming of Christ—millennial, post-millennial, amillennial, pretribulation, posttribulation—the form of the resurrected body, or the question of universal salvation). Ibid., 571–72.

6. Albert Schweitzer, *The Quest of the Historical Jesus: A Critical Study of Its Progress from Reimarus to Wrede* (New York: Macmillan, 1968), 328.

7. Karl Barth, *The Epistle to the Romans*, trans. Edwyn C. Hoskyns (Oxford: Oxford University Press, 1933), 314. It seems here that Barth is talking about the hope that saves us, the hope that sets everything toward the future.

8. Jürgen Moltmann, *The Theology of Hope: On the Ground and the Implications of a Christian Eschatology* (Minneapolis, Fortress Press, 1993), 16.

9. Paul O'Callaghan, *Christ Our Hope: An Introduction to Eschatology* (Washington, D. C.: Catholic University of America Press, 2011), 329.

10. Grenz, *Theology for the Community of God*, 571.

11. G. C. Berkouwer, *The Return of Christ*, ed. Marlin J. Van Elderen, trans. James Van Oosterom (Grand Rapids: Eerdmans, 1972), 9.

12. Trevor Hart, "Unexpected Endings: Eucatastrophic Consolations in Literature and Theology," in *Art, Imagination, and Christian Hope*, ed. Trevor Hart, Gavin Hopps, and Jeremy Begbie (Burlington, VT: Ashgate, 2012), 171.

13. As Stanley Grenz writes, "Eschatology is the exposition of the goal toward which the triune God is bringing his creation," in Grenz, *Theology for the Community of God*, 573. It is, to Grenz, "a goal which is ultimately cosmic in scope, one which envelops all creation." Ibid., 623.

14. As Paul O'Callaghan writes, "No created thing, no aspect of human life, 'is excluded from or eliminated in God's judgment.'" O'Callaghan, *Christ Our Hope*, 139–40.

15. Paul Ricoeur's *The Symbolism of Evil*, trans. Emerson Buchanan (Boston: Beacon, 1969), has elaborated the eschatological cast of even the foundational myths of the biblical text—the first chapters of the book of Genesis. Ricoeur notes how Abraham, before a second Adam in Christ has been conceived of, is already a response of hope and promise to the fall. He further explores how the meaning of the Abrahamic promise flowers into meaning that "had not been exhausted" in Joshua's Canaan, in Israelite history, etc., eventually tracing Christ's role as judge and coming king as further futures set in motion by the promise of the early myth (260–78). While Ricoeur does not particularly focus on the *textual*, he acknowledges the movement from oral to text in his reference to editorial additions and changes in a piecemeal biblical text, in which intertextuality and midrash are key ways the promise sets in motion the furtherance of meaning. Ricoeur's work setting forth a sort of biblical eschatology is by no means unique—it follows some of the dominant thinking in eschatology of the middle and late twentieth century. Ricoeur's

work is unique in its helpful contribution to how the symbols of the myth themselves give rise and place to the thinking about resistance, pardon, and redemption of evil.

16. Moltmann, *Theology of Hope*, 147.

17. See Richard Mouw, *When the Kings Come Marching In: Isaiah and the New Jerusalem*, rev. ed. (Grand Rapids: Eerdmans, 2002), for a discussion of how Isaiah's picturing of the repurposing of the ships of Tarshish in Isa. 60 figures into the theology of the eschaton, particularly how God purifies and transforms elements of culture for their purpose in the New Jerusalem.

18. Moltmann, *Theology of Hope*, 106, 107.

19. See Grenz, *Theology for the Community of God*, 624. Also, Han Urs von Balthasar's insistence in *Theo-Drama: The Last Act* (San Francisco: Ignatius, 1988) on a Trinitarian eschatology emphasizes the relationality of present and future being in Christ (57). For von Balthasar, this revelation is "being itself," "present . . . in every 'now'" (57). For Paul Fiddes, too, in *The Promised End: Eschatology in Theology and Literature* (Malden, MA: Blackwell, 2000), God's purpose for creation is communal, active, and open. God's plan is "to be satisfied by fellowship with personal beings who can, in love, make their own contribution to the relationship," or "the making of personalities in relationship with others and with God's own self," a creation "certain in fact and open in content" (174, 178).

20. Aquinas's writings on the supernatural virtue of hope also point out the extent to which others are involved in the becoming and courage-development of the individual.

21. Gabriel Marcel, "The Encounter with Evil," in *Tragic Wisdom and Beyond: Including Conversations Between Paul Ricoeur and Gabriel Marcel*, ed. John Wild, trans. Stephen Jolin and Peter McCormick (Evanston, IL: Northwestern University Press, 1973), 143.

22. Wayne Booth's *The Company We Keep: An Ethics of Fiction* (Berkeley: University of California Press, 1988) offers one vision of how this works: his argument centers around the relationships that we choose to have with texts—and their beneficial effects—and the evaluative process, coduction, by which we make those relational choices.

23. Alan Jacobs, *A Theology of Reading: The Hermeneutics of Love* (Boulder, CO: Westview, 2001), 90.

# Introduction: The End of Reading

"Do not interpretations belong to God?"
–Gen. 40:8

The Joseph of the book of Genesis is both a dreamer and dream-reader, and even the briefest page-through of his tale suggests that the latter is more useful—certainly more lucrative—than the former. In his early life, Joseph dreams two big dreams, the grasping subconscious desire of which is obvious—and offensive—to all those around him: one night, he dreams that his brothers' sheaves of wheat bow down to his sheaf, and another night, he dreams that the sun, moon, and eleven stars bow down to him. After the technicolor dreamcoat and its negative aftermath, however, Joseph stops dreaming and starts reading, and his dream reading—dream criticism, if you will—has much higher stakes and a much higher payout than his creative dreaming. It is dream *reading* that paves the way for his release from prison, grants him employment in government, and secures his posterity.[1] Indeed, if any biblical figure opens himself to the charge that his readings might be socially or economically instrumental, it is Joseph.

Joseph parallels the contemporary critic or literary theorist in the sense that he stands to gain a fair amount—in terms of

1

livelihood—from his reading work, though today's critics (particularly those at adjunct pay) may feel somewhat less well, or less dramatically, remunerated for their work. Falsely accused, Joseph is in jail when the royal cupbearer and baker dream their dreams. And when he gives the interpretation of impending release to the cupbearer, Joseph is sure to mention the use he hopes to make of his work: "But remember me when it is well with you; please do me the kindness to make mention of me to Pharaoh, and so get me out of this place. For in fact I was stolen out of the land of the Hebrews; and here also I have done nothing that they should have put me into the dungeon" (Gen. 40:14-15). He makes no such request of the baker, whose dream portends a fast-approaching date with a hangman—no use currying favor there—though that interpretation bears on Joseph's eventual release as well, since the cupbearer overhears it and mentions it to Pharaoh.

At the outset of what is undeniably instrumental reading, however, Joseph asserts another source, means, and end for his readings than the ones that seem most materially at work: God. He convinces the two men to share their dreams by appealing to a divine foundation for reading: "Do not interpretations belong to God? Please tell [your dreams] to me" (Gen. 40:8). And later, when Joseph's eerily accurate dream-reading skills have landed him an audience with the king, even though Pharaoh is ready to give Joseph the interpretive credit, Joseph asserts, "It is not I; God will give Pharaoh a favorable answer" and "God has revealed to Pharaoh what he is about to do" (Gen. 41:16, 25). This is not, of course, to say that Joseph doesn't make the most of the opportunity, laying out a response plan and suggesting a job description for himself, because he does and then some: "Now therefore let Pharaoh select a man who is discerning and wise, and set him over the land of Egypt. Let Pharaoh proceed to appoint overseers over the land, and take one-fifth of the produce of the land of Egypt during the seven plenteous years" (Gen. 41:33-34). Yet by this time, the conversation has fundamentally changed. When Pharaoh gives reasons for Joseph's appointment to the top post, he cites not Joseph's own gifts, as he had when he first consulted Joseph about the dreams, but God's presence in Joseph as the determining factor: "Since God has shown you all this, there is no one so discerning and wise as you" (Gen. 41:39).

In this story, readers see that God's purpose for the cosmos is the context in which human interpretations, naturally instrumental, occur. The precocious dreamer's disturbingly accurate interpretations become the means by which God preserves and protects his chosen people Israel from devastating famine. God's purposes and promises are preeminent; human readings and their uses are clearly subsidiary and, at times, beside the point (sometimes even downright dangerous or evil).

Present-day readers of Joseph's story, often enmeshed in our own reading patterns, may miss the larger context of the whole of Genesis, the Old Testament, or the Bible. We can tend to miss the forest of God's covenant promises of land and descendants for the trees of potentially useful ethical takeaways in Joseph's narrative: courage no matter what, persistence in integrity, perseverance in suffering, forgiveness of those who wrong you, and so on. Any church worker in children's ministry will have experienced innumerable instances of text as tool for virtue-ethics indoctrination.[2] Readings of individual Bible stories can be useful and may have some sort of moral value for children, though as a seasoned Sunday school worker, I sometimes doubt it. Such readings may also be incorrect and harmful (as is the reading of Joseph's dreams by his family). But when interpretation belongs to God and the fact of the larger story is taken seriously, even small acts of reading such as the interpretation of a dream in a prison cell may be part of the transformation of one family's drama into a story of God's saving of the cosmos, of his bringing the human family—so broken by the fall—into renewed fellowship with God.

This book is about putting reading—the human activity of textual interpretation—into the larger story of the cosmos, that is, into an eschatological, kingdom-of-God context. In Joseph's story, God's intentions redeem and reshape even the foulest of human behaviors: even the selling of a brother into slavery is transformed by the fact that God meant it for good. The larger context of eschatology likewise transforms our understanding of the practice of reading—our understandings of why we read, of how texts achieve meaningfulness, of how we interpret, and of how we may judge the value, merit, or morality of works.

Ultimately, this book investigates, from a theological perspective, why we read. For those privileged enough to have time, literacy, and access, reading may represent a great investment in an alarmingly finite life. Readers could be doing anything else: ladling sustenance at a soup kitchen, performing life-saving appendectomies, getting enough sleep for once, even praying. Why read?

### Reading as Means or End?

When people have thought about what we do as we read or why we do it, their ideas have tended to fit into one of two categories, which, as we will see, collapse into each other almost before we can make the distinction between them. Either we read with some purpose, in which literature is a means (to knowledge, escape, a particular sensation, entertainment, or even attainment of a kind of cultural authority), or we read for reading's sake, in which literature is an end unto itself. The history of literary study and, to a certain extent, that of broader popular reading of texts, reflects considerable confusion about reading as means or end, especially as readers make value judgments linked to each.

An instrumental use or purpose for reading might be, for instance, my reading of the entire Harry Potter series in the summer of 2007. It is difficult to admit this when Harold Bloom calls people who "devour J. K. Rowling" lemmings who "race down the cliffs to intellectual suicide in the gray ocean of the Internet."[3] But I couldn't help it—stress and anxiety left me in major need of an escape: I was working the tenure track, buying our first house, moving, helping my husband put in an entire house worth of floors within a month of purchase so that the bank would give us a mortgage, and chasing an eighteen-month-old around the construction zone. Noting that the seventh Harry Potter book was scheduled to come out on my thirtieth birthday, I consumed—yes, Harold—the entire series during the nights over just a few weeks so that I would be ready to stand in line at midnight on July 21, when the final book was released. Unlike those youths who had grown up with Harry Potter and savored each book, my reading at that time was voracious and unabashedly escapist. I was using the Harry Potter series of books to get a mental break from grown-up work and stress.

Reading for its own sake might involve activities associated with the aesthetic contemplation of the work itself. Rather than finding the work's meanings in its particular uses, whether escape, emotional healing, or forwarding of politics, reading noninstrumentally seeks the meaning of the text or narrative in the tracery of its own making and structure. A noninstrumental reading resists assigning value to a text based on its plain content, rhetorical power, or sociopolitical effects alone. Instead, it pursues an often slower and savored interaction with the text's form and meanings. Nowadays, noninstrumental interaction with texts is often thought to be associated with academic or high literary culture, though Andrew

Delbanco, in *Required Reading*, has termed the interaction with form and meaning a "fundamental *literary* pleasure from which almost all varieties of criticism have become estranged."[4]

Pleasure, of course, has been attributed to both instrumental and noninstrumental reading—though presumably the pleasures have been diversely valued and saddled with various moral or intellectual judgments. One may read *merely* for pleasure, the book scooted under the bed or slipped into a drawer; or, one may tout the pleasure as reaching the coffee-table heights of humanness, which will, in giving us what Harold Bloom calls "difficult pleasure," provide us with "the only secular transcendence we can ever attain."[5]

These two understandings of reading, as means and as end, tend to be tied to definitions of what literature in fact *is*, structure and function. Structural definitions tied to reading reach back to antiquity and persist in various lineages and permutations through the nineteenth century, the main currents being literature as *fictional* language (imitations neither true nor false) and literature as an *autotelic, stylized system* of language that is inwardly focused, intransitive, and nonfunctional, often aimed at beauty.[6] Under these definitions, literature is the thing that can be read through self-referential, systematic, and connotative analysis in a nonfunctional, perhaps academic environment. The only purpose of literature under a noninstrumental understanding would be that of aesthetic pleasure in the rich trove of deep meanings made discernible through careful attention to the text. Instrumental reading relies on a functional understanding of literature as types of discourse with discernible effects. As Tzvetan Todorov points out in "The Notion of Literature," though, one benefit of considering literature according to the functional definition "types of discourse" is that such types can be linked to discernible—and perhaps far more regular—structural patterns than an amorphous entity such as "literature."[7]

It is, of course, impossible to deny—and we see it already in Todorov's 1973 essay "The Notion of Literature"—that these notions of reading and their attendant definitions collapse into each other. What, after all, could be more instrumental than the passionate, carefully analytic reading that a graduate student does for her Ph.D. prelims? My grueling summer of twelve-hour-or-longer days of reading—despite inalienable, irrevocable delight studying Wallace Stevens's "Sunday Morning," as I paced around the neighborhood quoting aloud—was pretty much entirely in service of securing the foundational knowledge in my field that would yield me entrance into the dissertation stage of my doctoral work. Rita Felski, in *Uses of Literature*, has called out academics on just this score, writing, "I am always bemused . . . to hear critics assert that literary works serve no evident purpose, even as their engagement with such works patently showcases their critical talents, gratifies their intellectual and aesthetic interests, and, in the crassest sense, furthers their careers."[8] The sense of credentialization and increased confidence that I experienced through reading for prelims and in their lovely professional payout will attest to the furthering of my own career, anyway.

Perhaps we are in the last stages of the time when literary critics can ground their readings on an unmasking of the ideological underpinnings of reading for its own sake. We have harbored doubts with those suspicious about the hermeneutic of suspicion, and we have seen—and tutted—the myopia of close-reading. The means-oriented use of texts by lay readers has been noted and even championed through a scholarly focus on the cultural and historical activity of reading, fueled by unparalleled digital access to popular literacy materials and periodicals.[9] A heft of theoretical and cultural studies work has offered the discipline an opportunity to acknowledge uses that have been present through even the most high-falutin' moments that centralized reading for its own sake.

Perhaps as a result of these studies, but more likely for a broader range of reasons, it seems less possible than ever to define literature as a "noninstrumental language whose value resides in itself alone," except in some rarified subgroups.[10] This seems especially the case when our time's enabling structure for noninstrumental reading, the liberal arts institution, is fast achieving a snooty rarity sometimes explicitly related to its noninstrumental (that is, nonvocational) status.

I suspect, however, that the pendulum will swing back—or perhaps we will simply acknowledge the agonism that characterizes the division between reading for use and reading for its own sake as a sort of shadow boxing. Into the idea of reading for its own sake always worms the notion that reading accomplishes something—just something that seems larger or more fundamental than whatever use is deemed provisional (the acing of a test, say, or the procuring of a particular sensation or employment). We have innumerable examples of the unreserved soaring into rhetorical flight at the noble, but still undeniably use-oriented, value of reading and literature, some emerging from scholars seeking to resist the consumer-driven, pragmatic, or means-oriented university in which they have found their life's work and living. In the last decade or more, there has arisen what amounts to a textual industry of defense, where we find innumerable diagnoses of the book under threat or the humanities under threat or the reading mind under threat—or even the life of the (humanities-reading) mind under threat.[11] Seemingly far from crassly material uses, these suggest that reading can do everything from giving us friends to saving our souls.[12] Mark Edmundson has referred repeatedly to literature as our secular Bible. Even Harold Bloom, who claims blatantly, against all ideology, that literature will neither "save any individual" nor "improve any society," hopes that canonical literature, represented most centrally by Shakespeare, will form the self from a place of loneliness and "teach us how to accept change, in ourselves as in others, and perhaps even the final form of change."[13]

Not only do nonutilitarian, aesthetic, and academic readings collapse into instrumental uses, but instrumental use soars into grandiose flights of idealism that mirror the reach of the noninstrumental. For those that passionately defend use can remain remarkably amorphous about what exactly those uses actually accomplish. Todorov, for instance, traced the development of literature as a concept in "The Notion of Literature," primarily to disabuse the field of the concept of literature, which had been developed so recently and persisted so contradictorily that it seemed at least unhelpful, if not downright deceptive.[14] Todorov suggested that taxonomic value was rather to be had in "types of discourse" than "literature," since the former have discernibly shared and usefully denoted characteristics, whereas the latter is hopelessly diffuse. This, for Todorov, was undeniably a step toward the use-oriented and perhaps, too, a jointure with a primarily rhetorical understanding of language—at least as employed in literary study. Yet, in 2007, when *New Literary History* reprinted his original "Notion of Literature" with the new essay, "What Is Literature For?," he seems to put a point on the difficulty of the ends of his original recategorization of literature into "types of discourse."[15] Contemporary literary education, as he has observed it in French schools, suffers from an overemphasis on the technical skills and tools for reading, rather than on the works and their meanings, which for him, he says, were always paramount: "[N]ever should the study of these *means* for entering the literary work be substituted for the study of meaning, which is the goal."[16] Yet, of course, this trips back into the difficulty he pointed out and critiqued in the earlier essay—that the definitions we have for literature and the ends to which literature aspires don't actually help us that much in reading them. Meaning, which is the goal for Todorov, is a large, swooping, lovely thing but hard to delineate. He writes movingly but abstractly in favor of what literature can do:

> [L]iterature helps me live . . . literature does not replace lived experiences but forms a continuum with them and helps me understand them. Denser than daily life but not radically different from it, literature expands our universe, prompts us to see other ways to conceive and organize it. We are all formed from what other people give us: first our parents and then the other people near us. Literature opens to the infinite this possibility of interaction and thus enriches us infinitely. It brings us irreplaceable sensations through which the real world becomes more furnished with meaning and more beautiful. Far from being a simple distraction, an entertainment reserved for educated people, literature lets each one of us fulfill our human potential.[17]

The difference pointed out here—between distraction/entertainment for an educated elite and the fulfillment of human potential more broadly—appears in terms of class and scope. While Todorov's ends of literature are spirited, they deal in abstraction. Literature's ends, to Todorov, are human self-understanding, self-fulfillment, self-enrichment, and sensation: not so clear. And what's all this self-understanding, self-fulfillment, self-enrichment, and sensation for? The means-oriented approaches that Todorov sees in schools, which, I would argue, had been, by implication, supported when he sought a more useful delineation of text or language through "types of discourse," seem to be insufficiently meaningful—insufficiently specific, perhaps, for addressing the ultimate purpose of a life or self, for addressing "human potential."

The pervasion of the means in reading—whether in Todorov's astute observations of French schools (which will as easily apply to the Common Core in U.S. education), everyday reading, or professional literary study, even of a Bloomian variety in which use is expressly anti-ideological and unapologetically individual ("to strengthen the self, and to learn its authentic interests"[18])—has led to a more widespread, if sometimes unacknowledged, abstractness in the ends to which it points. Rita Felski's *Uses of Literature* describes four modes of textual engagement—recognition, knowledge, enchantment, and shock—where each contains "multi-leveled interactions between texts and readers that are irreducible to their separate parts" and that "are woven into modern histories of self-formation and transformation, even as the very variability of their uses militates against a calculus that would pare them down to a single political purpose."[19] This rightfully complicates what might be oversimplified or even denigrated use. Yet she, too, turns the end of such uses into something insubstantial: "While ordinary intuitions are a valuable starting point for reflecting on why literature matters, it is far from self-evident what such intuitions signify. The mundane, on closer inspection, often turns out to be exceptionally mysterious."[20] Even when the best literary critics highlight the issues surrounding the means and uses of literature, they seem to reach toward the higher mysteries. There seems to be no end to making books, and much study of them brings weariness to the flesh rather than bringing the hope for which the discipline seems to be looking.[21]

## Help from Ellul; Help from Augustine

Jacques Ellul's diagnosis of contemporary society (or what passed for contemporary society in 1969 and 1987, anyhow) in *The Presence of the Kingdom* shares the vocabulary of means and ends; it offers a bracing exhortation to the kingdom citizen, whether reader or no. He writes that we have so altered the arrangement of means and ends in our world that bearing witness to the presence and future of the kingdom of God—glorifying and enjoying him forever, as the Westminster Catechism puts it—is impossible.[22] Ends are completely abstract and thus absent, he argues, and "the world is wholly given up to means."[23] Everything is required to be useful to the community and is slotted for production, technology, efficiency, and success. The means of this world, Ellul argues, have become its meaning, and they justify themselves. For Ellul, the triumph of means and the obscuring of ends constitute a totalitarian control over the individual, under which conditions, "it is impossible to live one's faith."[24] But Ellul does offer comfort. While "the end, as well as the means, has been taken away from us, and we hesitate as we look at this way which lies open before us, whose end we cannot see; we have only one certainty, and that is the promise which has been made to us of a certain order, which God guarantees: 'Seek ye first His Kingdom and His righteousness, and all things shall be added unto you' (Matt. 6:33)."[25] Ellul reminds us that "the central point which we can already know, and which is already real, is the lordship of Jesus Christ,"[26] and "in the powerful presence of the Holy Spirit we receive the answer to this work of God, and we are bewildered because we are no longer very sure about the way forward, which no longer depends upon us."[27] The promise of the kingdom of God, eschatology, is both the end and the means to the end.

I propose that texts are not exempt from this, that the promise, and its presence in the world, is that God works his will in texts and in their reading. But how may our reading—its confused rendering of means and ends—bear witness to the promise and presence?

Augustine's distinction between use and enjoyment in *On Christian Teaching*, commonly referred to as the *uti/frui* distinction, seems to offer further insight into how we might unpack the swirl of intertwining means and ends—in texts and more. Augustine suggests that all *things* in this world—and texts (or signs or words) to him are things with meaning attached to them—may be either used (*uti*) or enjoyed (*frui*).[28] If we enjoy (*frui*) a thing, Augustine says, we "hold fast to it in love for its own sake," without any other purpose.[29] When we enjoy (*frui*) things, we place our hopes in them.[30] If we use (*uti*) a thing, on the other hand, we apply our love for it toward—or refer our love for it to—the one thing we really enjoy. That is, we position what we *uti* in relation to what we *frui*.

According to Augustine, we should enjoy for its own sake (*frui*) only what is eternal, namely God, the Trinity in relationship, Father, Son, and Holy Spirit, "which is a kind of single, supreme thing, shared by all who enjoy it."[31] This world and the things of it, says Augustine, should be *loved* but must not be enjoyed—at least not enjoyed as he describes enjoyment (*frui*). The things of this world (including ourselves and others we love) should be positioned in relation to God: "So if you ought to love yourself not on your own account but on account of the one who is the most proper object of your love, another person should not be angry if you love him too on account of God."[32] Things in the world must always be related to the eternal things so that people may love them (*uti*) in God. If we enjoy and love God for his own sake, all other things can be related to God without the love decreasing at all: "So a person who loves his neighbour properly should, in concert with him, aim to love God with all his heart, all his soul, and all his mind. In this way, loving him as he would himself, he relates his love of himself and his neighbour entirely to the love of God, which allows not the slightest trickle to flow away from it and thereby diminish it."[33] People enjoy God together, and love each other in relation to God.

The key here is relatedness. To Augustine, *uti*, proper use, relates things to God. That is, to the love by which we ought to be loved by others, the love that puts all our loves in their place. Even God loves us with *uti*, insofar as he puts his love for us in relation always to his own goodness.[34] God relates us to his own goodness; that is the measure of his *uti*. His *uti* clarifies what use ought to be for us, emphasizing that proper *uti* is Trinitarian relation-making, a putting of things in relation to the Trinity. All things, whether loved or not, ought to be placed in relation to the supremacy of the eternal Trinity. This is an ordering by which God is preeminent.

If a text is a thing, and we love it for its own sake alone—as an end in itself—doing so would be a misapplication of Augustine's *frui*, a failure to relate our love to that of the Trinity. For Augustine, if we *frui* things that ought to be *uti*, we are constrained in our ability to love and enjoy the things we ought to, the Trinity, say. But it seems likely that, in the present context (discussed above) of confused means and ends, pure *frui* of literature isn't reached—it's more of a vague ideal. In the case of *Why Literature Matters in the 21st Century* by Mark Roche, the *ultimate* ideal that literature offers could only reach as high as a timeless morality that, though placed in a realm of the absolute, is yet not precisely the interrelation of God. And as Ellul points out, ideal and timeless morality—along with its systemization on earth—is precisely the wrong orientation for all of life: "It is in the light of this Kingdom that the Christian is called to judge present circumstances, and these circumstances cannot be judged according to their moral content or their individual political outlook . . . but simply according to their relation, which always exists, to the *Parousia*," that is, to the coming of God.[35]

Most often, literature is used, as is perfectly natural. For Augustine, use is fine, so long as the use of it would be *uti*, as he puts it, to love "the thing which must be enjoyed [God] and the thing which together with us can enjoy that thing."[36] It would be a problem, in fact, an abuse, in Augustine's—and Ellul's—view, to use literature to do other than manifest the presence and future of the kingdom in some way.

This sentiment seems, at minimum, a bit extreme, and more likely offensively outrageous: texts should have no other use than to manifest the presence and future of the kingdom? I suspect the offense of the idea emerges because literature and language seem to us such human, provisional things and so open to all manner of uses and ends. But what if we took it seriously? What would it look like to put all things—texts, even—in relation to the kingdom of God? The next chapter will seek to put text upon a Trinitarian foundation centered in Jesus the incarnate word that proceeds from the Father and is brought into fulfillment in the Spirit. For the moment, however, Augustine's *uti/frui* and Ellul's diagnosis of confused means and ends offer several critiques of both functional and structural definitions of literature—of both reading for use and reading for reading's sake—that give a sense of the problems of reading on those foundations.

## Idolatry of the Ends: Eschatologically Insufficient

I have been suggesting that arguments for noninstrumental reading often rest on the idea that a larger or more personally formative end can keep reading from being too immersed in the round of consumer-driven means to ends. Bringing Augustine and Ellul to bear upon these arguments suggests that reading literature for literature's sake, the autotelic structure for literature that is implied by the methodology, is an insufficient eschatology.[37]

Arguments for reading for its own sake, however mistaken they might be about the possibility of avoiding use, value literature *contra mundum*, against the world of ideology, of technology, of fleeting fame, of educational pragmatism. In so doing, they are asserting that the literature itself either offers transcendent value of its own or assists readers in being able to choose their own transcendent values. They are trying to beat back the self-proclaimed despair of the discipline by making literature and the experience of literature a value that will stand against moral and intellectual decline; reading, then, is a stay against confusion, a ballast. Reading is functional hope. As Andrew Delbanco describes reading American literature in particular, despite the inevitable political connection of literature, it is "[t]hrough this *literary* experience . . . we can partake of the democratic faith in the capacity of all human beings to perform the miracle of creation."[38] And, if literary texts are indeed structurally autotelic too, then they both functionally and structurally presuppose their own, nondivinely originating eschatologies. In short, in reading for reading's sake, literary form generates an eschatology unto itself.

This process, of course, may not be direct. Roche, for example, suggests that the hope that is offered for literature and literary criticism, that is, *Why Literature Matters in the 21st Century*, is that the forwarding or unpacking of literary form in noninstrumental reading may offer moral guidance. In the final assessment, he substitutes the moral for the religious—setting up the permanence of particular values above the purpose of God. He writes, "Morality is not one subsystem among the others, such that there is art, science, religion, business, politics, and so forth, *alongside* morality. Instead, morality is the guiding principle for all human endeavors."[39] And, to the extent that literature or literary criticism fails to "fulfill [or attend to, in the case of critics] certain universal conditions of beauty or to address the specific needs of the technological age," it will be morally unable to "garner a window onto an ideal sphere."[40] In Roche's view, the final purpose for literature is to be a moral force for beauty.

Contrastingly, Glenn Arbery's *Why Literature Matters* obliquely hints toward a Christian eschatology in his suggestion that literature is "waiting for completion from elsewhere,"[41] a "pure receptivity"[42] that is part of the literature's "promissory joy,"[43] rather than building its own road to the eternal elsewhere. His work falls back into the same sort of auto-eschatology as Roche's, however, with the assertion that, if a work does not achieve the status of literature through permanent honor-worthiness, it can do none of the aesthetically revelatory work that will come to it from the outside as revelation. The honor-worthiness comes from meeting particular formal standards: "A novel that does not succeed at being literature cannot fruitfully address the actual condition of the world. Why? Because it has not addressed, with sufficient awareness and care, its own actual condition as a made thing."[44] Arbery has required the sacredness of the work to come from within its structure and form. Without the standards of rule-following, in which genre and tradition are the foremost standards, "There is no reason to trust [the work] as wisdom, and its inflated contemporaneity will eventually hit a low pressure trough and drop into the waters where not even the *Rachel* will be looking for orphans."[45] So, though he gives some space for a work to become what it will be finally through an outside source and—as does Roche—has room in his ideas for the community of literature, he yet requires a work to *be literature* before it may have access to what Roche would call the ideal or what Arbery might call "divine form."[46] It must be all in all to itself before it may be an agent of revelation and made what it is by some transcendent force.

Often, those who advertise noninstrumental approaches to texts are driven, perhaps by crisis thinking, toward the very instrumentality they repudiate.[47] This instrumental thinking is elevated, however, and differentiated from vulgar use by moral illumination or even divine form—but this amounts to autotelic eschatological rhetoric. In fulfilling the form of the eschatological and the desire for it, however, they remain insufficient, for a few reasons.

First, instead of the expanding love of the Trinity visible in the community of the new creation, these authors' works seem to offer literary form. Only excellent literature (for Arbery, that which achieves honor through formal excellence; for Roche, that which possesses substantive content, sensuousness of style, organic coherence of substance and form, and supertemporality[48]) accomplishes the salutary effects that they promise, the ends to which literature itself is, in their view, noninstrumentally wedded. Putting aside the common relativist objection to arguments like this, namely that standards of literary or formal excellence are by no means universal or supertemporal, it seems that these eschatologies of literature, these divine uses to which literature is put, require that works of art generate their own worthiness. It is by no means self-evident, however, that particular standards of worthiness are required for texts to accomplish particular goods—even eternal ones. For the effects of literature are by no means easily controlled, as teachers are often chagrined to find. And if, indeed, as in Arbery's case, works are waiting for something outside themselves, something divine, to complete them, then it seems plausible that texts might not be completed from an already aesthetically perfect state to their most full being. There seems to be no space in Roche or Arbery under which literature—like people—may be redeemed, or, if you will, under which criticism may exist in a culture of grace. By understanding literature as centripetally arranged and autotelic according to a particular and universal standard, positions like Roche's and Arbery's might seem to handicap God from choosing and using whichever text God pleases to do kingdom work.[49]

Second, noninstrumental approaches, as they seem known to us through available arguments, tend to offer insufficient space for literary becoming. Roche does insist that literature is inexhaustible in meaning and to that extent not static; Arbery, too, finds some way for literature to become in its ultimate receipt of divine transformation after waiting for heavenly consummation. But such positions prematurely fix literary texts in eternal states. Such canonization seems at odds with a robust theology of the kingdom of God, particularly the present site of the already/not-yet kingdom and its advancement in time.

Third, noninstrumental reading eschatologies also seem to rely overmuch on certainty as to the greatness of some literature. That is to say, they delineate worthiness in artistry and communication—prejudging works with all confidence and almost falling into presumption by usurping the judgment of God.[50] Both Arbery and Roche assert that some literature has achieved, and definitively so, the lofty ends—the illumination of the ideal or the lasting honor of fame. They assert that the good critic knows and preaches that literature. Yet, if, as in both these cases, the ideal to which the text aims is eternal or divine, it seems that God would be the judge of that.

In various versions of the argument for noninstrumental reading of texts, there is an aspirational quality, a winsome call for "further up and further in" that can easily be seen as an opening to transcendence, to something eschatological in shape. In that sense, it can be seen as a glint of very recognizable and human hunger after the shape of the kingdom. Yet, this seeking of transcendence in reading can turn, like the tower of Babel, to self-ordained, self-justifying grasping. George Steiner, author of *Real Presences* and *After Babel* and practical priest for what is classic and transcendent in literature (and human achievement more broadly), has suggested that the great ones, "a Socrates, a Mozart, a Gauss or a Galileo . . . in some degree, compensate for man."[51] It is a turn of phrase no doubt somewhat hyperbolic—James Wood calls this tendency in Steiner a "melodrama of transcenden[t]" greatness.[52] Hyperbole itself is an eschatological turn—a too-strong statement that needs its verification and correction from elsewhere; hyperbole casts its net as wide as the sea for the Christ to fill. However, Steiner's statement nonetheless demonstrates a sense (however doomed) of human self-justification through the treasures of canonized achievement. For Christians, though, the canon can never be solely human; and the human can never solely save itself—through the canon or any other thing. Noninstrumental theories of reading tend to try.

## Idolatry of the Means:
## Insufficiently Eschatological

Instrumental uses of reading have been considered, if not gauche, certainly a bit shabby, lumped into a sort of dirty rhetoricality outclassed by higher textual encounters.[53] The residuum of this line of thinking still grates uncomfortably along the sometimes-unacknowledged divide between the literature and composition-rhetoric halves of many English departments. Then again, instrumental use has never been as strongly championed as in a set of more recent historical and cultural literary studies clarifying and redeeming the role of various kinds of reading heretofore ignored as vulgar use. Reading for escape, absorption, enchantment, or self-recognition—only a few among many possible uses of literature—has been earnestly and variously defended, perhaps as earnestly defended in the present as denigrated in the past. And consequently, the ideal of critical distance, with its traditional disapproval of absorption and escape, immersion and self-recognition, with their supposed attendant loss of discernment, has had its assumptions called into question. Studies of popular reading and its history have found evidence that immersed, absorptive reading and even escape have offered strategic and intellectual benefits to the reader and have even impacted—or, in some views, made possible—the public sphere from which they were supposed to have retreated.[54] Other uses are being recognized for their, well, usefulness, too: studies of self-recognition and identification to a certain extent made possible through immersive reading have begun to yield scientific evidence of particular social, intellectual, and moral benefits that seem broader than the individual.[55]

As should by now be abundantly clear, this book does not intend to critique instrumental uses from a morally superior position of non-use or commitment to particular canons of greatness—no latter-day Professor Teufelsdröckh here proclaims "Close thy [Dan] Brown and open thy [Robert] Browning!" Nor, however, does this argument intend to reclaim or celebrate the instrumental use as its own end, as is the sometime-fashion of the scholarly world—however compelling. Instead, this section argues that a look at instrumental reading opens up as clearly to the kingdom of God and eschatology as noninstrumental reading. Reading for any purpose—for escape, self-identification, or knowledge, as means (and all reading is a relating that may be called means-like)—opens up a vast space of desire that highlights the not-yet and, as I shall argue in the next chapter, is metonymically connected to the eschaton through the future of the word of God in Christ.

As I mention above, Felski's uses for literature—recognition, enchantment, knowledge, and shock—end in mystery much higher than their presumed strategic purposes would indicate, and her very words betray the point. Her language offers symptomatic glints of the eschatological consequences of reading for use. Reading for recognition, she writes, "comes without guarantees; it takes place in the messy and mundane world of human action, not divine revelation,"[56] that it is "ultimately driven by division and self-loss . . . far from synonymous with reconciliation."[57] When we read to recognize ourselves in literature, Felski shows, we find out what we don't have yet, but we do so only partially and limitedly. Our unified self is not yet, and what we truly need—connection with others—is certainly not guaranteed through reading, even as we seek to make connections through it. This sense of partiality and unfulfillment that reaches toward fulfillment is what I am pointing to as eschatological. Regarding enchantment, Felski's language is even more suggestive of the religious: she writes of the magic of understandings of reading as enchantment skirting "dangerously close to the edges of secular thought."[58] These snippets of language are perhaps metaphorical, or illustrative, but the religious speech genres and spheres on which they touch lend an eschatological quality to Felski's discussion: even when discussing mundane reading, we see reading as reaching into the transcendent, being willed there, perhaps, but pushing beyond somehow.

The theory and practice of reading for escape or absorption will show its eschatological reach. Scholarly positions on absorption appropriately understand it variously:[59] some figure escape or absorption as a dramatic drive through a text that explodes the details of language with the unconcern of a movie audience for the other cars smashed in pursuit of the bandits—so much collateral damage. Others suggest, contrarily, that absorption causes stronger attachments to language itself. The cold, distant clinician may be drawn, perhaps unwillingly, into tenderness for the subject, meeting full passion through slow exploration of a text's intricacies in almost a timeless dreamscape. As Charles Bernstein has understood absorption as a sort of artifice, absorption may be an effect of poetic language too, a way for a poem to extend beyond its devices.[60] It may even be visible, say, in the effect of poetic stuplimity (Sianne Ngai's term) produced by the seemingly endlessly iterable snippets of Gertrude Stein that produce a sublime stupefaction combining shock and boredom, which is in itself a sort of absorption that lends an alternative to mundane consciousness.[61]

My own experiences of absorptive reading and escape began very early; I began to figure out my need to escape and be absorbed in a text just at the moment when literacy made it possible: at five years old when I was diagnosed with stage three muscle cancer. After hours of chemotherapy but before the aftermath—just in the body's break between receiving the medicine and repulsing it with long periods of violent vomiting, my mother, sisters, and I would visit Flower Memorial Library, submerging our sorrows and the seats of our car in books. Two years of chemotherapy established something of a habit with us of a kind of excessive escape—we measured out my life in inches rather than pages of Andrew Lang's Coloured Fairy Book spines—buttressed by grocery bags full Trixie Belden and Nancy Drew on loan from friends.

It seems perfectly honest to admit that reading for escape—no matter what sort of absorption is described—is probably only metaphoric. Reading books never made me less cancerous, a fact I consider often when I reflect on my career choice. All sorts of use demonstrate, above all, the needs that set the use into motion—needs that point always to the eschatological end, which is, of course, found at the beginning. Escapist, absorptive reading, however, sets as paramount the desire or need for escape, while self-identification in a text—the recognition and self-critique that one finds in some useful reading—highlights a need for connection and community. Purely mundane use of text is illusory, some flimsy utility hole cover; if we are nosey, we may lift the cover of our own use and gaze into echoing spaces of longing. When we escape into a book, become absorbed into it, are magically transported, nothing becomes more visible, upon our return, than the edges that confine, the inescapable problems, the unabsorbable fact, the intransigent present. They become only so much more visible as under the x-ray—the indomitable ribcage, the recalcitrant tumor. Reading is thus primarily an acknowledgment that escape is fundamentally impossible. To read for escape, or stress relief, or relief of some other kind is, at bottom, rife with longing.

In the winter of 2013, I heard the poet Jon Woodward give a reading from his book *Uncanny Valley*, a longer poem called "Huge Dragonflies" that stands out for its use of what might be considered extreme repetition—134 instantiations of or variations on the line "Hope dwells eternally there."[62] Listening, I found myself in an absorptive, escaping space that concurrently registered in self-identification and attention to the texture of the litanied language. It was an in-between place: between the slide through a text that would be part of reading for plot and a very attentive absorption into textual effects. On the one hand, I surely wanted to know what was going to happen, and in the tension of the language, I was waiting as the repetition stacked up for the payoff. On the other, the repetition, as it extended, made me work to be sure that I wouldn't miss even the tiniest of variations. Within the poem, the "Hope dwells eternally there" line accrues errors—as if the language itself mutates at a cellular level and stutters itself forward. In attending to a kind of eternality through and beyond the creation of tension within variation amounting to plot, I found myself wondering about how to find eternality in language through degeneration and mutations. While listening, I wrote in a journal, "I don't seem to stop needing him to keep saying it." In the line itself was the tension between time—or hope, which seems to require time—and eternity. In this absorptive experience of reading through hearing, and, later, in rereading the text in the volume I scooped up from the book table, I found myself hyper-aware at the same time I was absorbed in the poem. Even my absorption was never escape.

In listening to Jon Woodward's poetry, the experience of absorption paralleled, too, what I have experienced as more often recognizably instrumental escape. The dual inattention and attention effected by the poem oddly freed me for my own riffs on and applications of the words. I was more aware of my own life—which I normally would have sought to escape—while listening to the poem create its own space. This is partially because of the iterability of the language of the poem—the space that it holds for the habitation of the listener or reader, whose mind is freed to make whatever use seems meet. Yet, I also felt, at the same time, an obligation to surrender to the text itself, rather than using it as a tool for processing my feelings about having just submitted the book proposal for this work to a publisher. In the end, I had to let go of both my concerns and the concerns presented by the text because of the length and burden of the unexplained repetition. In a way, the burden of the experimental language in poems like Woodward's is so great that it in fact parallels the burdens we bring to Christ. We have to let them go such that, like the yoke of Christ, the word carries the burden itself, easy and light.

And yet, as so many impassioned defenses of absorption or immersion or enchantment have noted, there is a much more action-oriented hopefulness imbedded in the process of escape or absorption. Such an idea, that reading for escape is hopeful, may be defensible: Ricoeur, for instance, argues that fiction provides possible worlds as an imaginatively functional hope of the remaking of one's own world through the envisioning of alternatives to it. Mark Edmundson's more recent *Why Read?* offers to a broader audience the idea that encounters with texts can yield testable versions of life transformation to readers, and scholar teachers in the university can purvey them to students. Edmundson argues passionately that "[l]iterature is . . . our best goad toward new beginnings, our best chance for what we might call secular rebirth," and that "in literature there abide major hopes for human renovation."[63] For Edmundson, literature gives us options that our families and upbringings never could, a wider array of possibilities for our lives—hope for our future—if we will use them thus. Of course, Edmundson points out what Ricoeur does not, that for him, literature is a "*secular* Bible"[64]—it may remake the world of the reader without recourse to a theocentric eschatology. It is, for Ricoeur, a useful metaphor, the functional provision of possibilities.

Most often, I have found that when I have sought escape in books, my mind zeroes in on connections between it and the outside world. This exacerbates the distance between the two, highlighting the need for rescue. In my experience, literature thus does not, as in Kierkegaard's formulation, which Ricoeur takes up, grant me a passion for the possible but rather a passionate response to the impossible. The experience of magic and wonder at the world prompts various degrees of longing, as when the desire to really fly, after reading the missives of fairy land, cannot in real life be satisfactorily pretended, no matter what one's mother constructs out of pantyhose, hangers, elastic, glitter paint, and the like. What seems truest about escape and self-recognition—at least in my experience—is their longing shape. Something seems present to our touch, yet also recedes from it, pointing to the insufficiency of our experience and the need for the rescue of the word. Escape, absorption, and enchantment are a sort of paradox: on the one hand a removal from something—whether it be body or mind or circumstances—and on the other hand, an enthrallment to a text that highlights our need for rescue rather than escape. As does the plaintive singing of "I'll Fly Away," the practices of absorption and enchantment in reading reinforce, at times, the jarring return, the need for redemption.

Both instrumental and noninstrumental ways of reading—which, after all, are but uses—crack open an eschatological gap. They highlight a desire for the future of the world in the future of the word. Ellul unflinchingly insists that "we have only one certainty, and that is the promise" found in Matt. 6:33 to seek first the kingdom of God.[65] And our necessarily ultimate relationship with God reveals both kinds of reading as potentially idolatrous. Reading for its own sake risks raising the book as a brick in Babel, the library as a luciferian reach toward its own ultimacy. Instrumental, everyday reading, for the most part, plows east of Eden, this side of Paradise, without seeing the larger story, yet each furrow bears witness to the need out of which it beseeches the cursed ground. In making human readers the primary users of literature and their uses into the ends of literature, we limit use to an accomplishment of the human person or psyche when it ought to be understood that it is ultimately divine use that matters. This book, somewhat perversely for the demands of the discipline, places debates about use within the wider framework of God's purpose for the world and its cultures. In other words, if instrumentality is a problem in our understanding of reading, then the problem is not how the instrument is played or whether the use is worthwhile. The real problem is whether the instrument is being played by the right person. The end or future that matters is the future of the word of God—that is, Christ. It is in this future where the end and future of all our words—and our reading—will be found. To this ultimate end, text is neither means nor end. For our words participate in the word of God; they are metonyms of the end who is also the means, the spirit of Christ, the word of God.

## Notes

1. "He had him ride in the chariot of his second-in-command; and they cried out in front of him, 'Bow the knee!' Thus he set him over all the land of Egypt. Moreover Pharaoh said to Joseph, 'I am Pharaoh, and without your consent no one shall lift up hand or foot in all the land of Egypt.' Pharaoh gave Joseph the name Zaphenath-paneah; and he gave him Asenath daughter of Potiphera, priest of On, as his wife. Thus Joseph gained authority over the land of Egypt" (Gen. 41:43-45).

2. See John Walton and Kim Walton, *The Bible Story Handbook* (Wheaton, IL: Crossway, 2010).

3. Harold Bloom, *The Anatomy of Influence* (New Haven: Yale University Press, 2011), 10.

4. Andrew Delbanco, *Required Reading: Why Our American Classics Matter Now* (New York: Farrar, Straus & Giroux, 1997), 209.

5. Harold Bloom, *How to Read and Why* (New York: Scribner, 2000), 29.

6. See René Wellek and Austin Warren, *Theory of Literature*, 3rd ed. (New York: Mariner, 1984), chapter 2.

7. Tzetan Todorov, Lynn Moss, and Bruno Braunrot, "The Notion of Literature," *New Literary History* 38, no. 1 (2007): 1–12.

8. Rita Felski, *Uses of Literature* (Oxford: Blackwell, 2008), 8.

9. A few of very many recent examples of this might include Rita Felski's *Uses of Literature*, Joan Shelley Rubin's *Songs of Ourselves: The Uses of Poetry in America* (Cambridge, MA: Belknap, 2007), Leah Price's *How to Do Things with Books in Victorian Britain* (Princeton: Princeton University Press, 2012), *Fever Reading: Affect and Reading Badly in the Early American Public Sphere* (Durham: University of New Hampshire Press, 2012), Lynn S. Neal's *Romancing God* (Chapel Hill: University of North Carolina Press, 2006), Margaret Willes's *Reading Matters: Five Centuries of Discovering Books* (New Haven: Yale University Press, 2008), along with Mark Edmundson's *Why Read?* (New York: Bloomsbury, 2004).

10. Phrase describing this view in Todorov, Moss, and Braunrot, "The Notion of Literature," 5.

11. See the following: Anna Kamenetz, *DIY U: Edupunks, Edupreneurs, and the Coming Transformation of Higher Education* (White River Junction, VT: Chelsea Green, 2010); Naomi Schaefer Riley, *The Faculty Lounges: And Other Reasons You Won't Get the College Education You Paid For* (Chicago: Ivan R. Dee, 2011); Victor E. Ferrall Jr., *Liberal Arts at the Brink* (Cambridge, MA: Harvard University Press, 2011); Andrew Delbanco, *College: What It Was, Is, and Should Be* (Princeton: Princeton University Press, 2012); Mark William Roche, *Why Choose the Liberal Arts?* (South Bend, IN: University of Notre Dame Press, 2010); Martha Craven Nussbaum, *Not for Profit: Why Democracy Needs the Humanities* (Princeton: Princeton University Press, 2010); Richard P. Keeling and Richard H. Hersh, *We're Losing Our Minds: Rethinking American Higher Education* (New York: Palgrave Macmillan, 2012). Other, broader looks at the state of reading in the United States, such as Mark William Roche's *Why Literature Matters in the 21st Century* (New Haven: Yale University Press, 2004), point to technological explanations alongside literary critical ones for the decline. Nicholas Carr has suggested in *The Shallows: What the Internet Is Doing to Our Brains* (New York: W. W. Norton, 2010) that the Internet age in which we live has rewired our brains—and that the online reader, whose brain's plasticity has responded to the medium, though able to process a lot of information quickly, can't think as deeply or thoroughly as before. Alan Jacobs's *The Pleasures of Reading in an Age of Distraction* (New York: Oxford University Press, 2011) suggests that reading still has a lively following in a technological age but that distracted readers have lost their confidence.

12. Works that defend noninstrumental reading have tended to function as responses to conditions where the value of literature is threatened. Most famous among these, perhaps, are any number of works by Harold Bloom, who says blatantly in *The Western Canon* (New York: Harcourt Brace, 1994), "The flight from or repression of the aesthetic is endemic in our institutions of what still purport to be higher education"; he is unequivocal: "To read in the service of any ideology is not, in my judgment, to read at all" (23, 29). In *Why Literature Matters in the 21st Century*, Mark William Roche asserts that, in a technological age, we must "preserve, against all attempts to reduce art to the sociopolitical and ideological, that aspect of art which is purely without purpose" (206). Roche cites the challenge of technology and offers literary criticism as a means by which literature may be seen as an agent of timeless and timely wholeness that will grant an inexhaustible well of meaning to the dedicated reader. Another, *Why Literature Matters: Permanence*

*and the Politics of Reputation* (Wilmington, DE: ISI Books, 2001) by Glenn C. Arbery, opens by repulsing what the author terms the "literature industry" and cultural studies, the materialist values of which are tantamount to the "loss of literature itself"—a point made more stringently by George Steiner, whose blatant disgust with the rabbit-like increase of critical works is well known, especially in works such as *Real Presences* (Chicago: University of Chicago Press, 1991) (xi). Roche asserts that while the reading he espouses is an end in and of itself, it nonetheless retains an end*less* sort of quality, a journey rather than a destination—in which the reader has access to truths that are timeless, though in no way, to his view, separate from the world of the now. For Roche, art is useful but not shabbily usable because it "is removed from the merely temporal and is potentially of supertemporal significance" (39). These approaches undeniably support noninstrumental, aesthetically focused reading by making noninstrumentality and aesthetics in some way valuable or useful. For Arbery, good reading is always "anagogical"—a spiritual knowledge, which must relinquish "the habit of trying to extract, by the quickest means, the usable gist of people and experiences; it requires a recovery of the inner nature of time" (149). Language, for Arbery, is a tool for thinking, a sort of weighty and important knowledge that is made knowable by form. Roche emphasizes that, "the sensuous dimension of literature [form] reinforces the value of the literary experience as an end in itself" rather than "for practical purposes" (29). Yet, he also gives literature a value from its use, that it gives "us great insight into the logic of human behavior and the consequences of given positions" and that it can critique reality, counter it with an alternative vision, or even "directly evoke a normative ideal" (20, 21). It may even in its "moral dimension" "perform an edifying function based on its integrity as an artwork . . . meaningfully affecting its recipients" (39). For Roche, this edification avoids abusive instrumentality because of literature's autonomy, where literature's distinctiveness is an autotelic structure. In reading, Roche suggests, a "mechanical means-end thinking disappears, and various vital impulses that are their own intrinsic end remain" (39). Because the impulses that Roche sees literature engendering are ones he sees as timelessly vital for humans, the use of literature for these purposes seems defensible to him. For Bloom, "The reception of aesthetic power enables us to learn how to talk to ourselves and how to endure ourselves" (29–30). In more than one book, Bloom, pooh-poohing larger claims for literature's salvific power, instead suggests that literature prepares us for change—most centrally for the change of death, which is inescapable. Along with a number of somewhat traditionalist defenses of noninstrumental reading from a literary studies standpoint, there have also been interdisciplinary research studies that link the methodologies usually associated with noninstrumental reading and beneficial popular or educational ends. Christina Vischer Bruns's recent book, situated on the borders of education, psychology, and literary study, *Why Literature Matters: The Value of Literary Reading and What It Means for Teaching* (New York: Continuum, 2011), advances the claim that literature is instrumental in personal identity formation and that teachers may assist students in identity formation through helping them to attach to books as transitional objects through which they may work out questions and issues of their own development. The psychological research of Raymond Mar and Keith Oatley in the last five to ten years on "deep reading" and the development of empathy in readers is one example of this (e.g., "The Function of Fiction is the Abstraction and Simulation of Social Experience," *Perspectives on Psychological Science* 3, no. 3 [2008]: 173–92). Further, the pressure of the scope of information and available material stretch the plausibility of use's plethora of possible claims regarding cultural and textual history. Maurice S. Lee's 2012 article "Searching the Archives with Dickens and Hawthorne" (*ELH* 79 [2012]: 747–71) helpfully points out how problematic New Historicist methodologies can be when enacted within and upon such vast electronic archives: we can find documentary evidence supporting just about any conceivable argument. Lee's fascinating case study of library and information science and literary study—of electronic archive research under the current conditions of documentary proliferation—have led him at least to swing back toward more formal and aesthetic standards: "A crucial unintended consequence of the New Historicism in an age of total information is that it highlights the need for aesthetic judgment when searching through documentary chaos" (750). Aesthetic judgment, though a traditionally nonutilitarian approach to addressing the form or structure of a text, ends up being a kind of means to discern the most helpful approaches to texts.

13. Harold Bloom, *The Western Canon: The Books and Schools of the Ages* (New York: Harcourt, 1994), 31.

14. Tzvetan Todorov has helpfully traced this definitional history in "The Notion of Literature."

15. Tzvetan Todorov and John Lyons, "What Is Literature For?" *New Literary History* 38, no. 1 (2007): 13–32. This essay took part in a special issue of the journal *New Literary History* on the topic, "What Is Literature Now?"

16. Ibid., 22.

17. Ibid., 17.

18. Bloom, *How to Read and Why*, 22.

19. Felski, *Uses of Literature*, 14–15.

20. Ibid., 15.

21. As Mark Edmundson has worded it in *Why Read?*, "What's missing from the current dispensation is a sense of hope when we confront major works, the hope that they will tell us something we do not know about the world or give us an entirely fresh way to apprehend experience" (46).

22. Jacques Ellul, *The Presence of the Kingdom*, 2nd ed. (Colorado Springs: Helmers & Howard, 1989), 64.

23. Ibid., 52.

24. Ibid., 63.

25. Ibid., 78.

26. Ibid., 42.

27. Ibid., 78.

28. Saint Augustine, *On Christian Teaching*, trans. R. P. H. Green (Oxford: Oxford University Press, 1997), 9.

29. Ibid.

30. Ibid., 25.

31. Ibid., 10.

32. Ibid., 17.

33. Ibid.

34. Ibid., 24–25.

35. Ellul, *The Presence of the Kingdom*, 42.

36. Saint Augustine, *On Christian Doctrine*, 27.

37. Another counter to aesthetically driven, noninstrumental reading has emerged in Richard Viladesau's *Theological Aesthetics* (New York: Oxford University Press, 1999): noninstrumental uses of literature, which pride themselves on a supposedly non means-end thinking that facilitates a rich, unhurried engagement with literary form, risk an idolatry of the word that is tantamount to the worship of images. Such a critique, of course, is as old as Plato's Allegory of the Cave, as Viladesau has pointed out. Viladesau has further suggested that, as noninstrumental as self-consciously aesthetic

pursuits seem, they may fold into the vices of other, more pragmatic concerns as well, concerns that deny others while fulfilling the self: "the pursuit of beauty (like any form of human self-fulfillment) may serve as a vehicle of escapism, fostering an egotistical occupation with pleasure and providing a distraction from the love of neighbor" (199). The tacitly self-fulfilling nature of supposedly noninstrumental uses of literature makes them as idolatrous as more blatantly grasping uses, such as those outlined and defended so sensibly in Rita Felski's *Uses of Literature*. And not only for the sake of its threat to practical kingdom-work in the world would such noninstrumental uses of art be potentially sinful. The critique here is not only of any presumed inactiveness in the work of creating art but also of the refusal of self-sacrifice that the pursuit of one's own conception of beauty presupposes. The issue here, of failing to love others and loving the self more, which would be a problem attendant on uses of texts, is one of failure in love, a failure in the act of self-sacrifice that is central to the Christian faith—the taking up of one's cross in imitation and discipleship of Christ. Viladesau's own work has sought to link the arts with theology, particularly of the cross, under which banner the primary uses of self-love may, in fact, be concomitant on escapism or recognition. Viladesau points to this as a particularly Protestant problem, an iconoclast's ironic attempt to avoid idolatry by simply switching the target of idolatrous affection and ending up in the same boat as more instrumental uses of literature, which amount to a sort of magic transport via the Reading Rainbow or Super Why's leap into a book.

38. Delbanco, *Required Reading: Why Our American Classics Matter Now*, xi.

39. Roche, *Why Literature Matters in the 21st Century*, 8.

40. Ibid., 259.

41. Arbery, *Why Literature Matters: Permanence and the Politics of Reputation*, 228.

42. Ibid., 229.

43. Ibid., 230.

44. Ibid., 19.

45. Ibid.

46. Ibid., 229.

47. I have so far in this chapter argued that arguments in favor of noninstrumental reading of literature lean toward eschatology—problematically to the extent that they rely on autotelic texts, and insufficiently insofar as they give presumptive judgmental authority to

critics. Other critiques of earlier versions of noninstrumental criticism have arisen—more attached to the particular ideologies at work in, say, New Criticism. The sources I particularly deal with aren't meant to be more than representative of a kind—instantiations at a particular moment. Larger, more famous critiques of particular noninstrumentality exist. For example, Susan Sontag's famous "Against Interpretation" (in *Against Interpretation and Other Essays* [New York: Farrar, Straus & Giroux, 1966]) suggests that "interpretation" itself, in its systematization "presupposes a discrepancy between the clear meaning of the text and the demands of (later) readers" (6): the transformation of form and content into intellectually consumable bits, "makes art into an article for use, for arrangement into a mental scheme of categories" (10)—which again, though part of a schema explicitly aiming at noninstrumentality in its very schematization, functions as use. She suggests an erotics of art instead, which might be found in the desire for literature or the love of it—perhaps something along the lines of what Alan Jacobs is after when he seeks charitable reading and whimsy as guiding principles of interpretation in books such as *Theology of Reading: A Hermeneutics of Love* (Boulder, CO: Westview, 2001) and *The Pleasures of Reading in an Age of Distraction* (New York: Oxford University Press, 2011).

48. Arbery, *Why Literature Matters*, 19. Roche, *Why Choose the Liberal Arts?*, 251.

49. Thus also does Roche require morally exemplary critics, a requirement only slightly less daunting than Arbery's, which requires that critics must know the playlist of God's favorites in a world in which the making of books will have no end. Critics, for Roche, must "exhibit the virtues that they discuss in their interpretations with students and others, critics embody the existential worth of literature—not only the value of the existential relationship to literature but also appreciation of literature as an end in itself and recognition of those virtues elicited in aesthetic experience but neglected in modernity" (257). Criticism will, in so doing—if its critics attend to aesthetics and those questions inspired in a technological age—"earn its place among the disciplines that deserve support" (259). This is a meritocracy of books and of criticism—it is the secular academy and though easily associated with the eschatological in its idealistic cast, is not in the same key as the grace—the costly grace—central to the kingdom of God.

50. Arbery, for instance, unironically writes, "Of all the poems in the history of the West, actual Scripture aside, but including the *Divine Comedy*, *Paradise Lost*, and all the devotional lyrics ever written, God loves the *Iliad* most" (151).

51. George Steiner, "The Archives of Eden," in *No Passion Spent* (New Haven: Yale University Press, 1996), 275.

52. James Wood, *The Broken Estate: Essays on Literature and Belief* (New York: Picador, 2010), 160. Wood's mellifluously written assessment of Steiner in "George Steiner's Unreal Presence" proceeds along the same lines as the argument here, pointing out the eschatological hunger of noninstrumental reading: Wood suspects that what Steiner offers in works such as *Real Presences* is a making universal of the greatness of some works, in fact, the making universal of some tastes: "[W]hat Steiner is asking us to believe in is not the presence of the divine but the easier presence of undefined greatness. The test is easy to apply. Were Steiner proposing a doctrine of *meaning* it would have to be a universal doctrine. That is, if great work incarnates a Real Presence then minor or even bad work must do so also, for the divine cannot choose merely to be present in masterpieces. This is what a theory of meaning is: it is universal" (167). It might not be too much to say that proposing a universal doctrine of meaning in which the divine is present in minor, and even bad, works is more or less what this book is trying to do.

53. For an overview of such, see the introduction to Felski, *Uses of Literature.*

54. For a very few examples of what is really a much wider, and theoretically rich, phenomenon, see works such as Caroline Levine's *The Serious Pleasures of Suspense: Victorian Realism and Narrative Doubt* (Charlottesville: University of Virginia Press, 2003); Robert Darnton's *The Case for Books* (New York: PublicAffairs, 2010); Michael Millner's *Fever Reading: Affect and Reading Badly in the Early American Public Sphere* (Durham: University of New Hampshire Press, 2012). See also note 10 above.

55. For example, see David Comer Kidd and Emanuele Costano, "Reading Literary Fiction Improves Theory of Mind," *Science* 342, no. 6156 (2013): 377–80.

56. Felski, *Uses of Literature*, 50.

57. Ibid., 31.

58. Ibid., 57.

59. The variations described here ought not be understood only agonistically, however; it makes complete sense that absorptive reading might have varieties, as available ways of reading have varied over community practices. As Robert Darnton has pointed out in *The Case for Books*, some sorts of reading from the early modern period onward were never very absorptive

or even linear but distinctly piecemeal. Texts were cobbled together into commonplace books as one's own self and life were composed in the lines or even partial lines of another, not even always selected by oneself, but also by friends participating in the making of a self and a life (149–50). This, of course, is a different sort of making use of reading than specifically escape or absorption, in which one connects one's life events to the passages, but it too participates in the eschatological.

60. Charles Bernstein, "Artifice of Absorption," in *Artifice and Indeterminacy: An Anthology of New Poetics*, ed. Christopher Beach (Tuscaloosa: University of Alabama Press, 1998), 3–23.

61. Sianne Ngai, "Stuplimity: Shock and Boredom in Twentieth-Century Aesthetics," *Postmodern Culture* 10, no. 2 (January 2000): accessed November 24, 2013.

62. Jon Woodward, "Huge Dragonflies," in *Uncanny Valley* (Cleveland: Cleveland State University Poetry Center, 2012), 1–7.

63. Mark Edmundson, *Why Read?*, 3.

64. Ibid., 124.

65. Ellul, *Presence of the Kingdom*, 78.

# 1

---

# The Future of the Word

O Lord, bring me to perfection and reveal
to me the meaning of these pages. . . . Do
not desert your gifts, and do not despise your
plant as it thirsts.
–Augustine, Confessions

The writer of Matthew understands Jesus' life in terms of texts.[1] In
his gospel, the writer links all of the major events, many of the major
speeches, and several of the parable sequences to Old Testament
scripture passages. Apparently, Jesus' life is all about fulfilling
scripture. Sometimes the writer explicitly uses the term "fulfill"—as in
the fulfillment citations—and sometimes other formulae, such as the
"you have heard that it was said . . . but I say to you" passages. In both,
Jesus embodies the word, reinterprets the word, and sets forth the
future of the word. Matthew pictures a Jesus who reshapes the future
of Israel in terms of the kingdom of God through a pattern of what
Brandon D. Crowe has called "eschatological reversal."[2] Matthew's

Gospel constructs Jesus out of the future of the word, a savior, who, in renewing the word, renews the nation of Israel in the kingdom.

As the future of the word, Jesus is interpreter of the word and the kingdom. Indeed, the text shows Jesus positioning himself throughout the Sermon on the Mount as a new sort of scribe, one who has interpretive authority over the central texts of Jewish faith. Jesus describes his reading and interpreting practice as fulfillment: the bringing forward and expanding of the written word. He uses again and again the pattern, "You have heard that it was said . . . but I say to you," to help listeners reread ancient commands in light of the kingdom of God that Jesus announces (Matt. 5:21-22; 5:27-28; 5:31-32; 5:33-34; 5:38-39; 5:43-44). He has authority over the meanings and purposes of the texts he interprets. And Matthew acknowledges it: the Gospel tells us Jesus "taught them as one having authority, and not as their scribes" (Matt. 7:29).

In Matthew 13, the authoritative scribe appears again, this time fulfilling the word by telling parables, wherein lies instruction about the expanding kingdom of God. The parables themselves, their very proclamation, are "to fulfill what had been spoken through the prophet" (Matt. 13:35). In Matthew 13, parables work not in the same formula but still according to the same pattern as the "you have heard that it was said . . . but I say to you" of the Sermon on the Mount: they are another fulfillment of sorts—a future of the text—and they deal almost meta-textually, insofar as they are futures of the text that are about the expansion of the kingdom of God. The parables of Matthew 13 make more explicit the kingdom-expansion taking place in Matthew 5: the parables of the sower, the wheat and tares, the mustard seed, and the treasure hidden in the field—all of these picture how the kingdom expands and flourishes despite various obstacles. The future of the kingdom (told by and through the future of the word) is embodied in stories (words) about the future of the kingdom.

Jesus explains parables a great deal in this section, and at the end of the chapter, even shares a parable about someone who tells parables or reads them, a person Jesus calls the "scribe who has been trained for the kingdom." In this parable, Jesus as new scribe opens to others a place among his kingdom's scriveners: "Therefore every scribe who has been trained for the kingdom of heaven is like the master of a household who brings out of his treasure what is new and what is old" (Matt. 13:52). The scribe for the kingdom is, of course, Jesus, the master of the world who brings out his word anew in what is old. Yet, as Jesus explains the scribe "trained" for the kingdom, a posture that he has modeled by bringing out the new meanings from the old scriptures and stories that he reinterprets, he also extends that capacity to his listeners: we too may be scribes for the kingdom, whose reading and interpreting advance the future of the word.

Yet Jesus' fulfillment is not his termination of the word—and all the fulfillment language actually extends the future of the word rather than giving it the sense of an ending, though it maintains the idea of purpose. Two major meta-critical moments of the book demonstrate this. In the Sermon on the Mount, Jesus says, "Do not think that I have come to abolish the law or the prophets; I have come not to abolish but to fulfill. For truly I tell you, until heaven and earth pass away, not one letter, not one stroke of a letter, will pass from the law until all is accomplished" (Matt. 5:17-18). Given that heaven and earth do not pass away when Jesus dies and is raised from the dead, one presumes there is a further fulfillment, a further future of the word through the resurrected Jesus. The end of the book reaffirms this: in Matthew 24, in a long discourse thoroughgoing with eschatology—the future of the kingdom of God—Jesus takes things even further than the law and the prophets. In fact, he expands the force of the future of the word of God to include his own words: "Heaven and earth will pass away," he says, "but my words will not pass away" (Matt. 24:35). The future of the words of Jesus in this passage is marked out as continuing on in fulfillment—not ending.

The future of the word that Jesus embodies and extends through his resurrection and inauguration of the kingdom of God is a future that potentially infuses all words—all texts. In the introduction, I argued that contemporary understandings of reading literature, whether instrumental or not, fall into one of two problems: they are insufficiently eschatological or eschatologically insufficient. In this chapter, I will seek a surer eschatology for literature by grounding the future of texts in the future of the word of God, that is, in the future of Jesus. The future of Jesus Christ gives texts meaning, and the eschatological implications of this fact affect our understanding of how texts mean. The future of the word of God, Jesus, gives texts eschatological purpose and signification.

## The Theology of the Future of the Word

God created everything by the word, that is, by Jesus, the second person of the Trinity, the incarnate one. The Gospel of John tells us, "In the beginning was the Word, and the Word was with God, and the Word was God. He was in the beginning with God. All things came into being through him, and without him not one thing came into being. What has come into being in him was life, and the life was the light of all people" (John 1:1-4). This word, Jesus, with God and in being God, is the creator. And, as chapter 1 verse 14 reminds us, "the Word became flesh and lived among us."

Two things are important to note here. The first is that God's creation is by the word *in relation*. "The Word was with God and the Word was God" stresses the Trinitarian nature of creation. The fellowship between the persons of the Trinity, what some have called the perichoretic dance, is inter-reception, which involves motion or action. Because God is love, God is interactive in the Godhead. Creation *ex nihilo* is a production of their active, expanding, and plentiful fellowship: the Trinity's love creates. When the Trinity's love expands outside of the Godhead and God creates, the fellowship extended to creation does not subsume the creation into the Godhead, but rather, expands God's love outside of himself. As Athanasius writes in *Contra Gentes*, "[H]e envies nobody's existence but rather wishes everyone to exist in order to exercise his kindness."[3]

In addition, God's creation of all things is enacted by the word of God that *became* flesh. That is, by the Jesus who, through the incarnation, has the human quality of becoming. Jesus' coming and his choice to become—words used no fewer than nine times in the prologue to the book of John—is the becoming of the word.[4] It's not, of course, that the word becomes the word of God—for the word is always already the word of God. But as the word, Jesus becomes. And as the resurrected incarnate word of God, Jesus is *still* becoming—*still* has a future: as Jürgen Moltmann has written, "all statements and judgments about him must at once imply something about the future which is to be expected from him."[5] That is, Jesus has a future—his creating, like his word, is not over or done with; it proceeds according to the eschatological purpose that he has set forth for the cosmos.

In the becoming of Jesus, which is an action emerging out of the generative love of divine perichoresis, we find a way of understanding the creation, too, as becoming. The world, says Athanasius, is "called into existence by the Word's advent [*parousia*]"—or, to put it in other terms, the world *becomes* by the word's *coming*—and perhaps we are back at the wordplay of the prologue to the book of John.[6] Colin Gunton has argued that "[t]here is . . . no creation 'in the beginning' without an eschatological orientation. . . . Creation is 'out of nothing' in that it is made both to be and to become something."[7] Our existence, being created out of the love of the Trinity, is fashioned to become toward the Trinity's love; our existence in time is eschatological in shape because the word creates us and gives us a future. In fact, the creation itself is in the word, as Origen's commentary on the book of John notes: "It is because God thus established Wisdom that every creature is able to exist, for each participates in the divine Wisdom, according to which all were made. For according to the Prophet David, God made all things in Wisdom. There exists a great number of creatures thanks to participation in this Wisdom, but without their grasping the one by whom they have been established in being; very few understand Wisdom, not only in what concerns themselves, but also insofar as it concerns other things, for Christ is complete Wisdom."[8] Because of the creation's participation in the word, in divine wisdom, its coming to be is made possible. So rather than becoming being merely a function of Jesus' condescension to humanity, the coming to be of all things is a function of Jesus' wisdom. Becoming is thus divinely sourced.

Our becoming is an even-now and not-yet expression of God's community of the new creation, since our becoming occurs in time and through the formation of community. Our time is the time of God's revelation, as Karl Barth has emphasized, but further, our time is a shadow of God's relational time in the Trinity, a shadow longing to participate in the substance. And the consummation of time, devoutly hoped for, is that for which all creation "waits with eager longing" (Rom. 8:19).

We see an eschatological shape in the whole of scripture, in the way that God's sustaining creation is not static but generative. For example, in the text of Jeremiah's book of consolation, the prophet marks out the sustenance of generation as emerging out of the word of God:

> Thus says the Lord,
> who gives the sun for light by day
> and the fixed order of the moon and the stars
> for light by night,
> who stirs up the sea so that its waves roar—
> the Lord of hosts is his name:
> If this fixed order were ever to cease
> from my presence, says the Lord,
> then also the offspring of Israel would cease
> to be a nation before me forever. (Jer. 31:35-36)

The fixity of the word sustains creation; it guards generative nation building—the offspring of Israel that will yet persist, despite their sin-ridden and guilt-laden state, because of the goodness of the Lord.

Creation, as I've been describing it, is an act not only of invention or of development, but also of *signification*. That is to say, the word of God's creation out of the generative love of the Trinity is also an *ordering and arranging of perfect judgment*, such that creation has significance according to God's purposes. God's presence is a discernment and arrangement and judgment of creation; these are, in fact, part and parcel of the creation itself—and certainly part of the ongoing activity by which creation is upheld. "Being the Word," Athanasius writes, "he was not contained by anyone, but rather himself contained everything. And, as being in all creation, he is in essence outside everything but inside everything by his own power, arranging everything, and unfolding his own providence in everything to all things, and giving life to each thing and to all things together."[9] Augustine muses in *The City of God* that "the good and right judgment of God" would have been the means by which the creation could be "maintained" even if there had been no sin and Adam and Eve had lived "in eternal blessedness."[10] So, when granting meaning, God is both the maker and interpreter of what he has made.

The authority of God over his creation is the comprehension of God, and his granting significance to the cosmos is both creation and salvation. When God creates the world, it is out of nothing; his arrangement is the defeat of chaos. In a parallel way, when God rescues the world from sin, he rescues it from what Josef Pieper calls "the orientation toward nothingness and the reduction to nothingness,"[11] that is, the true nature of sin—or what Paul calls being "subjected to decay" (Rom. 8:20). For sin may be understood, as in Athanasius, as humans "despis[ing] and overturn[ing] the *comprehension* of God."[12] Sin is a movement toward both nothingness and meaninglessness; but the salvific, creative word of God is a sign, an interlocution of the Trinity that pours something—meaning through love—into nothing. The salvific word of God refuses de-creation and meaninglessness in his saving power. Thus the incarnation preserves the legibility of us all.

Understanding Christ's identity as *logos* is particularly important to understanding his incarnation as signification; indeed, the term as it is used in the Gospel of John establishes Christ's signifying power. The meaning of the biblical use of *logos* differs in part from Greek understandings, though there is, naturally, some commerce between these, since *logos* is, in John, the primary conceptual means of connection between Greek philosophy and Christian doctrine.[13] In Greek philosophy, the word carries massive weight; it is "symbolic of the Greek understanding of the world and existence."[14] The root contains the ideas of reckoning, by means of gathering or separating; the word itself evolves toward narration, and even definition: as Walter Bröcker has written, the Aristotelian sense of the term looms large—the "causing of something to be seen for what it is, and the possibility of being oriented thereby."[15]

Understanding Jesus as *logos* in the way John does establishes Jesus as generative and interpretive creator. In John is the idea that Jesus' creative power comes not only through invention but through the reckoning and bestowal of meaning. Further, though, the use of *logos* in John's Gospel shows the word of God as both interpreter and *interpreted* creator; ongoing interpretation of Jesus—from inside and outside his circle—seems fundamental to John's establishment of Jesus's divinity.

One common scholarly view suggests that the New Testament *logos* emerges from ideas about wisdom in the Old Testament, because of the association of both Jesus and Wisdom with creation. This would link the *logos* of Christ with divine wisdom in Proverbs 8, which emphasizes not only creation by wisdom, but the ordering and reckoning of that creation.

> I was there when he set the heavens in place,
> when he marked out the horizon on the face of the deep,
> when he established the clouds above
> and fixed securely the fountains of the deep,
> when he gave the sea its boundary
> so the waters would not overstep his command,
> and when he marked out the foundations of the earth.
> (Prov. 8:27-29)

According to this connection between word of God and wisdom, then, titling Jesus the word of God is, for John, tantamount to an assertion that Jesus both establishes, and in fact *is* the significance of the created order, an idea whose implications echo the Christ hymn of Colossians 1. As Stanley Grenz articulates it, the idea of Christ as word "refers to what is revelatory, to what reveals the significance of an event or even reveals the nature of God."[16] Jesus, the word of God, creates the world and has the power to grant significance.

But the word's signifying creation goes even further—as I hinted above, Christ's signification is also participatory and becoming. John Ronning in *The Jewish Targums and John's Logos Theology* suggests that John's use of the term *logos* to refer to Jesus is the result of the influence of Jewish targums—Rabbinic paraphrases and interpretations of the Hebrew Bible in Aramaic—and their references to the word of God. His carefully argued assertion is that the targum linkage to the *logos* title for Jesus in John has a particularly Christological payoff; Ronning suggests that it allowed Jews to make textual connections (via translation, an idea that I will return to in chapter 2) that facilitated their understanding of Jesus as fully God and fully human.[17] A targumic source also, Ronning argues, allows John's Gospel to reread—and reinterpret—targumic references to the word of God as unwitting messianic prophecies. Understanding the targumic source for the Johannine *logos* thus makes John's use of the term *logos* and his use of the scripture itself into something multivalent over time. John thus could be considered, in the targumic view, but also in several other views of the Johannine *logos*, to understand the divine significance of the word as inherent within earlier texts and brought forward to expanded significance in his interpretation in the gospel.

So Jesus grounds the world's significance, and through ongoing participation is ever more expansively understood as the word of God. But Jesus the word, also in fact *is* the particular significance of the world. His arrangement and unfolding of creation also reveal God, and he is the subject of the world's meaning. For Barth, the New Testament witness to revelation always demands Christ as the subject of its revelation, the only true subject, the arbiter by which all other concepts are comprehensible or bear any meaning at all. Nothing, he writes, no principle, narrative, ethic, or maxim "has any value, inner importance or abstract significance of its own . . . apart from Jesus Christ being the Subject of it all."[18] The biblical witness to revelation, for Barth, is the pattern for our response to the divine revelation of Christ. Now, the evangelical discomfort with Barth's assessment of scripture has its place here—perhaps the Bible has to do with other things than solely Christ—but I wonder if part of the difficulty might be solved by expanding rather than diminishing or dismissing this claim. For, significance itself is the predicate of the subject *Jesus Christ*, the act of the word of God with God. John Milbank has suggested, for example, that the significance of Jesus for the significance of the cosmos is tied to Jesus as language. He writes in *The Word Made Strange* that it is "*only* an insistence that the Son is also *logos* in the sense of language, that allows us to make any sense of this place at all."[19] Jesus, as the language-logos, is the Lord of sense-making who saves us by signifying. We might say, then—and perhaps I simply will paraphrase—that signification is found in no one else, for there is no other signification to be found in heaven and earth by which we must be saved.

Now, these three theological points have implications for how we think about text. Taking the part for the whole, we may say that texts are part of the created order and the qualities that apply to all creation also apply to texts. These theological points suggest that in considering texts, we ought not to seek an ontology of texts, nor even an ethics of texts, but rather develop an eschatology of texts.

## The Theology of the Future of the Text

Because text is a part of God's creation, it is a making by the word of God, and is sustained by him. All our words are words within the word of God, for he has unfolded himself in all things.[20] The texts, spoken and written, that emerge from people are, on the one hand, objects or actions of people's own wills, but on the other hand are also under the providence of God.[21] When humans speak or write, they do so under the authority of God, and, ultimately, the Authorship of God. As Barth articulates it,

> Our existence is real in so far as He wills it and posits it as real. It has an Author from whom as such it is absolutely distinct and to whom it is absolutely related, but not in such a way that it belongs essentially to this Author to have something really outside Himself, not in such a way that there is anything necessary for Him in this relation. It has an Author outside whom nothing is necessary. . . . It has an Author who calls into existence and sustains in existence out of free goodness and according to His own free will and plan. . . . It has—this is what all these statements are describing—a Creator. And it is as the Creator that Jesus shows the Father to us.[22]

This authorship of creation is also the sourcing of language: God is the ground of our actions and speech acts. First, God is responsible for the creation of the capacity for response-ability. Second, God is responsible for the pattern of responsiveness—giving response-ability by and in the Trinity and patterning response-ability in the manner of the Trinity. Third, God is responsible because he is pattern, subject, glorified object, and indeed, by the power of his Spirit, the means of our graced actions of responsiveness.

Yet this authorship under which we may author is not one of immanent determinism, but rather of what John Milbank has called a "simultaneous and risky openness both to grace and the possibility of sinful distortion—for which one is both responsible and not responsible."[23] God allows for us to have intentions, too, intentions that, subordinate to his sovereignty, are part of the inter-responsiveness of creator and created. Our intentions are not yet in accord with the will of God, or as Kathryn Tanner puts it, "Our will is not Christ's will in the way the human will of Christ simply is the will of the Son, without needing to be brought into correspondence with it. Instead, our lives are made over as a result of their being assumed [into the life of Christ]."[24] The interrelation complicates authorial intention as we may commonly conceive it.

The complication does not only extend to the moment of textual authorship either, wherein the permission of God sustains the author in her intentions such that a text is possible or bears a particular meaning. From the cosmic-level view, human intersubjectivity complicates all actions too—since every action is both distinct to an individual *and* a function of a whole history of webbed interactions. We are entirely responsible and entirely not responsible for all actions—which is what so necessitates faith in a meaning-making God: "If we attend to God," Milbank writes, "he will graciously provide us, out of ourselves, with appropriate good performances. The moral actor, since he *is* an artist, is as much at the mercy of 'the muse' (or the Holy Spirit) as the artist."[25] Milbank here considers human operation and action as fundamentally poetic, where humanity "quite gratuitously makes meaningful objects."[26] In Milbank's view, humanity inheres in sign-making, where action is a kind of language and language is action. And yet, language acts have an openness. They are subject to what Wilhelm Wundt calls a "heterogony of ends" in which the effects of any action or speech are beyond original intentions and thus craft new actions by the self and others.[27] Thus people are both responsible and not responsible for their speech actions' full perlocutionary force on both vertical and horizontal axes.

Further, not only creative speech acts or textual production, but also the reception and response to text are governed by the sustaining creation of the word. And as Bonaventure has pointed out, "we cannot" even "judge with certainty except in view of the Eternal Art which is the form that not only produces all things but also conserves and distinguishes all things, as the being which sustains the form in all things and the rule which directs all things. Through it our mind judges all things that enter it through the senses."[28]

In this way, in the tricky negotiation between the absolute authority of God and the intersubjective participation of people, God is the author of all text, and God's word is the word within which our own words are made.

God's word becomes toward his eschatological purposes—becomes as the word of God (though, of course, it doesn't become the word of God, for it already is the word of God)—toward the community of the new creation. This means that God's word works toward the kingdom. We might consider Jesus' explanation of his own ministry in relationship to God's word as the guiding principle. Jesus' pattern for language that becomes is ongoing fruition in a living, expanding, toward-the-community-of-the-new-creation way. Above I cited Matthew's pattern-speech in which Jesus says "You have heard that it was said . . . but I say to you"—as he brings Old Testament texts forward into ongoing life. This process is worked out again and again—outside of Matthew—for example, in the book of Acts, as the apostles, in various speeches, interpret the word of God toward the becoming of the community of the new creation. We may think of Peter and Stephen as early church masters of the reinterpretation that brings the text forward.

But how shall this apply to all text?[29] Romans 8 declares that the entire creation is "subjected to futility" and that it groans as with labor pains toward the revelation of the new community—"the children of God"—when it will be "liberated from its bondage to decay and will obtain the freedom of the glory of the children of God." The passage reaches out at this moment from its ostensible subject—freedom in Christ for believers—to the freedom in Christ that happens for the whole creation. This must include texts, too. Poet Fanny Howe has talked and written about the aspirational quality of language in a way that more distinctly shows how the structures of language, understood temporally, craft a discursive futurity for text that groans after this new creation. In an interview with Michael Brito, Howe said "I link letters and sentences with time; they are analogous to minutes and hours and aspire to a justice which is also analogous to our quest for the promised land."[30] Howe makes a related assertion in the essay "Work and Love," explaining more fully the kind of eschatological community to which sentences aspire:

> . . . there is a vision of a just world behind language, sentences, syllables.
>
> The evolution of a single word, into syllable, sound, amendment, assertion, tends towards justice. In every sentence you take measure of all the words in relation to each other.[31]

For Howe, the structure of language indicates both relationality and future hope. In the next chapter, I will identify possible ways that our participation may serve a text's becoming toward the community of the new creation. But for the moment, this idea may be clarified some by being put into play with some philosophers of language who have similar ideas about texts' futurity and relationality—because, as is no doubt obvious, the idea of language as inherently future oriented and/or relational (even if not exactly Trinitarian) is common. The idea of an eschatology of text has fruitful interplay with the works of several key theorists of language for whom futurity and relationality have some purchase.

Jacques Derrida's sense of language as future-oriented inheres in the motion and deferral of *différance*.[32] *Différance* for Derrida is the philosophical culmination of de Saussure's idea that signification in language is made possible by the difference of one signifier from another—that *cat* means *cat* fundamentally because it doesn't mean *bat*, *rat*, *hat*, and so forth. Derrida's contribution to this idea is his observation that the process of differentiation contains within it a motion or movement of deferral. The distinguishing between *cat* and *rat* (and all the other possible elements from which it may differ) is a "spacing and temporalizing," a "'historically' constituted . . . fabric of differences."[33] We see these differences in the sign—in writing, which may be said to bring to presence traces of the difference showing themselves to be effaced. Thus "the present becomes the sign of signs, the trace of traces . . . a trace of the effacement of the trace."[34] If meaning is deferred through temporalizing and spacing, then signification is future-oriented, insofar as the trace is always dependent on its relationship to past differences and hollowed out by its relation to future differences. The text is readable through the tracking of traces that makes a text both dead—a preserved inscription of traces—and alive—insofar as the trace is a track leading to more traces.

We may recognize what Derrida calls *différance* as inscribing a trace of the eschatological. At the end of "*Différance*," Derrida states that we can find a measure of what he calls "Heideggerian hope" in *différance*—the idea that the deferring and differing play of *différance* might fuel the quest for what Heidegger calls "the first word of Being" that suffuses everything.[35] It is a hope for "the proper word and the unique name," the "first word of Being" by the detour of *différance*. It is not impossible, Heidegger insists and Derrida quotes, "because Being speaks through every language; everywhere and always."[36] Heidegger and Derrida insist that "in order to name what is deployed in Being, language will have to find a single word, the unique word" with its absolute relation to the present.[37] Surely, the hunger here has some relationship to the groan after what Paul Fiddes has called the healing of time.[38] The unique word might, in the eternal, allow Being's trace to be sensible beyond logocentric systems. Though assumed to be against onto-theological systemization and thus pretty much fundamentally opposed to this argument, *différance* is yet susceptible to eschatology insofar as the eschatological always exceeds systemization and, indeed, representational language.

An eschatology of texts might also, for example, rehabilitate *différance*, insofar as it helps us through *différance's* nagging futility, alongside pointing out the nature of its hopes. In the temporalizing and spacing of *différance* is a relentless and possibly malignant fracturing of meaning. The quality of futurity—deferral—in *différance*, though itself opposed to every co-optation in service of power, generates conditions of possibility for such onto-theological discourse—whatever in us desires a realm, Derrida says. An eschatology of texts crosses—literally puts under the cross—the malignancy of this all-too-human power-grasping. It recognizes the possibility of God's reaching out into time—that God has time for us—affirming that the first word of Being, the unique name, is Christ. Not logocentric as Klages defined it and Derrida critiqued it, the eschatology of texts is *logos-centric* insofar as the *logos* himself is between presence and absence, is becoming, has time for us and is yet eternal. The God term here is not subsumed into the logocentric violence of human power structures. Indeed, the Trinity makes possible an upending of logocentrism, as the generative, creative, expanding love of the Trinity invites all to participate. It opens up meaning rather to a different sort of realm than the one Derrida is envisioning—one of hospitality and hope.

An eschatology of texts receives the resurrection's deposit on a future it guarantees and funds: a nonstatic, community-building future, which will not serve the "rulers and authorities" (Col. 1:15). It detours the record against us—the cooptation of meaning by power—nailing it to the cross. An eschatology of text, a jointure of texts' futures to Jesus' future, will always submit to the detour of *différance*, as the most basic example of scripture: in the gospels where the sign of the cross is turning an illocution of execution to a perlocution of promised, present, and future redemption. Derrida may be quite right that the onto-theological categories that turn into regulations in service of power are visible in the traces that mark language. But, an eschatology names these traces as "shadow[s] of what is to come, but the substance is Christ" (Col. 1:17).

Ricoeur has noted that from the moment language becomes semantic rather than semiotic—when it moves to the level of the sentence from the level of the sign, it contains within it the seed of discourse—the predicate, which grants it discursive-event status, a location in time. The nature of discourse as event, in its interlocutionary force, grants each utterance the weight of a question-generating response. These in turn generate future responses, and themselves craft a dialogic and conversational future for a speech act.

In a related manner, Hans-Georg Gadamer has discussed the way that the fusion of horizons in seeking understanding "allows something to 'emerge' which henceforth exists."[39] The understanding of writing, he argues, is "not a repetition of something past but the sharing of a present meaning."[40] The detachment of text from authorial intention leaves it open to the surplus of meaning available in discourse, what Gadamer describes as the freeing of text "for new relationships."[41] For Gadamer, then, these relationships between readers and texts create a future for the text in which the text is understood newly in every situation through the fusion of horizons between text and reader. It opens up a posture of questioning in the reader that is constituted by a vulnerability to the otherness of new relationships. Walter J. Ong has written about how writing is the death and resurrection of oral speech—and that writing may be a new life for speech, a life returned to speech (in some measure) within readers. For Ong, text, because of its passing through the death of writing into print, "becomes in countless ways more versatile than the purely vocal, living word. It can be freed from the surface, resurrected, variously."[42] For Ong, the fact that writing is a sort of death, that narrative is conventionally retrospective, raises special issues for the biblical text. He suggests that perhaps it may be important that the revelation of God through the Bible takes place in a spoken word carried through the death represented by writing and into the resurrected life of the printed word. Ong and James Nohrnberg posit a retrospective mode particular to narrative, but a special openness to the future in the biblical text that ends "Come Lord Jesus," rather than "The End."

Ong follows Ricoeur and Gadamer in his sense that interpretation is a bringing of an historical text into the present by means of appropriation. For Ricoeur, interpretation appropriates what was foreign; it "wants to . . . assimilate in the sense of making similar. This goal is achieved insofar as interpretation actualizes the meaning of the text for the present reader."[43] "As appropriation," Ricoeur writes, "interpretation becomes an event"—one not bringing forward the historical intention of the author (as in Schleiermacher), but disclosing "a possible way of looking at things, which is the genuine referential power of the text."[44] What we see in the text when we appropriate it is a referentiality that opens up future possibility in our own world. In this way, Ricoeur moves from reading as a making present of a text distanced in time from the reader, into the text as projecting a future—largely by means of metaphor and symbol that open up new ways of being. For Ricoeur, the temporal dimension of textual existence deeply impacts the world of the reader. The world of the text has an actual referential relationship to the world because the narrative is present in the real world of the reader, and opens up possibility through multiple interpretations and the polysemic twist of metaphor.[45] In Ricoeur's thinking then, narrative creates, in its multiplicity of meaning, a passion for the possible that is something like hope. It remakes the world of the reader.

My own argument grants the basics of Ricoeur's and Gadamer's ideas as far as they go. But as useful as they are in understanding our own position relative to text, these anthropocentric views misdirect the gaze. Must interpretation function as appropriation, even if Ricoeur's defense of appropriation holds—that far from being a kind of possession, appropriation becomes dispossession as the text offers a "new mode of being" to the reader? Even with this hedge, the argument's payoff for textual meanings is that they remake only my world as I fuse my horizons with the text and then appropriate them.[46] And here we are back again at the problem of reading for use. These hermeneutic ideas, rightly noticing the influence of context and limitation on our reading, still fail to acknowledge something that could be larger than that context or limitation. In short, by throwing off the yoke of authorial intention and the historical locatedness of that intention, the above arguments miss the thought of language as words within the word—the divinely intended, but also interrelational, word. The eschatology of the literary text must be more than that of Gadamer's or Ricoeur's understanding—it must believe that the "Come Lord Jesus" that characterizes the biblical text is in fact the "Come Lord Jesus" of *all* text and narrative—is in fact the groan of the entire creation, "Come Lord Jesus."[47]

## Text Is Significant through the Word toward the Community of the New Creation

If we pursue an eschatology of text, then the most important application of these points is that interpretation of text belongs to

Jesus. As the significance of the cosmos belongs to the word, so the significance of the text belongs to the word.[48] Hermeneutics and poetics as we experience them will differ in light of his sovereignty. For one thing, if interpretations belong to God, authorial intention cannot in any simple way—as we may be used to thinking about it—constitute textual meaning. Steven Knapp and Walter Benn Michaels's famous denunciation "Against Theory" relies on their carefully argued assertion that meaning and authorial intention are necessarily identical.[49] They demonstrate that a reader's designation of something as language entails an assumption of intention, and that any methods of reading based on a search for authorial intention are logically impertinent. Knapp and Michaels's argument represents the end of a long line of textual theorists who base their readings in authorial intention. They show how even alternate accounts of textual meaning that rely on larger structures of intention, such as genre, beg the question of authorial intention; in providing hermeneutical methodologies for discerning authorial intention, they've assumed it.

The argument I have been making has no problem with some of Knapp and Michaels's argument. If textual meaning is divinely ordained toward the becoming community of the new creation, then it may be okay to think about textual meaning as a function of divine authorial intention—and to assume that all text is constituted by that intention, though of course, I presume Knapp and Michaels would pose major objections to this argument. To assert this would be no simple transference of the theories of authorial intention into a theistic context, however. The God who possesses all interpretations and grounds all intentions has several uniquenesses over and against the human (or even machine) speech actor or textual intender. Perichoresis, for instance. The three persons in one are a qualitatively different authorial body than the possible authors entailed by Knapp and Michaels's argument. For the Trinity, intention is discursive, unified, but between persons in the mystery of the three in one, as in the "Let us make humankind in our own image" (Gen. 1:26).

The Trinity's intended meaning has a communal and becoming quality that makes it not simply identical with the sort of intention implied in "Against Theory." The idea that fellowship is the primary quality of the Trinity's perichoresis bears on the idea of intended meaning. It makes meaning eschatological. The Trinity's love is *expanding* betweenness—so, too, is divine authorial intention—thus textual meaning, too, must be becoming; it is toward the kingdom of God, it is becoming toward participation in God's community of the new creation. Thus, we might say, meaning is both between and becoming, rather than identical to a single authorial intention as Knapp and Michaels and others have understood it.

The author as we traditionally view her is a participant in the becoming-betweenness of meaning-making. The divine Author grants some measure of authority to human authors, insofar as they are intersubjectively responsible and not responsible for their words and works via context and community. But—and here we get toward the point of the whole book—God's role as not only inventing-creator but *also ordering- and interpreting*-creator offers readers, too, a chance to participate in the becoming-betweenness of eschatological meaning. The sovereign God allows meaning to be becoming between not only human and divine authors, but also between human and divine *readers.* Thus we may participate in how the meaning of texts moves toward the glory of God revealed in the resurrection of Christ and the love of the Trinity.

Some texts and readers will reveal the love of the Trinity by virtue of the judgment of the Lord. The problem of evil in reading and the problem of offense in text are topics that will be more fully addressed in chapters 3 and 4, respectively. Interpretations, as the story of Joseph rightly reminds us, belong to God, and his judgments are—as his love is—supreme. God's kingdom does not necessarily seek to preserve what humans judge as glorious, but to engender community, love, and the glory of God through strengths and weaknesses. In the light of eschatological hope, the judgment of texts will be a conversation, a participation—a bearing witness to the way that even failings have led to the triumph and the future of the word.

But if textual meaning becomes toward God's community of the new creation, then we might also say that bearing witness to the community of the new creation in the future of the word, has already happened and *is* happening in reading. In the same way that God works through the Body of Christ, that his kingdom might come, the Holy Spirit guides us into all truth, granting us participation in his revelation of the kingdom of God—a reading community and a significance that is already and not yet. For we are always reading God; we are always reading *with* God.

## Notes

1. Saint Augustine, *Confessions*, trans. Henry Chadwick (New York: Oxford University Press, 2008), 222.

2. There is an enormous body of literature on the relationship of Matthew to fulfillment and the Hebrew Bible. For a good overview on the positions of Matthew and fulfillment of OT scripture, see J. R. Daniel Kirk's "Conceptualising Fulfilment in Matthew," *Tyndale Bulletin* 59, no. 1 (2008): 77–98. Brandon D. Crowe's "Fulfillment in Matthew as Eschatological Reversal," *Westminster Theological Journal* 75 (2013): 111–27, is a helpful recent addition to the literature.

3. Athanasius, *Contra Gentes and De Incartione*, trans. Robert W. Thomson (Oxford: Clarendon, 1971), 115.

4. Frank Kermode, among others, has noted the tension between being and becoming in the prologue to the book of John in the *en/was // egeneto/became*

interplay, which has demonstrated the coming together of eternal being with human becoming. "John," in *Literary Guide to the Bible*, ed. Frank Kermode and Robert Alter (Cambridge, MA: Belknap of Harvard University Press, 1987), 440–66.

5. Jürgen Moltmann, *Theology of Hope* (Minneapolis: Fortress Press, 1993), 17.

6. Athanasius, *On the Incarnation*, trans. John Behr (Yonkers, NY: St. Vladimir's Seminary Press, 2011), 53.

7. Colin Gunton. *The Christian Faith: An Introduction to Christian Doctrine* (Malden, MA: Blackwell, 2002), 19.

8. Quoted in Richard Viledesau, *Theological Aesthetics* (New York: Oxford University Press, 1999), 75.

9. Athanasius, *On the Incarnation*, trans. John Behr (Yonkers: St. Vladimir's Seminary Press, 2011), 66–67.

10. Saint Augustine, *The City of God*, trans. Marcus Dods (New York: Modern Library, 2000), 711.

11. Josef Pieper, *Faith, Hope, Love* (San Francisco: Ignatius, 1997), 136.

12. Athanasius, *On the Incarnation*, 53.

13. Hermann Kleinknecht,"The Logos in the Greek and Hellenistic World," in *Theological Dictionary of the New Testament*, vol. IV, ed. Gerhard Kittel, Geoffrey William Bromiley, and Gregory Friedrich (Grand Rapids: Eerdmans, 1976), 69–136, 91.

14. Ibid., 77.

15. Quoted in Kleinknecht,"The Logos in the Greek and Hellenistic World," 80.

16. Stanley J. Grenz, *Theology for the Community of God* (Grand Rapids: Eerdmans, 2000), 301.

17. John L. Ronning,*The Jewish Targums and John's Logos Theology* (Peabody, MA: Hendrickson, 2010), 43.

18. Karl Barth, *Church Dogmatics I.2, The Doctrine of the Word of God*, trans. G. T. Thomson and Harold Knight (Peabody, MA: Hendrickson, 2010), 11.

19. John Milbank, *The Word Made Strange: Theology, Language, Culture* (Oxford: Blackwell, 1997), 3.

20. I am grateful to Brian Bantum for this phrasing.

21. Gerardus Van der Leeuw has argued that the purity of a particular art form is what makes it the servant of Christ, or its truth: "All music that is absolute

music, without additions, without anything counterfeit, is the servant of God: just as pure painting is, whether it treats religious subjects or not; and as true architecture is, apart from the churches it builds; and as true science is, even when it has little to do with theology, but busies itself with gases, stars, or languages" (quoted in Viladesau, *Theological Aesthetics*, 149). Here, though, I'm not particularly talking about the measured holiness or sacredness in the work of art as such, but rather the more fundamental argument of the precondition of God's making for the making of any language—what Pannenberg talks about as the *excessus* that preconditions our knowing of being, or what Derrida might call the *différance*. I'm referring to the Trinity's proceeding, expanding love, from which and in which all beings live and move and have their being.

22. Karl Barth, *Church Dogmatics 1.1: The Doctrine of the Word of God*, trans. G. T. Thomson and Harold Knight (New York: T. & T. Clark, 2004), 389.

23. Milbank, *The Word Made Strange*, 127.

24. Kathryn Tanner, *Jesus, Humanity, and the Trinity: A Brief Systematic Theology* (Minneapolis: Fortress Press, 2001), 57–58.

25. Milbank, *The Word Made Strange*, 126.

26. Ibid., 125.

27. Wilhelm Wundt, *Ethics: The Facts of Moral Life* (New York: Cosimo, 2006), 330.

28. In Viladesau, *Theological Aesthetics*, 113.

29. Many scholars have pointed to the future or afterlives of some kindsof texts. One example is Mark Knight, in *An Introduction to Religion and Literature* (New York: Continuum, 2009), arguing that "because of their involvement in God's creative activity, religious myths have an afterlife that brings with it space for other texts to continue the open-ended stories of their predecessors and narrate the story of the world in new ways" (24).

30. Manuel Brito, *A Suite of Poetic Voices: Interviews with Contemporary American Poets* (Santa Brigada, Spain: Kadle Books, 1992), 101.

31. Fanny Howe, *The Wedding Dress: Meditations on Word and Life* (Berkeley: University of California Press, 2003), 133.

32. Any number of scholars have understood Derrida's work in relation to the religious—some suggesting that it is only possible to read the peculiar logic of Derridean thought through the language of religion—but we may talk here

of Kevin Hart, Amy Hungerford, Hent de Vries, and John D. Caputo. The haze of language, reflected perhaps in the difficulty of summarizing the idea of *différance*—or the *pharmakon*, or the supplement, or any number of names by which the nexus of ideas has appeared in Derrida's work—has led some toward considering Derrida as in some way proceeding by apophatic avenues toward transcendence. Derrida's work becomes an admirable religious nonreligion without the ontological violence of messianism—as in Caputo. Or from another, less approving angle, this implicit religiosity is the stain of transcendence on Derrida's work that "evacuates" the material implications of his ethico-political project—as in Arthur Bradley's critique in "Derrida's God: Narrating the Theological Turn," *Paragraph* 29, no. 3 (2006): 21–42 (22). When I write about Derrida here, though, I'm less interested in saying something about Derrida than in saying something about how an eschatology of texts may be therapy for *différance*—that *différance* might have an eschatology, too.

33. Jacques Derrida, "Différance," in *Literary Theory*, ed. Julie Rivken and Michael Ryan (Malden, MA: Blackwell, 1998), 385, 393.

34. Ibid., 403.

35. Ibid., 405–6.

36. Ibid., 406.

37. Ibid.

38. Paul S. Fiddes, *The Promised End: Eschatology in Theology and Literature* (Malden, MA: Blackwell, 2000).

39. Hans-Georg Gadamer, *Truth and Method*, 2nd ed., trans. Joel Weinsheimer and Donald G. Marshal (New York: Continuum, 1999), 383.

40. Ibid., 392.

41. Ibid., 395.

42. Walter J. Ong, "Maranatha: Death and Life in the Text of the Book," *Journal of the American Academy of Religion* 45, no. 4 (1977): 419–49, 436.

43. Paul Ricoeur, *Interpretation Theory: Discourse and the Surplus of Meaning* (Fort Worth: Texas Christian University Press, 1976), 92.

44. Ibid., 92.

45. Ibid., 55.

46. Kevin Vanhoozer's *Biblical Narrative in the Philosophy of Paul Ricoeur* (New York: Cambridge University Press, 1990) has a great line where he

paraphrases Ricoeur's take on how narrative remakes the world of the reader: "fictions remake the only world that matters, the only world that I care about—*my* world" (89).

47. It seems worthwhile to note the expansion, in the last twenty-five years, of the category of aesthetics to include a much wider range of materials beyond those that aim at beautiful representation (e.g., Kant) or produce aesthetic abstraction (e.g., Gadamer, though he worked to restore art to concrete situations; see Viladesau, *Theological Aesthetics*, 143). Within and beyond Gadamer's reinclusion of art in its horizons and contexts, Frank Burch Brown and others have noted a much wider range of the aesthetic altogether. This present argument, naturally, works toward as broad a conception of text as possible.

48. I'm pursuing this argument from within a few examples of literary theory and hermeneutics. For an angle more within the analytic philosophy of language, see Kevin W. Hector's *Theology Without Metaphysics: God, Language, and the Spirit of Recognition* (New York: Cambridge University Press, 2011) for an analytic theology of how meaning-making and truth in language are grounded in "God's being-with-us." One relevant section: "The properly theological meaning of a concept is the product of a normative trajectory carried on by a series of precedents which are themselves normed by God's being-with-us, and this normativity is carried on by Christ's normative Spirit—yet given that the Spirit is itself carried on through an ongoing process of intersubjective recognition, it follows that meaning's answerability to God is not incompatible with its answerability to human persons, since the norms implicit in one's recognitions have been mediated by, and in turn mediate, the normative Spirit by which meaning is to be judged" (145).

49. Steven Knapp and Walter Benn Michaels, "Against Theory," in *Against Theory: Literary Studies and the New Pragmatism*, ed. W. J. T. Mitchell (Chicago: University of Chicago Press, 1982), 11–30.

# 2

---

# Reading for the Future of the Word

In the last chapter, I showed how the book of Matthew depicts Jesus as bringing forward—cultivating, if you will—the future of the word, in part through the series of parables in Matthew 13. The last of the great assemblage that features the parable of the sower, the parable of the mustard seed, the wheat and tares, the treasure in the field, the pearl of great price, and the parable of the net is a diminutive sentence about "the scribe trained for the kingdom of heaven" (Matt. 13:52). The scribe, Jesus says, is like a "master of a household," who "brings out of his treasure what is new and what is old" (Matt. 13:52). The whole group of parables—but perhaps most centrally this last tiny parable—establishes Jesus as the model and authoritative scribe of the kingdom. Unlike the scribes of the day, Jesus has brought out the kingdom of the new community from within the promises set forth in the prophets. Jesus reorients and reenacts and reinterprets the prophets, expanding the kingdom in listeners' ears and hearts through the telling and interpreting of parables.

Those parables, particularly but not only the scribe for the kingdom, not only reveal the kingdom and its growth, but also offer the disciples a sense of the appropriate response to the kingdom: they should treasure it. Followers of the kingdom listen, seek understanding of the unfathomable, and, ultimately, sell everything to get it.

The treasure referred to in the parable of the scribe trained for the kingdom may find its source in Jesus' first experience of treasure. As a toddler, Jesus received eminent visitors, the magi, who opened *their* ancient treasures and offered them as a gift of worship, for the growth and nourishment of the newer-born treasure. Matthew tells us that "entering the house, [the magi] saw the child with Mary his mother, and they knelt down and paid him homage. Then, opening their treasure chests, they offered him gifts of gold, frankincense, and myrrh" (Matt. 2:11). The word "treasure" in the story, the same as the word in the parable of the scribe for the kingdom, is the felicitous Greek word *thesauros* from which we get our cognate, that treasure chest of words. The magi show the ultimate act of treasuring when they bring out their treasures, but give them up in worship for the greater treasure. They are perhaps the first scribes trained for the kingdom.

Or perhaps not the very first. Mary, explicitly mentioned as being with Jesus when the magi enter the house and open their treasure chests, had been treasuring and sustaining the Christ child with her own body for some time before the magi. Mary receives from God the treasure of the kingdom—through literal receipt of Christ's body within her own and through the receipt of the magic treasure. She stewards the treasure for the growth of the kingdom. Mary presents, along with the magi, a metaphoric image, what participation in the future of the word might look like. The Gospel of Luke links Mary's treasuring of the kingdom more directly with the treasuring of language qua language. Mary receives the angel's message of her impending pregnancy and then, later, the testimony of God's revelation to the shepherds, by carefully treasuring their words: she "was much perplexed by his words and pondered what sort of greeting this might be" (Luke 1:29), and she "treasured all these words and pondered them in her heart" (Luke 2:19). In the case of receiving the treasure of the magi, Mary presumably stewarded it with her husband for the care and nourishment of Jesus. With the verbal messages, Mary yet does something similar: she receives the revelations of language and values them through the careful stewardship of ponderous thought. Her own verbal response to the revelation, the Magnificat, might be, too, its own treasuring and cultivation of Old Testament text—the speech of Hannah in 1 Samuel 2.

This book seeks to make the claim that texts have futures in the kingdom of God, and that the kingdom of God ought to reshape how we think about what we do with and to text. In the introduction, I argued from a theological standpoint that some contemporary ideas about reading, both those that seek to avoid use or revel in use, open up an eschatological chasm—a hunger for a more ultimate future of the word to which we might relate reading. The first chapter developed that textual eschatology, showing how the future of Jesus makes possible the future of the world and the future of the text. In this chapter, I argue that the work of God in the world—both at creation and in the establishment of the church—undergirds human participation in the future of the word. I also offer several angles on that participation, picturing how the Holy Spirit might work through people in treasuring and cultivating the future of the word for the kingdom of God.

## Foundations for Participation:
## Anthropologies of Creation and New Creation

A theological anthropology may offer a window into people's participation in texts' futures for the kingdom of God. The anthropology of creation, the way humans are created by the triune God, warrants their participation in the development of the world, including (and particularly) texts. The anthropology of *new* creation, the way that God sets up the church as the body of Christ in the time of the not yet, shows how the Holy Spirit works in the world through people to make all things new, including (and particularly) texts. While believers will be especially affirmed in participation by the theology of the church, that theology does not exclude nonbelievers, for ecclesiology tells us about the work of the Holy Spirit, work that is of a piece with God's cosmic work. Ecclesiology is particularly pertinent here, though, because it gives us a sense of God's design for human relationship to the kingdom of God.

The cultural mandate is a starting point for an argument advancing our participation in the future of the word out of an anthropology of creation. Genesis 2:15, "The Lord God took the man and put him in the garden of Eden to till it and keep it," expresses the purpose for human presence in the garden, and for many, it founds the concept of human vocation.[1] The verse allots to humans a participatory role in the upkeep and development of God's created world, or, as I describe it in chapter 1, a role participating in the becoming betweenness of God's love as it bears up and bears upon and bears with the created world.

The divine plan for human participation is visible in God's prelapsarian gift of work to humans, namely, the garden's cultivation and upkeep. Scholars have suggested that the Gen. 2:15 mandate conflates agricultural and sacred labors; this leads to a sense that the caring for land, particularly sacred space, has a priestly and even cosmic function, that even the work and keeping of the ground has in this setting a grand purpose under God.[2] John Walton writes that "the point of caring for sacred space should be seen as much more than landscaping or even priestly duties. Maintaining order made one a participant with God in the ongoing task of sustaining the equilibrium God had established in the cosmos."[3] Reading Gen. 2:15 in the context of Sumerian and Babylonian creation myths illuminates how a Judeo-Christian conception of human engagement with the created world is sourced in and participates in the work of God who creates and sustains the world. The tilling and keeping of Eden's garden, as Claus Westermann has shown, is both like and unlike other ancient near eastern mythic conceptions of human work. Many ancient creation myths show humans tasked with maintaining the realm of the gods and perhaps of relieving the gods of their work. The key difference in Genesis is the extent to which human work is directed toward the flourishing of the *human* world (as sacred space, perhaps), rather than toward the flourishing of a separate, distinct realm of the gods.[4] In the Genesis myth, for humans to act such that the created world flourishes as sacred space to God's glory and to act such that God's inter-responsive love expands is in utter concert with God's ongoing upholding and involvement with his creation. God is omnipresent and omnipotent creator and sustainer, whose creation is pattern and source for human behavior—and God's Sabbath is only one example of this.

The sustenance of the cosmos in which humans may participate is never closed or static, but rather a continual making and making new—where people participate in the work of the creator. The verb for "keep" in Gen. 2:15 contains the sense of guarding, an active preservation. But, when the verse stipulates that humans *till* and keep, rather than just keep, it indicates that humans will be involved in facilitating new growth and fruitfulness for the world, rather than simply maintaining or preserving the creation.[5]

This pattern of receiving, sustaining, and responding naturally indicates how an *author* might participate in the becoming-betweenness of meaning-making. John Milbank has argued as much in *Being Reconciled: Ontology and Pardon*, summing up his position in a disquisition on *methexïs*, or performed participation, in the divine: "Not only do being and knowledge participate in a God who is and who comprehends; also human making participates in a God who is infinite poetic utterance: the second person of the Trinity."[6] The divine author, God, grants some measure of authority or making to human authors; they are intersubjectively responsible and not responsible for their words and works via context and community. But, as I argued in chapter 1, God not only makes, but also interprets and orders his creation. This, too, is work in which we may participate, and it is the work of reading. It is a way in which humans participate in the development of all creation toward that eschatological purpose.[7] The cultural mandate of Genesis offers us, I think, a few ideas about what participation in the future of the word may look like: (1) the causing of something to be fruitful in its cultivation—this as a dynamic process of making new; (2) the guarding of a thing for its possibilities of future fruitfulness.[8] Many activities associated with reading may lend themselves to these sorts of cultivating and keeping; in this chapter I'll offer thoughts about preservation, utterance, translation, and response.

The second foundation for human participation in the future of the word is an eschatological ecclesiology, or, an anthropology of the new creation. The work of the Holy Spirit in the church confirms that God's creative actions are ongoing: God's making of the church parallels God's creation in Genesis 1, for the church is called out of darkness (as the term *ekklesia* indicates) into God's light. Through the expansion of God's creative and community-building love, the church emerges as the new creation. The church is made possible by the new creation in Christ's blood, and it is also the sign and guarantee of the new creation, insofar as it is sustained (and constituted, as John Zizioulas points out) by the Holy Spirit.[9] The church is, by grace, a part of God's means for bringing the kingdom of God into future being and fulfillment. The Spirit's work in the church, so richly described in biblical texts, demonstrates God's ongoing commitment to human participation in the love of the Trinity. In biblical accounts of church, we find that our participation in the church contributes to the becoming of all creation, as God judges and purifies us—and all creation with us. As Grenz has written, "Insofar as the future is open, God summons humans to participate in his program in creating that future. God's future will surely come, but we are invited to be involved in his historical work, bringing it to pass."[10] For instance, when we obey the injunction from the book of Hebrews to not neglect the gathering together of believers for encouragement, we are drawn into that community's bondage-breaking and justice-making, and we accept God's invitation to be involved in God's work in the world.

Yet, as the eschatologically minded discourse of 2 Peter reminds us, our paltry participation in God's work in the world is far inferior to the power and holiness of God. Our joining in his work is so inferior to the divine as to be expressed in an interrogative rather than a declarative: "Since all these things are to be dissolved in this way, what sort of persons ought you to be in leading lives of holiness and godliness, waiting for and hastening the coming of the day of God, because of which the heavens will be set ablaze and dissolved, and the elements will melt with fire? But, in accordance with his promise, we wait for new heavens and a new earth, where righteousness is at home" (2 Pet. 3:11-13). Our participation is a hopeful action, a life of holiness and hopeful hesitation, a life of active waiting.

Fascinatingly, in Peter's account of the right sort of participation in the love and work of the Trinity, the interpretation of texts comes up. The active patience of the hopeful believer who is engaged in kingdom work is linked to the interpretation of texts—in this case the interpretation and misinterpretation of Paul's letters. Peter points out that "there are some things in [Paul's letters] hard to understand, which the ignorant and unstable twist to their own destruction, as they do the other scriptures" (2 Pet. 3:16). But, Peter continues, the beloved community should not do so, but should instead be maintained in stability by keeping on their guard and "grow[ing] in the grace and knowledge of our Lord and Savior Jesus Christ" (2 Pet. 3:18). Their own growth in the grace and knowledge of the word, Christ, will facilitate their reading the written word well. And in this case, reading the word well emerges out of *growing* grace and knowledge—the expansion of God's work in the world. Such growth in grace will help the church to interpret the Lord's delay in coming as patience and salvation effected by Christ, but also to "hasten" his coming by their own grace-given godliness and holiness. Interpreting well—particularly interpreting the revelation such that it causes the growth and becoming of the word in the body, what the text calls the "wisdom given" Paul (2 Pet. 3:15)—will be part of the church's future in the kingdom of God as they remain in the Spirit.

This idea of the church illuminates particular aspects of textual futurity, too, even beyond its general reinforcement of the not-yet, becoming quality of the whole creation. In particular, ecclesiology adds to our eschatological focus a more fully rendered theology of community. Beyond the created person's inherent exocentric openness to the world, a doctrine of the church as community invigorates and reorients our sense of how all of creation—and particularly how texts—become. It reinforces the communal nature of interpretive becoming—the becoming-between of the Trinity is invoked—metonymically—in the way that texts become between people. The world becomes, not just through the engagement of the individual human cultivator with it, but also through the communal engagement of the church in love. And so we must think about the communal mode of interpretation as central to a future of the word.

As a corollary to this, the doctrine of the church that begins at Pentecost with the arrival of the Holy Spirit suggests that the work of bearing witness to the revelation of God is profoundly diverse, translational, and radically expansive. As the church is always crossing boundaries in the act of breaking walls between people and building relationships between them, so also is—must be—reading's work of making meaning through the work of the Holy Spirit. The church's sign of the spirit, the sign of Christ's future in the word, is the sign of tongues in Acts. And the offering and interpretation of tongues is part of the proclamation and bearing witness to the glory of God in the world. Thinking of the doctrine of the church in this way helps us to think about reading, reorienting to the centrality of translation in its traditional and metaphoric senses for our understanding of how texts mean—in between people and also within and mediated by cultures. This means that the future of texts, which is always a crossing of contested territory, will be above all cultivated through reconciliation and peacemaking, as I will describe more fully in chapter 4.

So, ecclesiology, which shows us how God works in the world through the church, helps us think through the future of text, but the kingdom of God exceeds the church insofar as it has cosmic reach and insofar as it is prior to (and generative of) the church.[11] The Spirit's work in the world is of a piece with the work of the Spirit in the church, and so the ways that texts become toward their futures in the kingdom of God are visible outside the church even as they are visible through the theology of the church. That I'm arguing from an eschatological ecclesiology to emphasize the centrality of community in the becoming of the text should not be taken as an assertion that texts become only through readers in church book clubs—or only through Christians. Far from it. God's purposes for the cosmos are cosmic in scope. And while the church is the bride of Christ, yet the word that created all things is at work in all texts, just as the word that created all things sustains the viability of seed, regardless of the faith of the farmer.

Scot McKnight and others have taken a strong line against this sort of idea, asserting that there is no kingdom of God without the church—perhaps because of scholars too ready to label any politics they agree with as kingdom justice. The warning is fair: assigning various political movements or world events to the glory-of-the-coming-of-the-Lord category of events—and especially assigning them to the trampling-out-the-vintage-where-the-grapes-of-wrath-are-stored category of events—is a tricky business, and is liable to earn the rebuke meted out to Job's friends. Yet the kingdom of God responds to the groaning of all creation. God's divinely ordained meaning-making capacities in languages—the hum of multiplicity and more love in how language differentiates and cultivates significance—is something that many readers, Christian and not, can see.

The fact that we fail at seeing these things, that our interpretations may perpetrate violence against a text, and so on, is only more evidence of the Lord's grace is granting us participation in the love of the Trinity, through existence and in the body of Christ. That same grace is offered to us who are granted the privilege of literacy. Meaning-making through reading, after all, is another testimony of the attributes of the invisible God being clearly seen in what has been made (Rom. 1:20). That we fall into idolatry is undeniable—in reading and the rest of life: the image in Romans of exchanging "the glory of the immortal God for images resembling a mortal human being or birds or four-footed animals or reptiles" is as aesthetic and poetic as it is magic and earthen (Rom. 1:23). It harkens back to the idolatries of both noninstrumental and instrumental reading discussed in the introduction. God will bring the entire cosmos into the beloved community of the new creation through the purification and repurposing work of judgment—as idolatry and violence and sin and death become the nothing to which they have always pointed. God's judgment will differentiate those who seek the glory of God from those who seek the nothingness of their own glory. But text may be cultivated by anyone; its becoming gives glory to the God of all meaning-making regardless. The special office of the reader in the body of Christ is the express veneration of the word—is, in short, praise.

## Angles on Participation

This book seeks understanding of how reading may participate in the future of the word; it is not seeking to be especially normative or prescriptive or even innovative in proposing metaphors or methods for reading. These and other kinds of engagement with text already exist in the world, from a host of cultures, spaces, and theoretical commitments. They should be seen for what they may be: a cultivation and keeping of texts for their futures in the kingdom of God. The angles gathered here should be considered only an assemblage of possible connections, moments when we may keep our eyes open for the work of the Spirit as it broadcasts its call in the world. There is no attempt here to flesh out these ideas as fully as warranted, nor to systematize them into an ontology of becoming. These angles often overlap with one another, but each offers something to the discussion, if only by giving a sense of the extreme variety—and thus perhaps freedom—of approaches to the future of the word. Omissions are future opportunities. As for those present here, they share qualities of becoming, betweenness, and bearing witness.[12]

## Preservation

The dangers surrounding the futures of text can in part be articulated in terms of their survival or ongoing accessibility for reading. Franco Moretti's "Slaughterhouse of Literature," a fascinating Darwinian account of how detective-fiction authors' formal decisions played a hand in the evolution of the detective story as genre and the survival of their texts—in a way that they could not have anticipated from their lonely scrivening tables—states that the vast majority of literary texts are certainly lost to most of even the very interested and highly trained reading audiences. According to Moretti's conservative figure, 99.5 percent of nineteenth-century literary texts alone are basically absent from any safe canonical posterity of readership.[13] This means that not only grocery lists and outdated car repair manuals seem in danger of being lost to readers and meaning-making, but the very greatest number of books meant to be guaranteed some sort of stable ongoing existence in the world are, in fact, fast-tracked to loss and oblivion.

In the Gen. 2:15 mandate, the "keeping" part of "to till and keep" is a Hebrew term that involves the sense of guarding or protecting against danger. Preservation of the text may involve a range of actions against such loss, or against corruption of the text, and for community in the future of the text. These may include acts of scholarly service, such as textual editing or textual criticism, digital rendering and scanning, librarianship, or curation for various audiences, digital and otherwise. It may be more specialized, as in private collecting.

The link between librarianship and preservation of text for the future of the word has already begun to be noted by Christian librarians. Gregory A. Smith, in "A Rationale for Integrating Christian Faith and Librarianship," has argued that the work of librarians has benefited the propagation of the Christian faith—has, in a sense, nurtured the future of the word through preservation of texts.[14] Others link librarianship to the future of the word through to the concept of community—in that in libraries, communities share ideas and resources over time, which develop into the sifting and winnowing of truth and the growth of people and ministries.[15] In days of older library circulation systems, a record of the becoming of a text in a community might be read from the names and dates marked in the sign-out cards in the pockets of all the covers of the books. Community may even occur in what might be considered out-of-bounds behavior in libraries, the passing along of illicitly written marginalia. A consideration of librarianship as a sort of reading that facilitates the future of the word offers a sense that no collection is solely a repository of the past, which in a collection of texts is a space of hope and future through the building of community around and in text.

A retired librarian and rare book collector I know, Edward Blankman, would take issue with these scholars' valorization of the space of the library as a space for the preservation of books at least—community aside. With a collection that numbers in the many thousands of rare books, and a full career working in and with libraries and book dealers, Blankman is in something of a position to know about the fate of books in both circles. His last will and testament's stipulations for his large collection, he tells me, encapsulate his position: *none* of his books may ever end up in libraries. Libraries, he tells me darkly, and I envision his decades of at times painful curation of the collections at the local high school with students' grubby hands and errant pencils (including my own) defacing the treasures of the kingdom, libraries are where books go to die. No idealist, Blankman knows collections must be culled as needs of libraries and patrons change, yet, he says, there isn't sufficient knowledge among many to be able to know what to save when readers' tastes change. He tells me of being pressed into service at the Flower Memorial Library in Watertown, New York to thin their stacks, being horrified at what books had been placed on the chopping block. Blankman practices another sort of preservation in his collection of physical copies of rare books, in dust jackets, on subjects that interest him—and perhaps another sort of community, too, though perhaps the world of book buying and selling may be less a sharing than an economic transaction of sorts. Nicholas Basbanes's classic work on book collecting, *A Gentle Madness*, has demonstrated that the work of collecting had, in times before the vast proliferation of printed material, been almost certainly tied to the preservation of manuscripts or early printed copies against what seemed like irretrievable loss. Yet of course other, personal, acquisitive motives no doubt played a role as well. But even so, even infused with unflagging desire for possession, the work of collecting—in personal collections or libraries—*may*, despite this, concurrently make possible a work's future and becoming.

Alice Walker's storied pilgrimage to find and mark Zora Neale Hurston's gravesite offers a more particular example of preservation and the future of the text through the recovery of out-of-print texts. Walker's journey, even though her marker was less accurately than devotedly placed, revitalized interest in Hurston's texts and facilitated her work's entrance into the reading of the next generation. The act of designating and marking a grave for a human body—and then writing about it in a nationally circulating women's magazine—ended up facilitating a resurrection of the body of Hurston's works, the manuscripts of which had themselves been barely rescued from a clean-up fire by a police deputy a few days after her death.[16] The search for what Walker called elsewhere "our mothers' gardens," precipitated the widespread interest in the literature—and offered to generations since the great majority of Hurston's written works, most especially *Their Eyes Were Watching God*.[17] That novel is now routinely taught and read in American secondary school and college, even though Hurston was roundly critiqued during her own day by fellow writers, and even by her audience, for her politics, craft, and relationship to white patrons. Her work has been brought forward by Walker's act, which amounts to the preservation of possibility—the allowing of space and time for the text to be made replete with readings and meaning. And Walker's preservation, in solidarity with like acts by other scholars and writers, established a tradition of black women's writing. Now, Hurston's personal star may rise and fall—and it is certain that it is as an individual that Hurston sets her works forth for literary posterity. Views of the quality or centrality of her work may wax and wane; perhaps she is only temporarily set at the center of a canon of black women's or feminist writing. Hurston herself said—as one of her recent biographers noted, "God balances the sheet in time"—and that is true of all works.[18] Our reading isn't the salvation or damnation of a text, neither its end nor beginning. But we get to have a part in keeping the text going.

One of my colleagues has suggested from time to time in conversation with me that the number of important historical authors or texts to rediscover like that within literary history is—and ought to be remembered as—limited in number, especially for eras when the scope of education or leisure for minorities and women was more limited. There are, in this view, only so many literary discoveries or recoveries left to be made—or *worth* making. My colleague is right in that there is a theoretical limit on the number of recoverable texts, and I don't mean to suggest that we are all enjoined as scholars to recover texts this way. But to the extent that we do participate in such acts of recovery or preservation, the snippets of future that we offer to texts in our present remembering of them form spaces that fit into the larger unfolding of God's future for the text, for the reader, and for the world subject to his kingdom. And, our metrics for worth are by no means coterminous with divine standards. A pragmatic approach to time and valuation masks the utter upending and reversal within the divine economy of both.

There is, of course, a never-ending supply of texts that seem *meant* to be temporary (remember the issue of grocery lists and car repair manuals), which may contribute to the future of other writing. Examples of this might include drafts of a work, or the writing surrounding a piece of writing in progress. Flannery O'Connor, for example, is said to have written ten times as many pages as ended up in the books themselves. A novelist friend of mine has stacks of material in a file cabinet in her garage—preliminary material from pieces that she's written over the last fifteen years, untouched since the works' publications. Sometimes, in messy times, she considers divesting her family of the baggage. Her preservation of it functions as not only the future of the texts that she's written and published insofar as those materials may be useful in future to scholars. Even now, the presence of those materials also offers her the future of her own work, as it reminds her, through a physical obstacle, of the great volume of labor that goes into any finished piece. It forms a kind of encouragement toward perseverance, through the reminder of past efforts.

A special collections librarian once told me that one of the most important aspects of his job is to throw things away, so that representative examples of authors' papers and of historical material are visible and shaped and may assist others in their future works. There may be considerable debate as to whether keeping or discarding things may amount to better preservation and cultivation of the future of the text, yet it is possible that both actions have some share in the future of the word. And the librarian's position seems another angle on the thought that in textual editing or special collections, there may be as many variants or less-valuable material to be rejected as material to be approved and accepted. Yet the variants of a text may even be meaningful from within the mess that they make, establishing a record of possibility, reading, and even error for the text. These surely draw attention to an intoxicating textual liquidity, one even more meaningful in a digital age.

Even prior to a time when digital preservation is more or less assumed, in the work, for instance, of poet Marianne Moore, we see the preservation of variation as interpretively rich. Moore approved of multiple versions of her poems being in print at the same time, and even footnoted alternate versions of her famous lyric "Poetry" in her 1967 *Complete Poems*. Interestingly, she intentionally created the poem to be *in*complete in the final version by discarding material in a move that, for scholars, basically constitutes an invitation to find the missing pieces.[19] The final version was only three lines of a poem that was more than twenty lines in some versions: "I, too, dislike it. / Reading it, however, with a perfect contempt for it, one discovers in / it, after all, a place for the genuine."[20] The other versions of the poem, which exist in footnotes and other publications, actually function as interlocutors for the final version—so many ghosts that aren't actually lost or dead. Even the discarded material lives in the subtext of the poem and functions as a place for exploring the inter-resonance of the work. For Moore's work, textual multiplicity through variation was and is productive in its messiness. The poem's longer version insists on the importance of all the ephemera: that "'business documents and // school books' . . . are important," that "all these phenomena are important" provided that imagination is added to them.[21] Despite the annoyance of what could be made by half-poets, "Reading [poetry], however, with a perfect contempt for it, one discovers in // it, after all, a place for the genuine." The space surrounding the shortest version is packed full of words and things that don't ever really disappear. Moore was an inveterate collector of all manner of snippets and tidbits that made their way, scraplike, almost inexplicably, into poetry—and first into her notebooks: she scoured pamphlets, observations from scientific material in museums and books, and shards of conversation, sometimes with inexplicable or rabbit-trail-like attribution and citation. Everything could be important, could make itself into poetry. And poetry itself could be fluctuating, could have its own future-making. The energy of motion between the textual versions, between the material and the imaginative construction, is an energy for Moore, not so much of an unstoppable progress, but rather a sort of possibility that emerges in the conversation between the versions.

Yet how ought we proceed in deciding what to preserve? For Moore, the miscellany of her wide observation seems to be marshaled by her commitment to absolute precision in observation and a certain moral sense, perhaps joined with the stalwartness of a Presbyterian upbringing. Her choices seem, however, singularly personal as well, based on interest and inquisitiveness. Readers confronting the massively more available records, texts, and miscellany of all kinds from the past in a digital age may have as difficult a time knowing how to confront the amount of information for the work of preservation in reading and collecting as Moore had in writing the poetry. Alan Jacobs, in *The Pleasures of Reading in an Age of Distraction*, has suggested whimsy as one approach to managing the excess; I suspect Moore would approve.[22]

Even literary whimsy may be fruitfully placed into an eschatological context, as God deals out his kingdom-bringing grace and redemption to the world at large in and through individual predilection as well as networks of connection. As Walter Benjamin has written in "Theses on the Philosophy of History,"

> A chronicler who recites events without distinguishing between major and minor ones acts in accordance with the following truth: nothing that has ever happened should be regarded as lost for history. To be sure, only a redeemed mankind receives the fullness of its past—which is to say, only for a redeemed mankind has its past become citable in all its moments. Each moment it has lived becomes a *citation à l'ordre du jour*—and that day is Judgment Day."[23]

For, as Benjamin notes, "every second of time was the straight gate through which the Messiah might enter."[24] Theoretically speaking, any text at any time may implicitly offer the lineaments of the future of the word of God—or may serve as an occasion for the bearing of fruit of the kingdom. While human limitation will naturally bound what is desirable or possible in this regard, the omniscience and omnipotence of God redeems both time and text—the redemption, through transformation and judgment, of all texts.

It seems there is little reason to suspect that every jot and tittle are not accounted for by some means in the purposes of God. Our own accountings, riddled as they are with idolatry, corruption, and the exchange of power, are somewhat different. In the light of God's care for jots and tittles—the sparrows of language do not fall without his knowledge—we are enjoined to proceed with humility, to rely on the wisdom of the word, and to not neglect the community that may find in whatever language the revelation of the word.

## Utterance

With the word, God spoke the world into being, and in the death and resurrection of the word of God, God speaks forth the making new of all things. Likewise, in our own contexts, utterance, the speaking forth of the word, is a powerful avenue for the cultivation and keeping of the text, a making new, of time and place. Utterance is a saying or telling of a text, reissuing it in space or time. Quotation, in part or in whole; the conscious thinking of a text, planned or spontaneous; printing and reprinting: utterance is both a function of preservation and a making new, as contextual differences renew the word and world in the iterations of the text.

Leslie Marmon Silko's exploration of Pueblo storytelling as ceremony links utterance—even thought utterance—to the becoming of a world. Since a storytelling is a ceremony, even the imagination of a story is a making of that story into a community, making the community's future out of the past. The stories that create the Laguna people, she says, are constantly told and retold—not merely ancient stories, but more contemporary ones, too, and these are braided, past and present, into the mythic story that creates, sustains, and heals the community in its telling.

> So in the telling (and you will hear a few of the dimensions of this telling) first of all, as mentioned earlier, the storytelling always includes the audience, the listeners. In fact, a great deal of the story is believed to be inside the listener; the storyteller's role is to draw the story out of the listeners. The storytelling continues from generation to generation. Basically, the origin story constructs our identity—within this story, we know who we are. We are the Lagunas. This is where we come from. We came this way. We came by this place. And so from the time we are very young, we hear these stories, so that when we go out into the world, when one asks who we are, or where we are from, we

immediately know: we are the people who came from the north. We are the people of these stories.[25]

Silko's 1977 novel *Ceremony* is a telling, an utterance of the mythic story of Thought Woman, which includes not only the mythic world of Hummingbird, Fly, Reed Woman, and Corn Woman, but also the struggles of psychologically broken soldiers returning from WWII. The main character, Tayo, goes on a quest for healing; his story is inseparable from the story of the land and the stories of his people. Even the ugly stories, indeed, all the stories, are woven in. The story's telling is a ceremony of healing for Tayo, for the land, and for the Laguna people.[26]

Yet, Silko emphasizes, the telling is a lively, changing thing. The stories of contemporary or more recent history feed into the utterance of the larger story, which is kept alive and becoming as it keeps its people alive and becoming. In *Ceremony*, one of the wisest of medicine men, Betonie, offers insight into why the traditional skull ceremony hadn't worked to Tayo as the elders had hoped:

> [T]hings which don't shift and grow are dead things. They are things the witchery people want. Witchery works to scare people, to make them fear growth. But it has always been necessary, and more than ever now, it is. Otherwise we won't make it. We won't survive. That's what the witchery is counting on: that we will cling to the ceremonies the way they were, and then their power will triumph, and the people will be no more."[27]

Gertrude Stein has had something to say about how utterance or reading of a thing results in its becoming and differentiation. Her work offers another shade of utterance. Her experimental long poem, *Tender Buttons*, for instance, results from an occasion of utterance:

> And then, something happened, and I began to discover the names of things, that is not discover the names but discover the things the things to see the things to look at and in so doing I had of course to name them

not to give them new names but to see that I could find out how to know that they were there by their names or by replacing their names. And how was I to do so? They had their names and naturally I called them by the names they had and in doing so having begun looking at them I called them by their names with passion and that made poetry, I did not mean it to make poetry but it did, it made the Tender Buttons.[28]

This difficult passage, quintessential Stein, demonstrates the extent to which her reading of the relationship between language and things, her utterance of the names, offers a new way of seeing. The first "button" in the poem, "A Carafe, That Is a Blind Glass," refers to this new way as a "spreading" difference that will reorder the seeing of the whole system of language: "A kind in glass and a cousin, a spectacle and nothing strange a single hurt color and an arrangement in a system to pointing. All this and not ordinary, not unordered in not resembling. The difference is spreading."[29] For Stein, the calling of the thing by its name produces a new way of seeing that will cause everything to look new.

Stein's writing is famous—and infamous, even—for use of repetition, her views that also help us understand utterance as one avenue toward the future of the word. For repetition of a text is not the issuing forth of a static equivalent instance of the text, as might be assumed. In "Portraits and Repetitions," Stein writes a number of sentences that call into question assumptions about repetition:

> Is there repetition or is there insistence. I am inclined to believe there is no such thing as repetition. And really how can there be.[30]

Expressing any thing there can be no repetition because the essence of that expression is insistence, and if you insist you must each time use emphasis and if you use emphasis it is not possible while anybody is alive that they should use exactly the same emphasis.[31]

For Stein, repetition is, strictly speaking, not possible; every utterance is a making new. If we understand repetition as a tool of the writer for creating a dynamic work, we might also extend such powers to include the reader. The simple reading, silent or aloud; the quotation; the scan: these form a sort of emphasis that resists the closure or death of a work, even when the work itself seems to insist on such closure.

During the 1970s and 80s, several writers that literary historians have loosely grouped under the heading of the Language poets sought to, as Lyn Hejinian describes it, reject the closure implied by many sorts of text and seek the openness possible within language's materiality.[32] Hejinian strongly critiques what she calls the closed text—and recommends instead an approach to writing text that insists on the vastness of the undifferentiated world and then also differentiates within it: "What saves this from becoming a vast undifferentiated mass of data and situation is one's ability to make distinctions. The open text is one which both acknowledges the vastness of the world and is formally differentiating. It is form that provides an opening."[33] Hejinian critiques "[t]he coercive, epiphanic mode in some contemporary lyric poetry . . . with its smug pretension to universality and its tendency to cast the poet as guardian to Truth. And detective fiction can serve as a positive model, presenting an ultimately stable, calm and calming (and fundamentally unepiphanic) vision of the world. In either case, however pleasurable its effects, closure is a fiction, one of the amenities that falsehood and fantasy provide."[34] While I disagree with Hejinian's implication that an open text is at odds with truth—especially the ultimate truth of Christ—it seems to me that it is not, or not only, in *writing* that one makes an open text. Rather, it is the act of reading, construed broadly, that cracks open the text, that fuels its dynamism in and becoming. A text becomes experimental when readers experiment with it. Readers bring texts into new spaces and times and groups; techniques and styles, after all, flash in their pans. Utterance, even repetitive utterance, can never be sameness, even at the edges of stupefaction.[35]

Utterance may particularly contribute to the future of the word by means of providing a communally constituted refusal to halt a text in finality or totality. In every reading, provided the readings continue, we have a refusal of stasis or closure in meaning-making, a refusal of death or ending. That is, we find in reading the *repletion* that comes with an assumption of meaningfulness, but are not, reading, able to assess the *completion* of meaning. In the uttering or reading of a text, we may approach, at least metaphorically, what Emmanuel Levinas would call the *saying*. In *Totality and Infinity*, Levinas argued that the ontology, the work of determining the essence of things, registers a totalizing and violent force toward the other.[36] Ontology, being the foundation of totality, is the foundation of war itself. In *Otherwise Than Being, or Beyond Essence*, Levinasclarifies a bit how we may deal with the problem of ontology in our approach of the other through the complex interplay between the *said* and the *saying* in the act of communication. For Levinas, the *said* is the thematization of the other, the assignation of teleology. The *said* makes possible the ontological assertion of the judgment of the essence of a thing, or its monstration. The said may be—at least in part—associated with what is written, insofar as the written text has some qualities of boundedness and sign. The *saying*, however, is the inexhaustible surplus that arises out of the *said*. It is the posture of approach to the absolute otherness of the other, a posture that grants the other "signifyingness," but so much so that the signifying will exceed whatever significance might be particularly articulated or thematized in the *said*. Thus *saying* for Levinas is not a signing of the other, but an opening to the other in vulnerability. In *saying*, we are utterly responsible for the other in all the other's fullness, knowing that the repletion—indeed excess—of the other can never be something we complete.[37]

According to Levinas, when we read, we discover that "what [the text] is capable of saying goes beyond what it wants to say; that it contains more than it contains; that perhaps an inexhaustible surplus of meaning remains locked in the syntactic structures of the sentence, in its word-groups, its actual words, phonemes and letters, in all this materiality of the saying which is potentially signifying all the time."[38] For Levinas, exegesis is a way of freeing the significance that is in the *saying* of the sign. And yet, the sign itself contains the trace of the saying. Utterance itself, the continuation of it, resists the ontologizing violence and closed-downness of the said. Utterance may be prior to exegesis but display even greater revelation of the saying, for the act—the telling, the performance—amplifies the excess of the saying within the said and grants it a future. For Levinas, the *saying* itself isn't quite accessible, since accessing its particularity would only be an accessing of the *said* that houses the trace of the saying. But it may be that across time or space, the *saying* that I'm here linking with reading becomes the passivity, the noninsistence of patience that believers are enjoined to have in 2 Peter. Utterance may be our patience with the sovereignty of the Lord in the face of the other that we cannot know and yet may commune with in the love of the Trinity. As a form of participation in the future of the word, the patience of utterance allows that the completion of the text's inexhaustible surplus, the completion of the *saying* within its *said*, comes from the necessary rescue of the word of God.

## Translation

Lamin Sanneh has shown in *Translating the Message* that translation—both literal translation of the biblical message and figurative translation of the structures and contents of faith—has been historically and theologically bound up with the expansion and future of the Christian faith. He writes that the earliest translations and movements of Christianity were focused on the decentralization of the ethno-political dominance of Jewishness as the medium of the Christian faith as such and the destigmatization of the Gentile elements of Christianity. For Sanneh, Christianity's radical insistence on taking shape within specific contexts—multiple times, spaces, and languages—critiques ethnocentric insistence on the culture that brings the message, "a certain judgment" that involves a rethinking and a reshaping of closely held pieces of dogma.[39] It is also concurrently a balanced approval of whatever in the vernacular receiving culture provides a home to the gospel. Sanneh writes that "the gospel is capable of transcending the cultural inhibitions of the translator and taking root in fresh soil, a piece of transplanting that will challenge the presuppositions of the translator."[40] Indeed, the gospel is cultivated and kept within the spatial, temporal, and linguistic soils of the translated word.

Yet, in a way both larger and more primary, translatability is fundamental to textuality itself. Walter Benjamin has posited that translatability is part of the essence of some texts—that the better a work's language is, the higher the translatability. For Benjamin, translation brings to view the target language's aspiration to the pure language of truth and the ideation of language's ultimate relationality. If a text has no relation or relatability to the pure language, and is instead purely informational, pure language is obscured under the "utter preponderance of content."[41] For Benjamin, the realm of God's imagined translational power, the word made of pure unmediated language, is found most centrally in the prototypical interlinear translatability of scripture. Yet Benjamin's own argument is that the inability of some, most, or even all practitioners to translate a work does not mean that the work is essentially untranslatable, but rather that the translatability is located in another realm—in God's translational locus.

Benjamin argues that translation gives ongoing life to texts. Texts have life, he argues, nonmetaphorically (though inorganically), because they have histories: "The concept of life is given its due only if everything that has a history of its own, and is not merely the setting for history, is credited with life."[42] The more the text exists—not by way of content, but by way of distinction in language—the more it is alive, with its own history and ongoing future; that is, the more it is translatable. Yet, I don't think his argument that life is guaranteed by the possession of a history is enough to prove that "great texts" are more translatable than ordinary ones.[43] It supports a more broadly general argument about text. For if every event, without distinction, is citable in all its moments from the eschatological perspective of judgment day, as Benjamin argues in "Theses on the Philosophy of History," then every language event, every text, has its own history, whether or not anyone knows or cares about it. It has its history, and has its life in God. The text has its life in the word, within the future of the word. In chapter 1, I argued for the word's future within the future of the word of God. The text's being within the word of God, which by Benjamin's assertion is necessarily translatable because it is equivalent to revelation, would garner an essential translatability of texts.

Translatability is a locus for understanding how texts move into their futures in the kingdom of God. It is fundamental as a way that language becomes by movement in space, time, and community.

By means of translation, text expands its reach and life, through the renewal of the word. And, in the history of translation theory, the connection between translation and futurity is an evident theme. Arthur Schopenhauer, in "On Language and Words," argues that "new concepts are created during the process of learning a foreign language to give meaning to new signs."[44] Friedrich Schleiermacher assumes that the bringing of the German language into contact with foreign languages by translation is "just as our soil itself has probably become richer and more fertile, and our climate more lovely and mild after much transplanting of foreign plants, so do we feel that our language, which we practice less because of our Nordic lethargy, can only flourish and develop its own perfect power through the most varied contacts with what is foreign."[45] The adding of something to the language—"a new impulse in the life of the language"—is the goal of all written utterance, and translation of necessity must and does preserve this, but only by means of bringing together the reader and writer in an act that preserves what is foreign of the original without devolving into utter foreignness.[46]

Translation is a fraught, impossible, yet practicable sort of reconciliation founded in the word; it is always already not yet and illuminates the not yet; it brings glory to God in so doing. The word himself makes translation possible. God's eschatological purpose for the cosmos is to build the community of the new creation through the creative love of the three in one; translation of the word—spatial, linguistic, and temporal—is at the heart of the relational multiplicity of language through which the word becomes toward that community. From the multiplication of languages at Babel—providing for humility before God and an earth-wide spread of peoples and tongues to all nations of the blessing through Abraham—to the blessing of tongues at Pentecost, the biblical witness testifies to every tongue's participation in the word, confessing the Lordship of Christ.

But of course, this newness enhanced by translation is complicated by power and the inevitable error, gap, and difficulty of translation. As many tares as grains of wheat are sown in its practice. A reading of older translation theory shows how long this has been the case: Hugo Friedrich describes Roman translation practices, emerging from Quintilian, saying that translation is a striving with the original text: "The goal is to surpass the original and, in doing so, to consider the original as a source of inspiration for the creation of new expressions in one's own language."[47] In this way, translation may be seen as an almost vampiric conquering and feeding off of the lifeblood and language of other cultures that provides a reanimation of one's own language.

And yet, in the very movement from language to language, translation may be seen rather as the baptism of the word in the word, rather than as vampiric sucking, as the judgment of the target language chastens the grasping of the original. Or perhaps, translation is the reconciliation, the mutual repentance, and mutual glory of languages. It is always a penance for the false assumptions of Babel—a building together that is through the word, under the word of God, rather than a unitary falsity of grasping toward the idea that one reading or one way of words is enough. It is a plunging beneath the name of the Father, Son, and Holy Spirit after the tradition of being baptized. For the one that baptizes always also needs baptism : "I need to be baptized by you," John says (Matt. 3:14). And translation, like baptism, always prepares the way of the Lord. It is water baptism's reconciliation and conversion—but it is also the baptism of the Holy Spirit and with fire, a baptism of judgment and tongues. It illuminates language's blanks and blemishes, both rhetorically and propositionally. Bad translation would be a kind of false repentance: false submission, a grasp after power, an insincere apology. Good translation is a conversion and its outward sign—it is a falling in love and surrender. It points, above all, in the sacrifice and difficulty of its own act, to the need for, and possibility of reconciliation and forgiveness.

We may think of all reading as translation of texts. This, however, should not diminish a regard for translation in the frankest of senses as the rendering of one text into a different language and culture as the very concrete creation of space and future for text through a baptismal submission to the word. We are used to, in an American academic setting especially, offering a limited credit to translators for their great sacrifices in translating or retranslating less-available works. But from an eschatological perspective, translation must be among the most powerfully supported acts of cultivation—it is made necessary at Babel and in the tongues of fire in Acts, in the Vulgate and the King James and in the sacred committees at work on the biblical text.

In "Des Tours de Babel," Jacques Derrida makes the provocative comment about translation that the original itself is the first "debtor, the first petitioner" begging out of its own lack of meaningfulness for translation—and doing so all the while proclaiming the difficulty and impossibility of translation because of the uniqueness of its own proper name.[48] This idea—that texts under Babel both demand translation and declare it impossible—Derrida extends to God himself. God grants the divine name to the tower of Babel, according to Derrida, a name that both *means* "confusion" and, in its untranslatability, *causes* confusion. But God also pleads for the translation of God: "God weeps," Derrida writes, "over his name" and "pleads for a translator."[49] In the scattering of Babel's bricks, God pleads for a translator, but then, of course, in the next chapter of Genesis sets in motion the promise of the translator through which all nations on earth will be blessed. God sends a translator—or becomes one. Derrida does not refer to the incarnate Christ as such a translator, who, as word, can intercede through what Derrida sees as God's forbidding of translation at Babel. Yet, translation is the metonym for the reconciliation effected by Christ—it builds on the foundation of the scandalous cornerstone of Christ, making even the new Jerusalem from the clay that, though perhaps yet subject to the fault of being made without straw, yet in the words of Gerard Manley Hopkins is still "immortal diamond."

## Call-and-Response

The pleading of the word, of the text, for translation, overlaps with the idea of the word as *call*, to which any *response* is a synchronic jointure and a diachronic rejoinder. In the shape of call-and-response, we may consider the activities of interpretation, criticism, rewriting, and so on as activities in which the future of the word may hum from Babel to the challenge and reconciliation of Pentecost.

African and African American cultural histories offer multiple structures for thinking about call-and-response participation in the future of the word by bringing out the new and old of the treasure of the text. As Craig Werner has described it,

> Call and response begins with the call of a leader who expresses his/her own voice through the vehicle of a traditional song, story, or image. This call, which provides a communal context for exploration of the "individual" emotion, itself responds to a shared history that suffuses later stages of the process. If the community, as it exists in the ever-changing present, recognizes and shares the experience evoked by the call, it responds with another phrase, again, usually traditional, which may either affirm or present a different perspective on the initial call. Whether it affirms or critiques the initial call, however, the response enables the leader to go on exploring the implications of the material.

Rich in political implications, this cultural form enables both individual and community to define themselves, to validate their experiences in opposition to dominant social forces. When working most effectively, this process requires individuals not to seek a synthesis, to deny the extreme aspects of their own experiences, but to assert their subjectivity in response to other, equally personal and equally extreme, assertions of experience. Call and response, then, is African-American analysis: a process that, by admitting diverse voices and diverse experiences, supports a more inclusive critique than any individual analysis.[50]

In African American church tradition, emerging out of West African community relationships, call-and-response functions as a community builder that refuses to flatten difference. The call opens itself to challenge and contradiction, but continues both relationship and becoming through inter-responsiveness. When Werner emphasizes that response to a call "enables the leader to go on exploring the implications of the material," it becomes clear that the very continuation of the word or call itself is predicated on relational interchange. In African American Christian church and preaching traditions, we see the vestiges of call-and-response in choir/leader calls and responses during congregational singing, and also richly within the interchange between preacher and congregation. In sermonic call-and-response, the congregation's *Amens* and *Help, Lords*, while valorizing and valuing the preaching voice, also de-center the authority of the preacher such that the sermon becomes a collaborative response of people and preacher to the call of God on the church and community. Its willingness to validate even opposition, seeking not singularity, but multiple-threaded dialogue, marks this as a structure for navigating the future of the word in a compromised and complex environment.

Call-and-response is a helpful way to think about the relationship between works in African American literary traditions—an alternative to Harold Bloom's notion of anxiety of influence, though perhaps not entirely unrelated to it. Call-and-response may more broadly suggest how reading participates in a communal and becoming Trinitarian love within engagement of a text. Examples of the call-and-response here could be most obviously linked to the future of the word as African American authors provide their own responses to the biblical word, asserting themselves and the future of the word in tandem within retellings of biblical narratives that occur so prominently in African American literatures, including novels such as Zora Neale Hurston's *Moses, Man of the Mountain* or poems such as Anne Spencer's "Before the Feast of Shushan" or Frances Ellen Watkins Harper's "Vashti." Outside the African American literary community examples likewise abound, from Thomas Mann's retelling of the story of Joseph to Anita Diamant's retelling of the story of Dinah.[51] There are any number of models—ancient and modern—that share traits with African and African American call-and-response, such as Midrash, already implicitly present in discussions of biblical intertextuality or parallelism common to Hebrew poetry; more recent philosophy grounded in the western philosophical tradition has plenty of interest here as well, for instance in the work of Jean-Louis Chrétien, whose *The Call and the Response* suggests that language itself is always a call, is always the call of the beautiful to nothingness, a call that is creative and brings into being.[52] The first word of creation calls to nothingness and brings being itself into becoming, and human language from then on works as response and call together. The call itself is a pleading against termination and nothingness and silence; it is the elicitation and the crafting of a becoming and a community.

## The Redemption of Use

In this book so far, the uses of literature have come under negative scrutiny. There's nothing really new in that scrutiny, though. Barbara Herrnstein Smith noted in her 1988 book *Contingencies of Value* an anti-utilitarian strain that was then contemporary. Of course she and others note that anti-utilitarianism is susceptible to its own charges, is always already implicated in systems of valuation or use,[53] Rita Felski's *Uses of Literature* is only one of the many echoing Smith's critique; her manifesto seeks to revitalize literary theory by the power of everyday readers and their uses.

The present argument actually seeks to slip between. Against a claim that a humanist critique of use falsely thinks it escapes the vulgarities of embodied and economic uses, and against a claim that use is precisely the vigorous reinvention of theory that literary theorists or scholars need in the present, I am seeking an embodied kind of reading, aware of its own tendencies toward use to the extent that such self-awareness is possible, and yet fully insisting that there are yet higher uses—eschatological ones—to which literature may be directed. Reading in the body, through preservation, utterance in community, translation, call-and-response, or even other workable models not discussed here, seems to allow for an Augustinian use, the putting of reading in relation to the enjoyment of God—what this book refers to as the expanding and becoming betweenness of the Trinity in which we may participate.

I want to suggest that the *uti* of a text could be a cultivation—in which one might take great delight, and even some measured gain, but which would coincide with the cultivation and keeping of the God's kingdom. This is the redemption of use through the future of the word, its now and not yet. Preference in reading might be redeemed along these lines. With the future of the word in mind—the becoming and expanding repletion of the word in the Trinity—particularity, individual preference, and even disagreement in taste need not over-trouble us, nor sparring over the boundaries of the good or great.

In the plenitude of the Trinity's love, particularity in reading is a mechanism of creation and becoming. When grace restores us, our desires are reordered even in diversity, reaching toward the beatific, toward the kingdom of God. In this sense, the will's movement or the soul's affinity with the joys or revelations of particular texts will make concrete the expansion of the love of the Trinity, insofar as the expression of these affinities is an expansion of relational meaning-making. John Milbank argues that even free will itself, or preference, is a sort of grace, "the restoration of a good that we can only enjoy in common, and yet must receive according to our own unique affinities. To will . . . means to be moved beyond oneself toward a sharing and ontological distribution (according to real requirement not formal equality) of the inexhaustible common good. It is through this move that desire attracts once more to itself true vision and draws along with it new resources of power for self-realization."[54] The lower passions participate in the higher and all may be, in time, the time or space of the revelation of the infinite. Preference redeemed, valuation redeemed, use redeemed: all these add up to the restoration of gift exchange in reading, the openness or willingness to receive a text as a gift from God through and sometimes despite the peculiarity of our affinities. With the text as treasured gift, we bring out within it what is new and what is old through the plenitude of grace.

## Notes

1. For example, Claus Westermann, in *Genesis 1-11* (Minneapolis: Augsburg Press, 1984), writes, "It can be said that every human occupation shares in some way this tilling and keeping" (221).

2. John Walton, *The NIV Application Commentary: Genesis* (Grand Rapids: Zondervan, 2001), 172–73.

3. Ibid., 174.

4. For Westermann, this differentiation means a "demythologized" concept of work in Genesis, with humans possessing the ability to make "independent significance" outside the world of the gods (*Genesis 1-11*, 222). His wording, "independent significance," is correct and incorrect at the same time. On the one hand, there is a measure of meaning-making that occurs when humans engage with the world. But the participatory function is never independent of the world of God, insofar as he is always already sustaining it and keeping it, too. Westermann thinks of human dignity and such as flowing from the mandate for work—but that sounds a lot to me like independence rather than jointure. He writes that "human work . . . is a necessary part of the exchange between God and his people"—but this feels too economic (222).

5. Ibid., 220.

6. John Milbank, *Being Reconciled: Ontology and Pardon* (New York: Routledge, 2003), ix.

7. Colin Gunton, *The Christian Faith: An Introduction to Christian Doctrine* (Malden, MA: Blackwell, 2002), 19.

8. John Milbank and Catherine Pickstock too have conceived the participation of not just human making, but also of *liturgy, sacrament,* and *exchange* as the means by which the divine interparticipation of the three in one lays the foundation for the participation of cultural exchange in divine being and relationship. See Catherine Pickstock, *After Writing: On the Liturgical Consummation of Philosophy* (Oxford: Blackwell, 1998) and John Milbank, *The Word Made Strange: Theology, Language, Culture* (Cambridge, MA: Blackwell, 1997). See also John Milbank, *Theology and Social Theory: Beyond Secular Reason* (Malden, MA: Blackwell, 2006).

9. Stanley Grenz, *Theology for the Community of God* (Grand Rapids: Eerdmans, 2000), 481. See also John Zizioulas, *Being as Communion: Studies in Personhood and the Church* (Crestwood, NY: St. Vladimir's Seminary Press, 1993), 140.

10. Grenz, *Theology for the Community of God*, 656.

11. Ibid., 478.

12. In two earlier pieces, I searched for such postures of reading among mentors worthy of imitation, making the claim that a Christian sensibility would need to value appropriate imitation over the violence of a competition for innovation. In the present work, I suggest an orientation of renovation or rejuvenation—the expansion of the text into new contexts and situations—rather than the late-model scientific approach. See Tiffany Eberle Kriner, "Hopeful Reading," *Christianity & Literature* 61, no. 1 (2011): 101–31, and Tiffany Eberle Kriner, "Our Turn Now?: Imitation and the Theological Turn in Literary Studies," *Christianity & Literature* 58, no. 2 (2009): 266–72.

13. Franco Moretti, "The Slaughterhouse of Literature," *Modern Language Quarterly* 61, no. 1 (2000): 207. Moretti's tools for analysis seek to account for how the canon is formed by readers according to a market-based selection of formal criteria ascertainable only after the fact. In Moretti's view, the particular evolutionary path taken, the survival of particular formal traits in literature is not inevitable (audiences liked discoverable clues, but they might have liked something else), though the function itself, the survivability of some traits and not others, was and is inevitable. Moretti wants to see literary studies working with a broader range of methods to be able to better approach what Margaret Cohen has termed "the great unread" (*The Sentimental Education of the Novel* [Princeton: Princeton University Press, 1999], 23) in a way that can reshape the map of a much, much larger literary field. For Moretti, of course, close attention to the literary text is an impossible methodology for engagement in the exponentially larger literary field.

14. Gregory A. Smith, "A Rationale for Integrating Christian Faith and Librarianship," in *Christian Librarianship*, ed. Gregory A. Smith (Jefferson, NC: McFarland, 2002): 11–27.

15. David J. Pullinger, "Putting Librarianship under the Light." *The Christian Librarian* 32 (May 1989): 59–60. See also John B. Trotti, "The Theological Library: In Touch with the Witnesses," in *Christian Librarianship*, ed. Smith, 48–54.

16. Valerie Boyd, *Wrapped in Rainbows* (New York: Scribner, 2003), 436.

17. Alice Walker, *In Search of Our Mother's Gardens* (San Diego: Harcourt Brace Jovanovich, 1983).

18. Boyd, *Wrapped in Rainbows*, 438.

19. Her epigraph to the text is, "Omissions are not accidents."

20. Marianne Moore, *The Complete Poems of Marianne Moore* (New York: Macmillan, 1981), 36.

21. Ibid., 267.

22. Alan Jacobs, *The Pleasures of Reading in an Age of Distraction* (New York: Oxford University Press, 2011).

23. Walter Benjamin, *Illuminations* (New York: Harcourt Brace & World, 1968), 254. The French means "mentioned in the dispatches," as in "noted in the daily bulletin." It is a military citation.

24. Ibid., 264.

25. Leslie Marmon Silko, *Yellow Woman and a Beauty of the Spirit* (New York: Simon & Schuster, 1997), 50–51.

26. Silko also writes in "Language and Literature from a Pueblo Indian Perspective" (in *Yellow Woman and a Beauty of the Spirit*, 48–59), about how the utterance of story—especially the renewing stories that reinvigorate the myth and join contemporary times to mythic ones—functions as a renewal of the family and tribe, too: "Anthropologists and ethnologists have, for a long time, differentiated the types of stories the Pueblos tell. They tended to elevate the old, sacred, and traditional stories and to brush aside family stories, the family's account of itself. But in Pueblo culture, these family stories are given equal recognition. There is no definite, present pattern for the way one will hear the stories of one's own family, but it is a very critical part of one's childhood, and the storytelling continues throughout one's life. One will hear stories of importance to the family—sometimes wonderful stories—stories about the time a maternal uncle got the biggest deer that was ever seen and brought it back from the mountains. And so an individual's identity will extend from the identity constructed around the family—"I am from the family of my uncle who brought in this wonderful deer and it was a wonderful hunt." Family accounts include negative stories, too; perhaps an uncle did something unacceptable. It is very important that one keep track of all these stories—both positive and not so positive about one's own family and other families. Because even when there is no way around it—old Uncle Pete *did* do a terrible thing—by knowing the stories that originate

in other families, one is able to deal with terrible sorts of things that might happen within one's own family. If a member of the family does something that cannot be excused, one always knows stories about similar inexcusable things done by a member of another family. But this knowledge is not communicated for malicious reasons. It is very important to understand this. Keeping track of all the stories within the community gives us all a certain distance, a useful perspective, that brings incidents down to a level we can deal with. If others have done it before, it cannot be so terrible. If others have endured, so can we" (51–52).

27. Leslie Marmon Silko, *Ceremony* (New York: Penguin, 2006), 116.

28. Gertrude Stein, "Poetry and Grammar," in *Lectures in America* (Boston: Beacon, 1967), 235.

29. Gertrude Stein, *Selected Writings of Gertrude Stein* (New York: Vintage, 1990), 461.

30. Gertrude Stein, "Portraits and Repetitions," in *Lectures in America*, 166.

31. Ibid., 167.

32. Lyn Hejinian, "The Rejection of Closure," in *The Language of Inquiry* (Berkeley: University of California Press, 2000).

33. Ibid., 41.

34. Ibid.

35. See also the introduction's discussion of Jon Woodward's poem "Huge Dragonflies."

36. Emmanuel Levinas, *Totality and Infinity*, trans. Alphonso Lingis (Pittsburgh: Duquesne University Press, 1969).

37. Emmanuel Levinas, *Otherwise Than Being or Beyond Essence*, trans. Alphonso Lingis (Pittsburgh: Duquesne University Press, 1998), 37–51.

38. Emmanuel Levinas, *Beyond the Verse: Talmudic Readings and Lectures* (Bloomington: Indiana University Press, 1994), 109. Quoted in Julian Wolfreys, *Readings: Acts of Close-Reading in Literary Theory* (Edinburgh: Edinburgh University Press, 2000), 93.

39. Lamin Sanneh, *Translating the Message: The Missionary Impact on Culture*, rev. ed. (Maryknoll, NY: Orbis, 2009), 60.

40. Ibid., 60.

41. Walter Benjamin, "The Task of the Translator," in *Theories of Translation*, ed. Rainier Schulte and John Biguenet (Chicago: University of Chicago Press, 1992), 81.

42. Ibid., 73. For an expansion of Benjamin's ideas within contemporary comparative literature and contemporary translation studies, see also Bella Brodzki, *Can These Bones Live?: Translation, Survival, and Cultural Memory* (Stanford: Stanford University Press, 2007).

43. Ibid., 82.

44. Arthur Schopenhauer, "On Language and Words," trans. Peter Mollenhauer, in *Theories of Translation*, ed. Schultze and Biguenet, 34.

45. Friedrich Schleiermacher, "On the Different Methods of Translating," trans. Waltraud Bartscht, in *Theories of Translation*, ed. Schultze and Biguenet, 36–54.

46. Ibid., 38.

47. Hugo Friedrich, "On the Art of Translation," trans. Ranier Schultze and John Biguenet, in *Theories of Translation*, ed. Schultze and Biguenet, 13.

48. Jacques Derrida, "Des Tours de Babel," in *Acts of Religion*, ed. Gil Anidjar (New York: Routledge, 2002), 118.

49. Ibid., 118.

50. Craig Werner, *Playing the Changes: From Afro-Modernism to the Jazz Impulse* (Urbana: University of Illinois Press, 1994), xviii. See also John F. Callahan, *In the African-American Grain: Call and Response in Twentieth-Century Black Fiction*, 2nd ed. (Middletown, CT: Wesleyan University Press, 1988), 19–21.

51. Henry Louis Gates Jr., drawing from traditions surrounding the West African trickster figure of Esu Elegbra, offers another sort of response that unsettles, questions, and yet also brings forward the call: signifyin(g). Signifyin(g) is African American semantic play, the invoking and evacuating a given sign of its traditional, oppressive signified through a redeployment of a rhetorical figure. Signifyin(g) luxuriates in multiple associative references beyond those limited versions imposed by an oppressive syntactic system. In play, in the dozens, white time is suspended, white meaning suspended, and a revision offered. Gates insists that signifyin(g) is a synchronic opposition to the diachronic force of the sentence, but surely semantic play has a diachronic, temporal aspect too—surely signifyin(g) is dialogic, a subset of call-and-response. Henry Louis Gates Jr., *The Signifying Monkey: A Theory*

*of African-American Literary Criticism* (New York: Oxford University Press, 1988).

52. Jean-Louis Chrétien, *The Call and the Response* (New York: Fordham University Press, 2004).

53. Barbara Herrnstein Smith, *Contingencies of Value* (Cambridge, MA: Harvard University Press, 1988).

54. John Milbank, *Being Reconciled*, 12.

# Literary Scrivenings 1:
# Futures for the Living Dead

The three sections of this book headed *Scrivenings* bring out literary texts to play with the theology. Engaging questions of how reading might participate in the becoming, meaning-making, and community-building futures of texts, these interpretations try out the activities of the scribe for the kingdom—in a gloriously messy way. They map the myriad and manifold paths that reading takes outside of philosophical or theological argument, sometimes kicking against the pricks and sometimes seeming to take a turn themselves in the dance of the healing of time.

The previous chapter pointed to several angles on the future of the word—preservation, utterance, translation, and call-and-response; in this collection of scrivenings, I peer at a few literary works. How are they working the angles to offer meaning-making, futurity, and community to other texts? These texts, it is clear, are built out of their relationships with *other* literary works: *Pride and Prejudice and Zombies*, a contemporary utterance and parody of Austen's most famous novel, seems to both lampoon Austen's text and rescue it from twenty years of reductive, soul-killing interpretations; Frances Ellen Watkins Harper's "Died of Starvation" responds to a call from *Oliver Twist* to make it palatable to an American reading audience wary of Dickens's political and social agenda; Haruki Murakami's *1Q84*, an homage and literary translation of sorts, takes up George Orwell's *1984* again. Each participates in the making of a future for a text suffering what we might call, if we were to take a dramatic cue from *Pride and Prejudice and Zombies*, a living death. These three works revitalize literary, philosophical, and ethical problems in their source texts—problems to which literary posterity has been deadened. I believe these books cultivate the futures of their source texts. But they do not do so unproblematically.

## Pride and Prejudice and Zombies: *Utteringly Absurd*

If any work's posterity seems assured already, it's *Pride and Prejudice*, this most fawned-over and made-over text. Late in the year of the 200th anniversary of publication of Austen's novel, the theatre in my town was still showing *Austenland*, which portrays a woman so obsessed with Jane Austen that she heads to an eponymous immersive theme park to find her Mr. Darcy. *Pride and Prejudice* is *that* famous; it has its own trekkies who produce an alphabet of allusive bobble-heads, costumes, do-dads, fan-fictions, homages, movies, prequels, sequels, slash fiction, and even the recent popular vlog series, *The Lizzie Bennet Diaries*. And that is just the pop culture scene; any number of scholarly conferences are convened and papers presented and books published each year: they demonstrate what is a remarkably steady and ongoing interest in the novel. It would seem that I could simply suggest that the future of *Pride and Prejudice* is assured and marshal the resources of theology and literary studies for some other literary future.

But what if the cultural state of *Pride and Prejudice*, instead of being one of textual flourishing through ongoing meaning-building and community-building vitality, is actually infected and corrupt, its future gone awry? That is, what if *Pride and Prejudice*, instead of *living on* is really just the *living dead*? The very existence of Seth Grahame-Smith's parody *Pride and Prejudice and Zombies* seems to at least hint at the question—the blatancy of its parody pretty much trumpets it. The text is a mash-up of sorts, interspersing scenes of classic zombie violence and terror within the cut but mostly unchanged text of Austen's masterwork. Except for the obvious inclusion of ultraviolent zombie mayhem as a subplot unabashedly thrust into the structure of the original, the text of *Pride and Prejudice and Zombies* the parody is at many moments a verbatim utterance of *Pride and Prejudice*. Early in the novel, for instance, Grahame-Smith tucks in a quick battle with the "unmentionables"—his text's multivalent name for the zombies—during Elizabeth's walk to Netherfield Hall, the seamless effect of which on the plot is to give a more certain warrant for what the original text observed as her "face glowing with the warmth of exercise" when she arrives.[1] The ball at Netherfield is interrupted by a zombie attack, which demonstrates the social upheaval of the plague without significantly interrupting the advancing relationships that draw together the major characters in the novel. Grahame-Smith does alter the fates of some of the minor characters: Charlotte's choice to marry Mr. Collins has led to her being infected by the disease turning so many into zombies; Mr. Collins lets Lady Catherine behead his bride, but is so stricken by grief in the wake of this decision that he commits suicide. After Wickham elopes with Lydia, he is the victim of a mysterious accident and becomes paralyzed and incontinent, which leaves Lydia to care for him. But these decisions, ramping up the violence and zombie plot, actually exist largely in concert with the novel's ostensible views on the characters, though perhaps meting out a more eye-for-an-eye recompense to the characters for their decisions. All this is to say that the text is recognizable, though, like the characters infected with the zombie disease, corrupted and obviously incommensurate with the original. It is this attachment to the text itself that provides a starting point for thinking through the mashup as a reading that cultivates the future of the text through utterance, criticism, and call-and-response.

In a text made up so fundamentally of Austen's words, the corruption of Austen's text in Grahame-Smith's seems actually to point to the ways that Austen has already been corrupted even before this most egregious inclusion of zombie mayhem. The majority of popular readings in the Austen industry over the last two decades have positioned the text as a forebear to contemporary chick lit—a brilliant marketing decision, but perhaps less felicitous stewardship of the interpretive possibilities of the text. Readings of *Pride and Prejudice* have, by means of such texts and films as *Bridget Jones' Diary* and *The Jane Austen Book Club*, been largely blind to much outside interpersonal relationships and the achievement of happy marriage. Oddly enough, popular looks at Austen's text seem to have fallen into a somewhat less-considered reinforcement of what Austen was trying to critique: the actually non-universal truths made universally authoritative within particular economic and social systems.

In a chick lit setting, the romantic comedy plot largely deflects *Pride and Prejudice*'s economic and sociopolitical force. One obvious illustration of this would be the continuity of the character—and even actor—of Mr. Darcy across films associated with the novel. In BBC film of *Pride and Prejudice*, Colin Firth plays Fitzwilliam Darcy; he also plays Mark Darcy in the contemporary homage *Bridget Jones' Diary*. The qualities of the classic text most emphasized by this bringing forward of an actor/character in the burgeoning genre of chick lit, and, in film, the romantic comedy, are the nuances of the interpersonal relationship between Elizabeth Bennet and Fitzwilliam

Darcy. But, as *Pride and Prejudice and Zombies* demonstrates, there is a lot *else* going on behind the developing attraction, namely a pointed social commentary.

In *Pride and Prejudice and Zombies*, the shock of the original's satire comes back even more sharply through the device of zombie mayhem. The opening line shows how this works: *Pride and Prejudice and Zombies* begins, "It is a truth universally acknowledged that a zombie in possession of brains must be in want of more brains. Never was this truth more plain than during the recent attacks at Netherfield Park, in which a household of eighteen was slaughtered and consumed by a horde of the living dead."[2] This opening passage breaks from the original just at the moment the universally acknowledged truth is set to be announced. The laughable assertion about zombies draws attention immediately to its analogue, making the original opening commensurately mockable. The unstinting progress of *Pride and Prejudice* is toward marriage, as both Bingley and Darcy—with whatever ironies may lurk in the text only possibly visible to readers—march inexorably toward the altar. This tends to obscure in contemporary readers' minds the absurdity of the assumption about the supposedly universal truth. If in the context of contemporary romantic-comedy it has been mostly possible to read *Pride and Prejudice* popularly as if that maxim were profoundly true, then this opening cleaves the sentence in two as if it were the skull of an undead terror—quite literally splitting from the original just at the moment its faulty assumption begins.

Indeed, in both the quotation *of Pride and Prejudice* and in divergences from it, *Pride and Prejudice and Zombies* seems as interested in *preserving* the text for an audience as in mocking it or creating a credible zombie fiction. In the text, the strategy of the writer seems to have been to reawaken the power of Austen's sociopolitical and economic critique by using zombie mayhem as a stand-in for language that subtly parses social interaction as a function of class differentiation. This has the effect—for readers familiar with Austen's novel, which I believe the novel assumes—of raising the stakes of the often-overlooked parts of the text, namely economic concerns and social realities. Since the reader is always comparing the mash-up to the original, these critiques lately drowned in the rom-com deluge seem to revivify. When Mrs. Bennet wants to share the name of the new lessee of Netherfield Park with her husband, she presses her secret upon him: "Do you not want to know who has taken it?"—the original text lets Mr. Bennet say simply (with no commentary on tone or delivery), "You want to tell me, and I have no objection to hearing it."[3] This is a subtle indication of Mr. Bennet's only slightly masked contempt for his spouse. The zombie rewrite is less circumspect: "Woman, I am attending to my musket. Prattle on if you must, but leave me to the defense of my estate!"[4] In this way, the admittedly ridiculous dialogue of the zombie text makes much less gentle mockery of Mrs. Bennet, perhaps jarring a reader set for merely light comic tension between the senior couple. More importantly, it sets up the economic problem more clearly for an audience distant from social and class roles in late eighteenth- or early nineteenth-century England. For economics—the economic situation that Mr. Bennet finds himself in with five daughters and little to give them, say—is the primary, though faulty reasoning behind the universality of the universal truth that a single man in possession of good fortune must be in want of a wife. When in the zombie text Mr. Bennet says, "leave me to the defense of my estate," the word "estate" refers to his land (set to pass to someone outside of the nuclear family), his posterity, and the financial upkeep of his offspring, thus calling the reader's attention to the economic stresses that drive even the smallest interchanges between husband and wife. *Pride and Prejudice and Zombies* adds more substance, too, to Mr. Bennet's care for the living of his children—in the mash-up, he has spent significant time and money in preparing his daughters in martial arts and defense, skills key to their survival in a zombie apocalypse. *Pride and Prejudice and Zombies* states frankly at the end of the first chapter, "The business of Mr. Bennet's life was to keep his daughters alive"—and again, the zombie "business" stands in for the basically ignored "business" of the original: in *Pride and Prejudice*, economic necessity threatens the living of the women in the story, forcing them toward marriage.[5] The zombie plot raises the stakes of the economic concerns that are already present, preserving them for an audience more generically attuned to romance.

Even the social plot of Austen's text is made more cutting and pointed by Grahame-Smith's inclusion of the zombie plot. This unhinges the text from its contemporary happily-ever-after, situation-comedy frame. By exaggerating the interpersonal conflict between people—making the speech between characters more blatantly tense or rude—the zombie text ratchets up the audience's sense of the true cattiness and cutting that marks the social scenes in Austen. At times, the text simplifies or shortens speeches—not only to make room for the zombie plot, but also to emphasize certain emotions. The text shows Elizabeth physically rolling her eyes at Mary's long moralistic speeches—a tutorial for the reader that points out not only the insufficiency of Mary's platitudes, but perhaps more importantly the thin veneer of Elizabeth's graciousness. Mr. Collins's obtuseness is emphasized in the plot-twist in which Charlotte is infected with the plague and is turning into a zombie, but her husband completely fails to notice. In addition, the text flags every possible sexual innuendo that emerges out of the text—playing, for instance, on the multiple meanings of the term "balls," as "dances" and as "testicles," making jokes that, while poking fun at the propriety of the drawing-room civility as represented by Austen's text, also point out real sexual tension between Elizabeth and Darcy.[6] However, by making it so outrageous, the audience is mostly prevented from falling into the emotional pull of the romance between them, thus preserving the zombie text's alternate focus.

The zombie alterations may actually bring *Pride and Prejudice* forward into its future by drawing the reader back to the original. Though *Pride and Prejudice and Zombies* is, admittedly, almost a one-joke concept piece, what the author has called "absurd premise fiction," it not only richly engages the original, but even beyond utterance and contrast, implicitly enjoins rereading of the original at several points, making it concurrently an act of bastardization and preservation.[7] For, upon comparing the texts, despite years of reading and rereading *Pride and Prejudice*, I was surprised and chagrined to find that lines I thought were invented by Grahame-Smith were, in fact, original to *Pride and Prejudice*, particularly lines attributed to the Bingley sisters. By adding a few overdetermined lines to any scene, the parody and ironic force of any original lines are further highlighted.

The text of Grahame-Smith's zombie novel ends with discussion questions that are part of the artifice of the parody. They are common in book-club-selection-type novels, and even their inclusion is poking fun at the institution of chick lit and women's fiction. But while there are wonderfully juvenile questions, such as an inquiry as to whether scenes involving vomit in the novel have deep, symbolic meaning or are a gag (ha!) to get laughs, there are also questions pointing to minor characters that highlight Grahame-Smith's understanding of the novel's main critiques. One such is the pointed question surrounding Mr. Collins and religion in the novel: Grahame-Smith inquires, "How might [Mr. Collins's] occupation (as a pastor) relate to his denial of the obvious?"[8] Mr. Collins tends to be separated from thoughts of particularly religious critique in popular adaptations of the novel because of the overwhelming enthusiasm for Elizabeth and Darcy's relationship. Mr. Collins is just an idiot. Yet in the question, Grahame-Smith's choice to use the word "pastor," which is not in Austen's text, rather than "clergyman" (the term always associated with Collins in the original) shows Austen's critique of institutional religion in the original text, while also extending that critique to the present day where readers live in the twenty-first century. In light of this question, Wickham's early-intended career in the church points to the paleness of England's socioeconomic construction of the pastorate. For herself, Austen seemed rather more interested in theologically and experientially derived faith. As one of her letters to Fanny Knight in 1814 comments, "I am by no means convinced that we ought not all to be Evangelicals, & am at least persuaded that they who are so from Reason and Feeling, must be happiest & safest."[9] Yet readers of the novel awash in the deliciousness of Darcy's proposals may miss completely the novel's particularly religious critique. *Pride and Prejudice and Zombies* redresses this with the carefully overdetermined diction of its question.

The last discussion question points to the obvious joke of the whole text—but simultaneously to the sincere attempt in the reworking of the novel to preserve the original through the joke: "Can you imagine what this novel might be like without the violent zombie mayhem?"[10] In this way, the text of Seth Grahame-Smith's novel invites the reader to see anew the text of a work that has been shoehorned into a genre fiction context that fails to do justice to its complex interweavings. Of course, there's no way to make that critique without falling into one's own trap. But, by hyper-exaggerating the artifice of its own engagement with the text—blatantly ripping off the text and ripping it apart, *Pride and Prejudice and Zombies* can act as functional critique of the more egregious misreadings. The pleasure of this parody is that it realigns the audience for the text as much as it does the text for the audience.

*Pride and Prejudice and Zombies* thus, as odd as it may seem, works to both utter and preserve Austen's novel, even as it admittedly debases and corrupts it. The rich interactions that the genre-specific zombie elements have with Austen's text correct a reading pattern that hampers the possibilities of the text in its too-strong focus on the romantic resolution. It opens the already broad audience of Austen's novel to a broader set of revelations within the text—economic, religious, and social. Under these circumstances, zombie mayhem may highlight how *Pride and Prejudice* has something important to say about survival and humanness, even two hundred years later, even from the position of the walking dead.

Seth Grahame-Smith's website—and all the publicity surrounding his novel—claims that *Pride and Prejudice and Zombies* completes Austen's classic text with elements that attract today's reader. With a clever barb, the site suggests that in so doing, *Pride and Prejudice and Zombies* "transforms a masterpiece of world literature into something you'd actually want to read."[11] Yet, for all its trash-talking, my own experience, for one, will bear up the brag—for after reading *Pride and Prejudice and Zombies* the mash-up, I wanted to and did return to *Pride and Prejudice*, and the text was altered by my encounter with the "unmentionables," from a new sensitivity to elements in the original, such as the inexplicable presence of soldiers, to a keener eye for varied subtleties and themes. In expanding the capacity of the audience to experience the original novel in its fullness through an obviously excessive reading, Grahame-Smith seems to as much serve the future of the text as his own future. *Pride and Prejudice and Zombies* seems to be receiving rather its own set of preservations and utterances as well, though—and the fact that the novel was a runaway surprise hit confirms that. Naturally, Hollywood seems to be interested in riding the wave, responding to the call of the book, and there's a film in the works. And, of course, there are videogames, too, keeping the spirit alive. Admittedly, however, the zombie genre has its own better resurrections.

## Twisting Oliver or Seeing the Case?
## Francis Ellen Watkins Harper's "Died of Starvation"

The work of Frances Ellen Watkins Harper, a nineteenth-century African American poet and activist, was undeniably popular and political. Not as popular as *Pride and Prejudice and Zombies*, perhaps, but Harper's work, a bit like Austen's and Grahame-Smith's, engages sociopolitical monstrosities that seem unmentionable, that just won't die. Harper's vocation seems to have been using language (speeches, poems, novels, stories) to make possible and bring about what one of her books calls "a brighter coming day."[12] More than half of the poems in her first book are protest poems: they deal with slavery, poverty, the ravaging effects of alcoholism, and the unequal rights of women. Her 1854 volume *Poems on Miscellaneous Subjects* touted on the title page of the 1857 Philadelphia reprint that 10,000 copies had sold, a high sales rate for the time. As a poet, Harper was committed to making her poetry accessible to a wide audience—popular—and effectual for their good—political and religious. She spoke on national women's rights convention stages and lectured to packed houses wherever she went. By the early twentieth century, cities across America had set up F. E. W. Harper leagues and Christian temperance unions in her honor to engage women activists and public servants.

Yet Harper's work was not blithely in service of the political and economic causes she championed, nor was her work constructed without consideration of poetic and linguistic choices. Some of her poems tell stories that present, in sentimental language, the loss and heartbreak linked to the injustice of slavery or poverty, which are crafted to elicit emotional and political responses from readers; others are quotable, rhythmic anthems that raise the spirit. All are in service to Christian faith, her aesthetics dedicated to clarity of message and audience-connection.

Harper's 1854 poem "Died of Starvation" draws on her Christian faith and her interest in drawing attention to poverty and social ills as it retells and responds to a chapter from the work of another famously popular and political work, Charles Dickens's *Oliver Twist*, which was popular in its melodramatic sentimentality and political in its critique of Britain's New Poor Laws. "Died of Starvation" appeared in Harper's volume *Poems on Miscellaneous Subjects* with a footnote saying, "See this case, as touchingly related, in 'Oliver Twist,' by Charles Dickens."[13] The poem was also placed in the *Provincial Freeman* in 1857, accompanied by her essay on Christianity and an introduction to her work. The poem retells an early scene in the novel: Oliver is initiated into the brutal undertaking business by accompanying Mr. Sowerberry to measure a corpse for a casket—the corpse of a woman who'd starved to death. On the job, Oliver and Mr. Sowerberry encounter the woman's grief-crazed husband Bayton alongside her mad, aging mother and destitute children. Harper's poem cultivates the future of Dickens's text by both uttering its story and making the utterance a response to the story that wrestles with the issues the original raises.

It may seem like Dickens, whose popularity in America is an accepted fact of American literary history, and Oliver Twist, whose "Please, sir, I want some more" has become a catchphrase, would have no need of Harper's fan-poem utterance and response. That is true, to a certain extent, for Dickens's works were exceedingly popular even while he was living. But literary history seems to indicate that in the United States, *Oliver* among all of Dickens's works needed some public relations support. Robert McParland's investigation of nineteenth-century sources reveals that though popular and much read, *Oliver Twist* had negative connotations for American readers, even while they sprinkled its phrases and characters into their correspondence indiscriminately—especially in comparison with the far more droll *Pickwick*.[14] In more formal venues, conservative reviews that appeared on both sides of the ocean, *Oliver Twist* had been critiqued for its ugliness—its violent, low subjects—and its explicit politics. A review in London's *Quarterly Review*, reprinted in the U.S. in the *Southern Literary Messenger* in 1839, strenuously objected to the novel's focus on "the outcasts of humanity, who do their dirty work in work-, pot-, and watch houses." In such foci, the review argued, "the happy ignorance of innocence is disregarded. Our youth['s] tender memories are wax to receive and marble to retain. These infamies feed the innate evil principle, which luxuriates in the supernatural and horrid." "We object," it continued, to "familiarizing our ingenuous youth with 'slang'."[15] *Oliver Twist* readers were potentially wont to claim that the abuses Dickens highlights in the novel "in nineteen cases out of twenty do not at all exist."[16] The reviewer at the *Quarterly* disapproves: "[W]e regret to see him joining in an outcry which is partly factious, partly sentimental, partly interested."[17] Dickens had also received criticism, especially in the American South, surrounding his 1842 visit to the U.S. and the memoir of that visit, which despite lacking a full, detailed observation or depiction of slavery, yet unflinchingly denounced it. Dickens and Oliver seem to be too much for some audience members—too full of violence and horror, too pointedly political, and perhaps even too sentimental in support of particularly progressive politics.

In the early 1850s, when Harper's book came out with her poem on *Oliver Twist* in it, Dickens was facing profit problems with *Household Words*, his journalistic project, a self-consciously progressive repository of art and letters with a mission to even the poorest among people, to "rais[e] up those that are down," assuring "the hardest workers . . . that their lot is not necessarily a moody, brutal fact, excluded from the sympathies and graces of imagination."[18] The magazine, while explicitly targeting a broad readership, mostly reached the middle class, for whom it became on occasion the literary inspiration for various projects of social change. In the early 1850s, falling profits led Dickens to serialize another of his works, *Hard Times,* in the weekly paper, in order to bolster the sales of the periodical—a tactic that worked like a charm.

From what we know of Harper's work and interests, it seems little wonder she might take an interest in Dickens's text and amplify its causes for an American audience. She might have found in Dickens's work a penchant for the exposure and denunciation of injustice that coincided with her own. Perhaps Dickens's popularity could bring attention to issues she found dear. Or, if readers' sensibilities fell more along the conservative lines suggested by the *Quarterly Review*, then she might have opportunity to make the text's content and messages more accessible and effectual to them. And her own work also not infrequently responds emotionally and poetically to literary texts: she wrote poems engaging Harriet Beecher Stowe's *Uncle Tom's Cabin* and many biblical narratives.

"Died of Starvation" most fundamentally responds to *Oliver Twist* by making it possible for readers to focus on the vignette—such a small part of the novel—and really *see* it, see it so that they might respond. The poem does so by emphasizing seeing. The footnote, as noted above, urges the reader to "see this case." The poem also changes the point of view on the scene such that readers may see more clearly. The audience is less removed from the incident in the poem than in the novel, for the reader (or viewer) in the poem stands in as Oliver, who makes no appearance in the poem. Thus the reader-viewer bears witness to what Oliver himself "was afraid to look" at in the novel, to that which Sowerberry declared would be "nothing when [Oliver was] used to it."[19]

> They forced him into prison,
> Because he begged for bread;
> "My wife is starving—dying!"
> In vain the poor man plead.
>
> They forced him into prison,
> Strong bars enclosed the walls,
> While the rich and proud were feasting
> Within their sumptuous halls.
>
> He'd striven long with anguish,
> Had wrestled with despair;
> But his weary heart was breaking
> 'Neath its crushing load of care.
>
> And he prayed them in that prison,
> "Oh, let me seek my wife!"
> For he knew that want was feeding
> On the remnant of her life.
>
> That night his wife lay moaning
> Upon her bed in pain;
> Hunger gnawing at her vitals,
> Fever scorching through her brain.
>
> She wondered at his tarrying,
> He was not wont to stay;
> 'Mid hunger, pain and watching,
> The moments waned away.

Sadly crouching by the embers,
Her famished children lay;
And she longed to gaze upon them,
As her spirit passed away.

But the embers were too feeble,
She could not see each face,
So she clasped her arms around them—
'Twas their mother's last embrace.

They loosed him from his prison,
As a felon from his chain;
Though his strength was hunger bitten,
He sought his home again.

Just as her spirit linger'd
On Time's receding shore,
She heard his welcome footstep
On the threshold of the door.

He was faint and spirit-broken,
But, rousing from despair,
He clasped her icy fingers,
As she breathed her dying prayer.

With a gentle smile and blessing,
Her spirit winged its flight,
As the morn, in all its glory,
Bathed the world in dazzling light.

There was weeping, bitter weeping,
In the chamber of the dead,
For well the stricken husband knew
She had died for want of bread.[20]

While Dickens uses gruesomely vivid details to establish the scene's darkness and poverty, Harper uses wordplay and the motif of seeing to emphasize the moral imperative to see the scene. Harper adds dialogue between the man and his guards that begs them to let him "*seek* [his] wife." The wife is worn from "watching" for her husband.

She longs to "see" each face of her children. And more than these direct references, Harper includes imagery related to sight, such as the light that bathes the morning world. Instead of helping the woman see her children, however, that light reveals the woman's death and its causes—material need, rather than sickness: the systems of social oppression have imprisoned an innocent man and caused the death of a beloved and devoted wife and mother. Harper's text cultivates Dickens's text by recognizing its imperative to see, articulating that imperative, and explicitly generating and communicating the moral insights available within the situation.

Now, it is not untrue that Dickens's text also reveals such moral insights, but it does so in a far more ambiguous—and long-form—manner. The poem thus cultivates the text by interpreting and ordering its moral, social, and theological import in a short-form manner. Harper orders the narrative's moral logic in her poem, shaping the chaos of grief and poverty and assigning them causation. Out of the incoherent testimony of the speaker in Dickens's text, Harper crafts a chronology, beginning with the man in prison for the crime of begging. The poem's structural frame—the title, a mention of bread at the beginning and end of the poem—foregrounds the moral frame. The oppressive social system figured in the poem binds individuals and families in poverty. The plain truth is that the woman's starvation and death were absolutely preventable.

Harper reorients Dickens's text by highlighting faithful, sacrificial, moral family relationships as contrary to the oppressive social context. In *Oliver Twist*, the hero sees the destitute people in the scene as "so like the rats he had seen outside," while Harper helps her audience see in the animalistic creatures the seeds of humanity that Dickens plants in his novel.[21] While Oliver sees dehumanization, Harper shows her audience common, though idealized, human kinship. She makes the woman an ideal mother figure in an expanded deathbed scene. In Harper's version, the "gasping out [of the children's] names" in the rasping dark is the woman turning the bleak scene into an opportunity for embrace and blessing and prayer.

Harper reads the text according to her vision of Christianity's moral center—bringing from the textual details a meaning, which, while faithful to the text's protest of conditions for the urban poor, change it in length and focus. In so doing, she brings it into contact with other audiences—audiences who may be put off by the roughness or vulgarity or length of Dickens's novel. Harper's reading is not solely a sanitizing move to take out the naughty or distressing bits, though she does a bit of that. It moves the audience, to whom these characters might seem untouchable, to understand the story with charitable sympathy for the characters. The Dickens scene includes the bereaved husband's profane warning for all comers to keep back from the corpse; Harper omits this, but, interpreting it in her poem as a sign of the man's fidelity to and protectiveness of his spouse, replaces it with his prison cry, "Let me seek my wife!" In Dickens's narrative, the man's haggard physical weakness is foregrounded as he faints in retelling the story, and at his wife's burial; in Harper his weakness is occasion for moral fortitude: "He was faint and spirit-broken, / but rousing from despair / he clasped her icy fingers, / As she breathed her dying prayer" (70–71). Harper sees in the Dickens characters' physical weakness the moral strength that would overcome a broken body and broken spirit and rouse a man to be by his wife's side as she dies an innocent death.

Harper reinterprets not only morally or socially but also theologically. The Bayton scene in Dickens pictures a man raging against a cruel God who would look on while a woman dies of hunger. The man is shown grieving in dramatically ironized biblical postures. He commands all the viewers to "kneel down" to the dead woman—rather than to God.[22] When he tells the story of the scene, he avers, "I swear it before the God that saw it! They starved her!" and his language and posture invoke the demon possession of Mark 9 as he falls "with a loud scream, rolled groveling upon the floor: his eyes fixed: and the foam gushing from his lips."[23] By contrast, Harper's poem places the terrible scene within a biblical narrative that understands spiritual struggle as part of God's saving history. Using hints of King James language, Harper shapes biblical allusions so that the man's experience, rather than being linked to blasphemy and demon possession, is linked with positive biblical characters instead: he is Jacob in his struggles wrestling the angel, he is the Christ "tarrying" (as in John 11:6) inexplicably before going to Lazarus. He is "loosed" like Lazarus to go home. He is the faithful believer, "watching" and praying (as in Mark 13:33) for the coming kingdom as his wife gives up her spirit with a prayer. These images place this story in the anti-type future of the word of God. Rather than being afraid of what one reviewer calls Dickens's "muscular agony," Harper gestures to the Bible to expand the meaning of the man's suffering.[24]

Is Harper's reading a too-easy twisting of the vignette from *Oliver Twist* into a story of sentimental redemption? Is it stunting rather than expanding the meanings of the text, even as it puts the text into a particular theological context? It may seem to, in part because of the literary strictures to which the poem conforms, which tie up the dirty horror of the scene into neat quatrains. It seems undeniable, however, that the Harper and Dickens texts share a sense of the intolerability of the situation—an intolerability that they hope will be irritatingly motivating for audiences of their work.

And, "Died of Starvation" unravels the potentially quaint theological bow-tying of the middle of the poem. Rather than in hope of heaven, the poem leaves readers, as Oliver is left, to think through the blunt, ridiculous truth of death by starvation: "she had died for want of bread." This is perhaps an unexpected move by

Harper. More conventional would have been to end with the glorious deathbed scene made so much of in the middle of the poem, or perhaps with a reconciliation of the tragedy. Harper makes just such an ending in another poem of the same period—"The Dying Christian," published in the *Christian Recorder*. That poem ends thus:

> She faded from our vision,
> Like a thing of love and light;
> But we feel she lives for ever,
> A spirit pure and bright."[25]

By contrast, "Died of Starvation" does not end with the good death. Though the woman leaves this life with a blessing and a sure entrance into eternity, we end with bitter weeping rather than triumphant spiritual glory. This is an important writing decision, since, as a poet focusing on a very small narrative, Harper has complete freedom as to where she stops the story. Perhaps it was faithfulness to the text. Though the morning comes full of dazzling light, here, the light must read as ironic, for it sheds a light on the woman's dead body rather than her children's faces. Though this morning imagery would be a perfect location to invoke the resurrection, which Ann Douglas identifies as a signature move of the sentimental drive for power in the nineteenth century, neither the resurrection—nor even heaven—is the focus in Harper's work.

Instead, with brutal title, "Died of Starvation," the assertion of starvation in the first stanza, and the unshirking last line, "She had died for want of bread"—the poem asserts the physical, material need for more than spiritual bread. Spiritual sustenance seems assured in the family; what they need is material sustenance—the bread of heaven come down to earth. Harper weaves the food and hunger motif throughout her poem, indicating the bitterness of the material revelation most powerfully in ironic statements of consumption—"for he knew that want was feeding / on the remnant of her life," and "hunger gnawing at her vitals" as his strength is "hunger bitten." The simple, material, and preventable cause of the death makes bitter the laudation of spiritual riches of the family.

Harper's frank juxtaposition contrasts the glories of the spirit's future with the bitterness of the flesh's present reality; it is a difficult ending to parse. Perhaps Harper leaves the reader to wonder on responses that would make the bread of life (material) as available as the bread of life (spiritual). Her late poem, "Songs for the People," suggests that she wants her poetry to do this:

> Let me make songs for the people,
> Songs for the old and the young;
> Songs to stir like a battle cry
> Wherever they are sung.[26]

But she does not suggest any battle plans in "Died of Starvation." Or perhaps Harper seeks to offer some sort of comfort in her poem. She writes,

> I would sing for the poor and aged,
> When shadows dim their sight;
> Of the bright and restful mansions,
> Where there shall be no night.[27]

But if so, why end with the bitter weeping—refusing to be comforted? But then perhaps her poem will

> . . . soothe all [the world's] sorrow
> Till war and crime shall cease;
> And the hearts of men grown tender
> Girdle the world with peace.[28]

But, though we see a tenderhearted man weeping over the death of his wife here, his bitterness edges the tenderness—if we look back to Dickens—with the threat of violence rather than peace.

Harper's poetry in other settings and places does not shy from the pedagogical. Her poetry promotes a realized eschatology in which Christians

> . . . strive by high endeavor
> To make the world more bright;
> To change life's dull and rugged paths,
> To lines of living light.[29]

Surely in the poem from which those lines come, the "lines of living light" are metaphorical paths of good deeds and love. But any poet talking about figurative lines is talking about literal, poetic lines too. What would make the rugged path of Dickens's incident into lines of living light? A text's lines live when they are read and interpreted; when they make meaning. And perhaps Harper's injunction here is—the only aside to the reader in the poem, lodged in a footnote—"see this case." By wrestling herself with the text, giving space for it, responding to it in light of its context, the poem encourages us to see the case. That is what Oliver was supposed to do, but he is just a child.

The reading I'm doing here is one approach to popular and political poetry; through interpretation and faithfulness to the texts and contexts of the work, we find our way to seeing the text, wherever and whenever we are. This might sound obvious. But these qualities of Harper's work and person—of popularity and political focus—have perhaps threatened the posterity of her own work. The poems—and their aesthetic patterns—are tied to issues doubtless endlessly repercussing, but which, for many readers, seemed to be rendered less insistent by watershed events: the Civil War ended slavery; Prohibition and its aftermath ended what was Harper's hope for an alcohol-free America; the nineteenth amendment to the U.S. Constitution achieved what Harper would have wanted, a legal end to sex-based voting discrimination. Poems protesting these issues in sentimental terms might then seem less needful for or worth pursuing in ongoing reading—too directly tied to their time and place, perhaps. My students have trouble with it. One even dropped my class because of my inclusion of Harper's poetry: he wrote me that he refused to take a class with a professor who valued ugliness equally with beauty. My classes tend to divide fifty-fifty between on the one hand liking Harper expressly because she is political and accessible and on the other hating Harper expressly because she is political and accessible. Such are the tensions of working at a Christian liberal arts school, where Christian drives after social justice meet the aesthetic values of conservative or classical education. But both sides have pretty much left off actually seeing the case of her work with any attention. Those approving the message and accessibility trumpet the ease of its moral without investigating the richness or struggle within its "more abundant life",[30] those disapproving the message-making office on aesthetic grounds turn away their eyes from the scene altogether. But if lines of living light are to be had in Dickens or Harper, they must be had by seeing the case. Harper is trying to help her readers see the case even as she is wrestling herself with what she sees in Dickens. Scholarly readers are, more and more, trying to do the same with Harper, shedding some "lines of living light" on her posterity as well.

## The Translation of *1984*:
## Unpacking the Possibilities in Murakami's *1Q84*

George Orwell's *1984* is the author's last novel, written while Orwell was struggling with the illness that would eventually end his life. And as scholars have noted, a concern for posterity pervades the novel.[31] This concern is not merely personal posterity, the "sheer egoism" that Orwell says lends writers the "desire to seem clever, to be talked about, to be remembered after death."[32] A more general posterity—the future of the world—concerns Orwell. And his novel has certainly affected, as well as described, that future, at the least by contributing to the future of language by adding terms to the lexicon. It has, indeed, shaped discussions of looming totalitarianism through what must be the very essence of both personal and general posterity, namely the adjectival of the author's name—"Orwellian"—which is weekly thrown down as a gauntlet by news media pundits.

Orwell was concerned for the future; it also worried the main character of his novel, Winston Smith. Their concern for the future of the world, however, is expressed through a concern about the future and survival of text. Under the conditions of the changeable, erasable, or ignorable word, it seems that no possible communication or relationship with the future is possible—there is no way to learn from the past. The anxiety of textual survival first emerges when Winston writes the date of his first diary entry: "For whom . . . was he writing this diary? For the future, for the unborn. . . . For the first time, the magnitude of what he had undertaken came home to him. How could you communicate with the future? It was of its nature impossible. Either the future would resemble the present in which case it would not listen to him, or it would be different from it, and his predicament would be meaningless."[33] Winston seeks to utter truth that will reform the future, but his job at the Ministry of Truth, where he rewrites history and destroys evidence of the past, basically eliminates the possibility: "How could you make appeal to the future when not a trace of you, not even an anonymous word scribbled on a piece of paper, could physically survive?"[34] He answers but bleakly, "He was a lonely ghost uttering a truth that nobody would ever hear. But so long as he uttered it, in some obscure way the continuity was not broken."[35] Orwell the author likewise linked the future to text. Writing itself, he argues, comes out of "the desire to see things as they are, to find out true facts and store them up for the use of posterity."[36] The determination and utterance of truth is significant for the future, for both the author and his character.

When Orwell penned the date of Winston Smith's first journal entry, April 4, 1984 was in the future; when Haruki Murakami penned the April 1984 opening scene of his most ambitious novel to date, *1Q84* (2009–10 in Japanese, 2011 in multiple translations), that date was in the past. Yet Murakami's novel is no less concerned than *1984* with how writing may be related to the future. And it is closely linked to *1984*. Both texts investigate how to establish truth—on which the future depends—through history and memory, under conditions of the shifting text. Murakami is the respected and prolific author of cult favorites *The Wind Up Bird Chronicle* and *Kafka on the Shore*, and a standard entry on the Nobel short list. His *1Q84* translates Orwell's *1984* into a multiply layered, speculative fiction that shows how translation—across languages, cultures, and genres—might establish relationships that develop future possibilities for texts and people.

Translation is a reasonable approach to reading the relationship between *1Q84* and *1984* for a number of reasons. First, not only is Murakami a prolific translator of English literature, translation seems to be at the foundation and heart of his work. He tells the story of writing the first pages of his very first novel in English and then translating them to Japanese, "just to hear how they sounded."[37] Ted Goossen, one of Murakami's translators, has described the Japanese culture from which Murakami comes as "the culture of translation," where readers regularly search out titles not by author, but by translators, including the very popular Murakami, who receive top billing.[38] Furthermore, Murakami was engaged in his greatest and most important translation, of F. Scott Fitzgerald's *The Great Gatsby*, during the period he conceived of *1Q84*. His translation work on *Gatsby* changed his methods and theories about the task of the translator. In "As Translator, As Novelist," his translator's afterword, Murakami writes that *Gatsby* pushed him to put his "novel-writing experience to as good a use as possible" and "brought" his "imaginative powers as a novelist into play" as he found word-for-word equivalency insufficient to *Gatsby*'s sophisticated musicality and signification.[39] I suspect Murakami's mental jointure of novel writing and translation through the work on *Gatsby* affected *1Q84*. For the very title of *1Q84* points to itself as a translation of Orwell through a trick of wordplay. The Japanese word for nine ("kew") sounds the same as the word for the letter Q, and the titles of the two works would be pronounced the same in Japanese.

The basic story of *1Q84* (though there are many stories within it) surrounds a pair of what we might call "moon-crossed lovers" —Aomame and Tengo—in the year 1984. Aomame is a fitness instructor who moonlights as a paid assassin (she kills abusive husbands to rescue their battered wives); in the opening of the story, she climbs down an emergency stairway on the Metropolitan Expressway in an effort to get to a hit on time, only to discover later that the world has subsequently altered.[40] Aomame now inhabits what she comes to call 1Q84, and while she recognizes many similarities to the world she knows, she finds differences in history as well as in cultural and political arrangements (such as the escalation of armament for regular police officers in Japan) that cause her to question the realness of the world she now inhabits. The most significant sign of the change is that a new moon—a second moon—has appeared in the sky. Aomame's efforts to discern what sort of world she inhabits and how to navigate in it or out of it constitute the base action of the novel. The other major plot in the book is the story of Tengo, Aomame's long lost love, who has grown up from their childhood acquaintance to be a math teacher who also moonlights, but not as an assassin, as a writer. In the novel, Tengo is caught up in an effort to rig a major writers' contest by rewriting one of the submissions so that it has a better chance of winning. The submission, Fuka-Eri's *Air Chrysalis*, chronicles a young girl's experience in a world with two moons as she interacts with a religious cult animated by a strange, sinister force called the Little People. The story compels Tengo and his editor Komatsu, even though it is technically and formally flawed, and both men want to see it accomplish something in the world.[41] The problem is that the text is badly written—and the writer Fuka-Eri, in Komatsu's professional opinion, "has no future."[42] So, Komatsu hatches a plan to have Tengo, a careful though little-published craftsman, completely rewrite the manuscript. Rather than claiming it as his own, Tengo will step out of the way and let Fuka-Eri, take all the credit. *Air Chrysalis*, the story she has written—and that Tengo rewrites—is the story of the world that Aomame knows in the alternate 1984—1Q84. Murakami's novel follows the story of whether Aomame will be able to escape 1Q84 and return to 1984—and whether she and Tengo will be able to escape the malicious intentions of the religious cult and reunite under a single moon to pursue their long-lost love.

*1Q84* translates the message of *1984* to a new context, rewriting it in a move that both unpacks and expands its force, but also includes a critique. Murakami describes his purpose as follows: "First, there was George Orwell's *1984*, a novel about the near future. I wanted to write something that was the opposite of that, a novel on the recent past that shows how things could have been. . . . I had this feeling that I wanted to re-create the past, rather than re-produce it. I am always doubtful about whether this world that I am in now is the real one. Somewhere in me, I feel there is a world that may not have been this way. . . . I think people are gradually starting to understand and accept the realness of unreal things. To me, September 11 (2001) does not feel like an incident that took place in the real world. There must be a world somewhere that this didn't happen."[43] Murakami's rewriting of the past then, parallels what Winston Smith does in *1984* in the Ministry of Truth, rewriting the past in an effort to control the present and the future. Murakami's work, however, does so in ideological concert with, rather than against Orwell's anti-totalitarian mindset. Murakami has spoken about his commitment to always side with the underdog in and against the system—his Jerusalem Prize acceptance speech included a parable to that effect: "Between a high, solid wall and an egg that breaks against it, I will always stand on the side of the egg"; thus, his *1Q84* fictional rewriting of the past has all the effect of an anti-totalitarian dystopia in its own right, despite its different ending.[44] Murakami's *1Q84* offers an alternative vision for the triumph of love—rather than its defeat—against a totalitarian regime. He does this by recreating the recent past—1984 the year and *1984* the novel—to bring about an alternate future than the one we know as the past/present. This brings about for Murakami a real unreal, which remakes and reinvests the real with hope. And this, as Aomame says, "is what it means to live on. When granted hope, a person uses it as fuel, as a guidepost to life."[45]

The large structure of Tengo's plot of rewriting the unpolished work of Fuka-Eri mirrors both what Winston Smith does editing history at the Ministry of Truth ("You rewrite stuff," Fuka-Eri comments, after Tengo describes Winston's job as the rewriting of history) and what Murakami does when he writes 1Q84.[46] Tengo's rewriting of the story, which is a rewriting of events that have, according to Fuka-Eri, really occurred, is a rewriting of the past, something that Tengo devoutly desires, saying, "But if you rewrote the past, obviously, the present would change, too. What we call the present is given shape by an accumulation of the past."[47] Tengo may well be describing the project of the whole book—Murakami's desire to rewrite 1984 in order to rewrite 1984 and the disasters of the late twentieth and early twenty-first centuries—disasters promulgated in the name of extremist religion—such that they would not occur after all.[48]

A translation of 1984 within new contexts would require the resuscitation and recuperation—perhaps even regeneration of—the text's broad aesthetic and philosophical possibilities. For even Orwell knew that 1984 was by no means his best-written work. That he was hurrying through its writing besieged and distracted by illness has been amply commented on by scholars. Morris Dickstein has pointed out Orwell's letters as a source demonstrating the author's dissatisfaction with his work—particularly the ending—and has identified various unconvincing characters and stylistic effects poorly taken from other more prominent literatures.[49] Given his approaching death, there really was no more future for Orwell as a novelist than Fuka-Eri, though Orwell was, of course, at the end of his life rather than the beginning. And the legacy of 1984 has been almost completely ideological or content-based, rather than aesthetic. Though Orwell pointed to aesthetics as a major motivation—one of several—for his life's work, here, illness's disabling power leaves the text somewhat unidimensional, even considering the priority of the political—broadly conceived—in Orwell's work.

The way that Murakami's novel approaches Orwell's is to bring out in it, like the most careful translator, the strands and strains of the text that are lost in the shifts of time and language and lost in the simplification of the text that occurs in popular culture—perhaps even those missing because the author himself was unable to realize them as he would have wished. Like the *newspeak* that the novel discusses, the discussion surrounding the book has pared down its language to the most basic of terms. It is almost impossible to know now, from a survey of popular allusions, that the protagonist in *1984* is just as concerned about the nature of time, history, and reality as he is about the horrors of Big Brother and the Party. Orwell's novel has become Orwellian. As one of Murakami's characters articulates it: "[*1984*] was an allegorical treatment of Stalinism, of course. And ever since then, the term 'Big Brother' has functioned as a social icon. That was Orwell's great accomplishment. But now, in the real year 1984, Big Brother is all too famous, and all too obvious. . . . There's no longer any place for a Big Brother in this real world of ours."[50] Murakami translates and transports to the twenty-first century the richer engagement with the ideas and questions raised by the text. Today, surveillance culture is so ubiquitous as to provoke mostly nonplussed responses from the broader public. The single-word condensed concepts that contemporary readers link to *1984* do not offer as much on how we got here or how to manage within that culture of surveillance. So, in *1Q84*, the text figures the Little People, their shape shifting, and their ambiguous morality, as undermining us. Orwell's *1984* does put some ambiguity around Big Brother and the Party, but that ambiguity is mostly lost in the distillation of the text. Orwell's text actually presents a nuanced evil that undermines the protagonist from the inside. Murakami's novel brings the ambiguity to the foreground, expanding and unpacking it in a translation for the twenty-first century. It identifies insidious forces that fuel religious totalitarianism rather than political—a more twenty-first-century version of Orwell's problem. Further, it documents and indeed supports resistance to those forces.

Now, *1Q84* has received mostly positive reviews for its ambition and complexity, as well as for the way it uniquely bridges the genres of literary and speculative fiction.[51] Yet the text has also been criticized by some reviewers for its clichéd, overinflated language, and its expansive, potentially morally vacuous lacunae.[52] Compared to a more finely wrought *Kafka on the Shore*, the sentences of which, though just as unshowy, are remarkably vivid, the language of *1Q84* itself seems almost exhaustingly pedantic. It is a 925-page book (English edition), and many of the scenes contain a sense of being more than enough; even trying to quote it to write about it is difficult. Many critics have tactfully wondered if the prose is flattened by translation, and less tactfully suspected hasty composition, or the diminishing capacities of an aging writer.[53] I think that a closer look at the text does indeed pin the cause to translation—but Haruki Murakami's translation of George Orwell, not Jay Rubin's translation of Haruki Murakami. Kathryn Schulz writes in *The New York Times Book Review* that the formal expansion of *1Q84* after the magnificent opening of the text is a flaw: "Like our own universe, the weird world of *1Q84* begins with a big bang—and then, for good and for ill, just keeps expanding."[54] She finds no organizing principle or philosophical underpinning to the spinning expansion—a vortex in reverse—of the text. Yet is this not how translation itself works? David Ferry, National Book Award winner and veteran translator of Horace has remarked that translation sometimes demonstrates an expansion in quantity of words because translation itself may be viewed as an unpacking of possibility within the original—which often requires more words than the original.[55] Wilhelm von Humboldt, in his introduction to *Agamemnon*, has written that in translation language itself is "expanded into a greater representation of complexity."[56] If we consider *1984* as the philosophical and formal underpinning of the text, then it makes sense that the text expands in *1Q84*, because *1984* deals with innumerable questions about the relationship between time and text in a panopticon-world where significance, memory, or existence are threatened. The longer form, the continuation of meaning-making, is the fruit of the ur-text that *1Q84* cultivates.

In addition, the repetition and pedantry have thematic force; they function as the translation and unpacking of one of Orwell's main philosophical ideas, that under the totalitarian insistence on the manipulability of the past, the real is incredibly difficult to chart. Here's an example. In the space of any conversation in the text, there are several instances when one character exactly repeats the words of another. Chapter beginnings repeat the endings of previous chapters, too. In chapter 13 of book 2, Aomame is preparing to save Tengo by acceding to the cult leader's request that she assassinate him, even though his followers will try to seek revenge. The conversation between Aomame and the leader as he tries to convince her to kill him is laden with repetitions—it mimicks an over-the-top syllogistic *style*. The style functions to call attention to a chain rule of interaction whereby each statement is measured against the statement before it—questioning it—as a means toward the progression of an argument that seeks the truth. Narrative economy would demand something more luminous and powerful from the characters, but such repetitiveness in conversation has a flavor of the real.

And the real, of course, is exactly what Aomame is seeking with all her might to hold onto. The prophetic taxi driver who lets her out at the emergency stairwell on the Metropolitan Expressway at the novel's opening reminds her that after doing something out of the ordinary, "Things may look different to you than they did before. I have had that experience myself. But don't let appearances fool you. There's always only one reality."[57] But even he repeats himself: "'There is always, as I said, only one reality,' the driver repeated slowly, as if underlining an important passage in a book."[58] In this scene, Murakami points to repetition as an important stylistic factor in the book—one tied to reality. But is it? This taxi driver is patently wrong, as we discover in the aforementioned scene between Aomame and the Leader, and reality has switched tracks when Aomame descends the staircase. Repetition is insistence, the clutch after reality. The structure of Murakami's prose thus cases reality, exploring its knowability and limits, which is the broadly philosophical aim of *1Q84*. It is also what *1Q84* brings out of *1984*, a philosophical sense of the text missing from the more political understanding that has been handed down to the present day.

According to Lamin Sanneh, translation not only transplants and affirms a message in a new context; it also harbors a critique of the bringing culture and language. Murakami's translation brings out a less popularly recognized critique of Orwell—besides the perhaps implicit critique on the insufficiency of his writing—a critique of the misogyny and violence attendant on Orwell's vision of resistance to Big Brother. Yet it seems that this critique has not yet been fully available to readers. Schulz's review critiques *Murakami* for moral failure, not Orwell: "But where Orwell offered a bracing parable about the horrors of totalitarianism, the ethos of *1Q84* borders on incoherent. In *1984*, the story serves to convey ideas about power, injustice, and cruelty. In *1Q84*, power, injustice and cruelty are fantasy elements in service of a story."[59] The review assumes wide agreement on what *1984* is and does; it views Orwell's book as a simple, straightforward moral tale of doomed resistance to totalitarian government that amounts to a jeremiad against the political atrocities of the twentieth century. The misogynistic tint to Orwell's novel and its wild visions of rape and violence—like scenes that are so critiqued in this review's take on *1Q84*—seem to have become completely inaccessible in the public memory of a book that is not really visible or intelligible in the altered language of the contemporary period. Perhaps we may say then that *1Q84*'s sex and violence, not at all unusual among works by Murakami, yet represents something of an echo of *1984*.

For Orwell's *1984* is just as full as *1Q84* of uncondemned, amoral fantasy sex and violence—and a good bit of actual sex and violence, too. Winston himself confesses murder fantasies about his wife, Katherine, to which Julia heartily assents, saying, "Why didn't you give her a good shove [over the cliff]? I would have."[60] Winston confesses in his journal his vulgar purchasing of sex from a prostitute for two dollars just because she was painted, even though she was toothless and dirty. The novel repeatedly details his violent fantasies of hatred:

> Vivid, beautiful hallucinations flashed through his mind. He would flog her to death with a rubber truncheon. He would tie her naked to a stake and shoot her full of arrows like Saint Sebastian. He would ravish her and cut her throat at the moment of climax. . . . He hated her because she was young and pretty and sexless, because he wanted to go to bed with her and would never do so, because round her sweet, supple waist, which seemed to ask you to encircle it with your arm, there was only the odious scarlet sash, aggressive symbol of chastity.[61]

Winston admits to Julia that before she passed him the love note that begins their relationship, he had wanted to rape and murder her, to smash her head in with a cobblestone.[62] In the world of *1984*, the typical taboos—lust, fornication, sexual and physical violence, swearing, gluttony, and the like—are acts of resistance against a totalitarian regime, and are more or less condoned as such. If Winston decides ultimately *not* to murder his frigid wife, it is only because it would not do any good, not because there would be anything wrong with killing her.[63]

In the present, *1984* looks perhaps gentle in comparison to *1Q84* as the latter escalates the abhorrent quality of the sexual violence from rape to child rape, from passion-driven murder to cold-blooded assassination. Yet it is *1984*'s take that in a world of totalitarian control, any resistance would be permissible, if only it were possible, and the point is that resistance is useless. Is this really a bracing moral parable? The rebellion against the party stands to be as constraining or violent or misogynistic as participation in it, leading to a sense that there isn't anywhere a person can exist—which, I suppose, is the point, far more than the simple presence and evil of Big Brother. In the *New York Times Book Review*'s look at *1Q84*, the reviewer critiques Murakami's use of child rape and sexual subjects/fantasies, saying that in Murakami's text, the "moral status" of horrific acts "remains ambiguous."[64] It is true that in Murakami's book, it seems basically unquestioned for a time that vigilante justice through paid assassination is a legitimate action in response to the moral atrocities of the world in *1Q84*. I would argue, though, that this is the translation, an unpacking—with critique—of elements within *1984*. Murakami's inversion of Orwell's violence against women in his crafting of Aomame as assassin of abusive husbands brilliantly translates what is morally ambiguous about *1984*, opening it to critique. And the violence in *1Q84* does not actually remain as ambiguous as such violence remains in *1984*—for in *1Q84*, Aomame's love for Tengo and her reading of *Air Chrysalis* lead her to abandon the anger and hatred of her childhood: "[T]hose feelings were entirely gone. She was grateful for this. As much as possible, she wanted never to hurt anyone, ever again."[65] For Aomame, love and loyalty, the sacrifice that she will make for them, cleanses her hatred and in fact, brings her further on in a spiritual journey that allows her to move beyond the injuries of her childhood trauma as a member of a cult herself: "One time, as the cold wind blew and she kept watch over the playground, Aomame realized she"—unlike Winston Smith, who asserts even to O'Brien that he does not—"believed in God. It was a sudden discovery, like finding, with the soles of your feet, solid ground beneath the mud."[66]

In foregrounding both the ethics and methodology of rewriting someone else's text in translation, *1Q84* offers gems of commentary that, in light of the novel's relationship with *1984*, read as meta-commentary, a gloss on the ways that reading and writing work to bring about the futures of texts, the future of the word, and the future of the world. These resonant statements outline the ambiguous moral position and difficulty involved in participating in the becoming of a text, through translation or otherwise. For instance, when Tengo first considers Komatsu's proposal that he rewrite *Air Chrysalis* in an act of literary deception and cheating, Komatsu defends the proposal: "[T]he most important thing is that we are remaking *Air Chrysalis* into a much better work. It's a story that *should* have been much better written. There's something important in it, something that needs someone to bring it out. . . . We each contribute our own special talents to the project: we pool our resources for one thing only, and that is *to bring out that important something in the work*."[67] That project is arguably exactly what Murakami is doing for *1984*, and that these words come from Komatsu, never an admirable character in the book, demonstrates just how morally sketchy the project could be. Tengo's own statements and feelings about what he is doing for *Air Chrysalis* also reflect the complex relationship of stewardship, service, and his own creative cultivation of the text. When he proposes the project to Fuka-Eri, he says ambivalently, "I would be careful not to change the story but just strengthen the style. This would probably involve some major changes," thus giving with one hand and taking away with the other. He says "*Air Chrysalis* belongs entirely to you. . . . I could never make it mine," but also "I wanted to put my own stamp on the novella that you had written."[68] In reading's translation and expansion, which is always also a response, moral ambiguity abounds.

Murakami's ending makes it possible for the protagonists to escape the world of 1Q84. Unlike Julia and Winston, who are doomed in *1984*, Aomame and Tengo can escape the world of 1Q84, and they do so armed only with the texts that they are reading and writing to ward off "threats" and "dangers."[69] The world that we see in the novel, the world of 1Q84, is a world of incoherent morality and glib relativism where girls get raped symbolically, where cult violence, escalated police armament, and vigilante justice rule. Yet Murakami presents 1Q84 as a world that Tengo and Aomame may escape through their faithful love and sacrifice, and through their drawing attention to its sinister elements in writing—particularly the book within the book, *Air Chrysalis*, and Tengo's own unnamed novel. Murakami's answer to *1984*, his expansive textual response in *1Q84*, is that love could help you escape, through the creative and regenerative power of the word. Love makes reality. The reinvigoration of text that happens when Tengo rewrites it, a response, an utterance—a translation—fuels the love of lovers and the connection between people such that the sinister unreal can be escaped and a new real can be made by love's creative power. If this sounds too easy or even too cliché for an interpretive reading of Murakami, we may take comfort that it takes Murakami 900 pages in English to get there—and that perhaps criticism is an inferior brand of utterance for a page-turner like this, stylistic repetitiveness notwithstanding.

Readers of Murakami's work will recognize this sort of novel as quite a change for an author often very attentive to the individual in almost solipsistic isolation. In *1Q84*, Murakami expands the narrative vision beyond the isolate individual. And not only alternating between Tengo and Aomame, Murakami even extends the narrative perspective to allow readers into the perspective of the evil henchman of the text, Ushikawa. Orwell's text, then, and Murakami's translation of it have cultivated Murakami's future as well—by testing out another way of being and writing.

One could claim, of course, that *1984* does not really have any need for cultivation. In the United States, the 2013 NSA surveillance scandal caused an enormous spike in the novel's sales.[70] Even outside the English-speaking world, anything that smacks of the totalitarian revives interest in the text. Yet *1Q84* functions almost as meta-cultivation of the future of the word through its almost structural commitment to the translation, cultivation, and keeping of many texts, not just *1984*. Through a repetitive, almost obsessive invocation of a number of less-well-known texts within its pages, the novel has reinvigorated the ongoing life of numerous art works. The most obvious example of this would be *1Q84*'s multiple references to Leoš Janáček's symphonic poem *Sinfonietta*. The opening lines of the novel demonstrate how unknown the piece is: "How many people could recognize Janáček's *Sinfonietta* after hearing just the first few bars? Probably somewhere between 'very few' and 'almost none.' But for some reason, Aomame was one of the few who could."[71] The novel then proceeds to refer to the *Sinfonietta* more than twenty times in its pages, so much so that bookstores in Japan began selling recordings of the piece alongside the novel. And this is only the most obvious of such intertextual engagements. And if it is not fair to call Janáček's *Sinfonietta* a text, there are other texts aplenty: Chekhov's *A Journey to Sakhalin*, of which several pages are quoted in full, Proust's *In Search of Lost Time*, the Japanese *Tale of the Heike*, even the Bible. The lyrics of Bach's *St. Matthew's Passion*, themselves a cultivation of the gospel text, get a lengthy treatment. Each of these pieces has its allusive value in the text, but Murakami goes further than allusion. The texts themselves are translated (literally) and uttered, placed into unique narrative contexts—with significant quotations or discussion surrounding them. Rather than an inside joke or a display of intellectual prowess, Murakami's intertextual references constitute an invitation to the reader to move into the expansion and future of the text. To prod any of these texts even the smallest bit shows the power of the utterance—the Japanese *Tale of the Heike*, the quoted section of which deals with doom and acknowledgment of loss, is about the idea that nothing lasts—clearly a text conversant with *1984* and *1Q84*. Proust's *In Search of Lost Time*, which had formerly been translated in English as *The Memory of Things Past*, has two connections to *1Q84*, not just the coincident theme of memory and quirky obsession with time, but also the coincidence that *1984* and *In Search of Lost Time* are works with stylistic problems made more difficult by their authors' terminal illnesses. Murakami's *1Q84* unpacks these texts, translating their utterances and crossings, such that they create both an unreal real and the suggestion of a way to respond to the difference between the two.

The works taken up in these first scrivenings make their partial purpose the cultivation and keeping of other texts through utterance, call-and-response, and translation. In so doing, they create community between texts and also reforge the broken bonds of community between texts and their readers. At bottom, they participate in the futures of the texts they read. Doing so, however, is not without problematic aspects; these texts, in making their own utterances as well, offer no pure version of cultivation. And they are fraught with problems that warrant some consideration—either the ways that they may, in altering and judging the texts that they address, perpetrate violence against texts that they have otherwise hosted and brought forward, or the way that, in failing to ascertain or judge as they should, they may fall into the same failures and injustices as the texts they read. Evil in reading and in texts—and the reconciliation they require—thus becomes the subject of the next two chapters.

## Notes

1. Seth Grahame-Smith and Jane Austen, *Pride and Prejudice and Zombies* (Philadelphia: Quirk Books, 2009), 79.

2. Ibid., 6.

3. Jane Austen, *Pride and Prejudice* (London: Penguin, 1972), 51.

4. Grahame-Smith and Austen, *Pride and Prejudice and Zombies*, 7.

5. Ibid., 9.

6. Ibid., 21: ". . . balls are always a subject which makes a lady energetic" (21).

7. Carol Memmott, "Q&A with Seth Grahame-Smith, Master of the Mashup," *USA Today*, published March 3, 2010, http://usatoday30.usatoday.com/life/books/news/2010-03-04-grahamesmith04_ST_N.htm.

8. Grahame-Smith and Austen, *Pride and Prejudice and Zombies*, 318.

9. Jane Austen, *Jane Austen's Letters*, ed. Deirdre Le Faye (New York: Oxford University Press, 1995), 292.

10. Grahame-Smith and Austen, *Pride and Prejudice and Zombies*, 319.

11. "Books," Seth Grahame-Smith, published 2011, http://sethgrahamesmith.com/.

12. Frances Ellen Watkins Harper, "Iola Leroy," in *A Brighter Coming Day: A Frances Ellen Watkins Harper Reader*, ed. Frances Smith Foster (New York: The Feminist, 1990), 319.

13. Ibid., 69.

14. Robert McParland, *Charles Dickens' American Audience* (Lanham, MD: Lexington Books, 2010), 21-25.

15. Richard Ford, "Oliver Twist," *Quarterly Review* 64 (1839): 46–56. Google Books. Reprinted in *Southern Literary Messenger* 5 (1839): 704–5. Google Books.

16. Ibid.

17. Ibid.

18. Charles Dickens, "A Preliminary Word," *Household Words* 1, no. 1 (March 30, 1850): 1.

19. Charles Dickens, *Oliver Twist: A Norton Critical Edition*, ed. Fred Kaplan (New York: W. W. Norton, 1993), 47–50.

20. Frances Ellen Watkins Harper, "Died of Starvation," in *A Brighter Coming Day*, 69–71.

21. Charles Dickens, *Oliver Twist: A Norton Critical Edition*, ed. Kaplan, 47.

22. Ibid., 48.

23. Ibid.

24. Anonymous, "Oliver Twist; Or the Parish Boy's Progress. By Boz.," *Monthly Review* 1, no. 1 (January 1839): 40.

25. Frances Ellen Watkins Harper, "The Dying Christian," in *A Brighter Coming Day*, 67.

26. Frances Ellen Watkins Harper, "Songs for the People," in *A Brighter Coming Day*, 371.

27. Ibid.

28. Ibid.

29. Frances Ellen Watkins Harper, "A Poem," in *A Brighter Coming Day*, 269.

30. Harper, "Songs for the People," in *A Brighter Coming Day*, 371.

31. Morris Dickstein, "Hope Against Hope: Orwell's Posthumous Novel," *The American Scholar* 73, no. 2 (2004): 105. As Dickstein has written in *The*

*American Scholar*, "If Winston (like Orwell himself) already feels like a dead man, a corpse waiting to be interred, the book throws out a lifeline to some future time, a message in a bottle. Writing what he knows will be a posthumous novel, Orwell lends Winston his own sense of mission and purpose."

32. George Orwell, "Why I Write," in *The George Orwell Reader: Fiction, Essays, and Reportage* (New York: Harcourt Brace, 1956), 392.

33. George Orwell, *1984* (New York: Penguin, 2003), 7 and 32.

34. Ibid., 28.

35. Ibid., 73.

36. Orwell, "Why I Write," 392.

37. Roland Kelts, "Lost in Translation?" Page Turner: On Books and the Writing Life, The New Yorker, Condé Nast, accessed April 16, 2014, http://www.newyorker.com/online/blogs/books/2013/05/lost-in-translation.html.

38. Ted Goossen, "Haruki Murakami and the Culture of Translation," in *In Translation: Translators on Their Work and What It Means*, ed. Esther Allen and Susan Bernofsky (New York: Columbia University Press, 2013), 184.

39. Haruki Murakami, "As Translator, as Novelist: The Translator's Afterword," in *In Translation: Translators on Their Work and What It Means*, ed. Esther Allen and Susan Bernofsky (New York: Columbia University Press, 2013), 173.

40. Aomame's name, which means green peas, is explicitly annotated as such in the novel. Given the slightly misshapen, greenish second moon in the sky in the alternate-track *1Q84*, the name seems to link Aomame and the alternate world through the image.

41. Haruki Murakami, *1Q84* (New York: Alfred A. Knopf, 2011), 17.

42. Ibid., 18.

43. Yoko Kubota, "Surreal often more real for author Haruki Murakami," *Reuters*, last modified November 25, 2009, http://www.reuters.com/article/2009/11/25/us-books-author-murakami-idUSTRE5AO11720091125.

44. Haruki Murakami, "The novelist in wartime," *Salon*, last modified February 20, 2009, http://www.salon.com/2009/02/20/haruki_murakami/.

45. Haruki Murakami, *1Q84* (New York: Alfred A. Knopf, 2011), 641.

46. Ibid., 257.

47. Ibid., 308.

48. Compare Jonathan Safran Foer's *Extremely Loud and Incredibly Close*, a 9/11 novel in which the young narrator of the book seeks to play the images of the disaster—particularly those of the man falling or jumping from the towers, backwards.

49. Dickstein, "Hope Against Hope: Orwell's Posthumous Novel," 103–4.

50. Murakami, *1Q84*, 236.

51. Bill Ott, "*1Q84*," *Booklist* (15 September 2011); Kevin Hartnett, "*1Q84*," *Christian Science Monitor* (2 November 2011); Terry Hong, "*1Q84*," *Library Journal* (15 September 2011): 69; Brian Bethune, "*1Q84*," *Maclean's* 124, no. 45 (2011): 88–89.

52. Kathryn Schulz, "Murakami's Mega Opus," *New York Times Book Review*, last modified November 3, 2011, http://www.nytimes.com/2011/11/06/books/review/1q84-by-haruki-murakami-translated-by-jay-rubin-and-philip-gabriel-book-review.html?pagewanted=all.

53. Philip Hensher, "Parallel Lives," *Spectator* (22 October 2011). Hensher blames the translators for some of the issues but in the end sees Murakami as descending from the heights of his career: "But whose is the appallingly limp reflection—'And this other person was a police officer! Aomame sighed. Life was so strange'? Who is the source of the atrocious bathos when a character thinks, 'By the pricking of my thumbs / Something wicked this way comes' and immediately afterwards, 'Still, Shakespeare's skilful rhyme had an ominous ring to it.' Neither translator can write dialogue with any kind of convincing rhythm. But it is surely Murakami himself who hasn't envisaged the context for his conversations, how his characters realistically respond to each other, physically and verbally. They are always reported as 'sighing' and 'narrowing their eyes'—signs of a novelist reaching for stock gestures rather than looking freshly." In "*1Q84*," *Publisher's Weekly* (29 August 2011): 42, the reviewer writes a very positive review, but notes that "[t]he condensing of three volumes into a single tome makes for some careless repetition, and casual readers may feel that what actually occurs doesn't warrant such length."

54. Schulz, "Murakami's Mega Opus."

55. David Ferry, "Experiencing Translation" (public lecture, Lecture and a Poetry Reading by David Ferry, Wheaton College, IL, October 1, 2013).

56. Wilhelm von Humboldt, "Introduction to His Translation of *Agamemnon*,"in *Theories of Translation* (Chicago: University of Chicago Press, 1992), 57.

57. Murakami, *1Q84*, 9.

58. Ibid., 9.

59. Schulz, "Murakami's Mega Opus."

60. Ibid., 137.

61. Ibid., 15.

62. Ibid., 123.

63. Ibid., 138.

64. Schulz, "Murakami's Mega Opus."

65. Murakami, *1Q84*, 640.

66. Ibid., 742.

67. Ibid., 27.

68. Ibid., 49–50.

69. Ibid., 925.

70. Dominique Mosbergen, "George Orwell's '1984' Book Sales Skyrocket in Wake of NSA Surveillance Scandal," *Huffington Post*, last modified June 12, 2013, http://www.huffingtonpost.com/2013/06/11/orwell-1984-sales_n_3423185.html.

71. Murakami, *1Q84*, 3.

# 3

---

# Evil and Judgment

"But as there is no such thing as an innocent
reading, we must say what reading we are
guilty of."[1]
–Louis Althusser

This book has been lit by the idea that the eschatological purpose
of God for the cosmos includes texts, constituting and illuminating
them—in part through our reading—with expanding love and
meaning-making for the kingdom. But what about the dark side?
How does reading's glorious expansion of meaning and love through
the futures of texts square with evil? A reminder of evil makes the
future of the word as it has been described so far seem a naïve
universal salvation—the idea that no text or meaning will ever be
lost, or that meaning marches unflaggingly toward transparency at
Revelation's sea of glass. And how can an eschatology of texts that
demonstrates the expanding glory of the kingdom of God be visible
in works tainted by so much evil? Texts, after all, are insufficient,
inscrutable, illicit, ill-motived, ill-conceived, ill-formed, ill-finished.

They are occasions of—and for—sin, for the texts we make are co-opted for evil purposes of all scales—responsibility for which belongs to both the author and the reader. Evil even seems a foundation or precondition required for the texts we make. As Walter Benjamin has argued in "Theses on the Philosophy of History," cultural treasures "owe their existence not only to the efforts of the great minds and talent who have created them, but also to the anonymous toil of their contemporaries"—contemporaries that Benjamin figures as the conquered slaves in a Roman procession, "those who are lying prostrate" as "the spoils" are "carried along."[2] Edward Said says as much in *Culture and Imperialism* when he claims that Jane Austen's novels could not exist as they do without imperialism. And genocidal or racist ideologies not only spawn texts, but are spawned by them; individuals have found in texts the inspiration to abnegate personal responsibility or moral commitments. Texts both come out of and prompt more evil. Fallen people make them, and fallen readers read them. The next two chapters, and the scrivenings that come with them, have to do with these evils.

## The Wheat and Tares

Naturally, the mystery of evil in an age in which the kingdom of God has been expressly "at hand" is bigger than just texts. If Christ's incarnation, death, and resurrection inaugurate the kingdom of God on earth as it is in heaven, then why are there still evil, pain, suffering, and death? And what should people do about it? How should we be involved in the rooting out of evil?

After all, the banally pervasive experience of evil seems so antithetical to the image of the kingdom that Jesus sets up in the parables. In Matthew 13, for instance, Jesus tells parable after parable of the kingdom's expansion. The parable of the sower is only the beginning; it emphasizes most centrally a vision of a kingdom that will expand in rich fruitfulness among those who receive and pursue it. The series of parables show a kingdom as solidly present as the ground beneath our feet, massively growing, and worth everything. Listeners would have felt challenged to join in and receive the kingdom—to be good soil, to sell everything and get it lest they miss the vast riches of the rising kingdom. But if God's kingdom was so available, then what to do about evil that is mysteriously still present in the world?

The story of the wheat and tares seems to address directly that question of evil in a world in which the kingdom of God is at hand, but also not yet.

> The kingdom of heaven may be compared to someone who sowed good seed in his field; but while everybody was asleep, an enemy came and sowed weeds among the wheat, and then went away. So when the plants came up and bore grain, then the weeds appeared as well. And the slaves of the householder came and said to him, "Master, did you not sow good seed in your field? Where, then, did these weeds come from?" He answered, "An enemy has done this." The slaves said to him, "Then do you want us to go and gather them?" But he replied, "No; for in gathering the weeds you would uproot the wheat along with them. Let both of them grow together until the harvest; and at harvest time I will tell the reapers, Collect the weeds first and bind them in bundles to be burned, but gather the wheat into my barn." (Matt. 13:24-30)

In this parable, the questions of the source of evil and the solution to it loom large—into the middle of a kingdom where, as we have learned, fruitfulness is assuredly manifold, even though good soil is tough to come by. The poignancy of the question, "Master, did you not sow good seed in your field?" echoes in theodicy discussions spilling out of dorm and hospital rooms alike.

All parables, like the dough in the parable of the leaven, grow in the minds and conversations of their hearers as they are turned over and over and left to expand. But the text of Matthew seems to emphasize the way that this parable in particular houses ideas related to interpretation, which makes it particularly instructive, or at least illustrative for an argument about the eschatology, or kingdom purpose, of reading. Not only does the parable itself contain the questions and conversations of servants who try to interpret a set of signs and states of affairs, but the larger text of Matthew in chapter 13 pictures Jesus and the disciples in a situation very much like that of the master and servants in the parable, in which the conversation allows space for questions and responses relating to interpretation. Also, the gospel writer separates the parable and its interpretation by two more parables of the kingdom of God, the parable of mustard seed and the parable of the leaven, which assertion of context (as interruption) emphasizes the basic fact that the kingdom of God is about growth, expansion, and rising—even irruption. Matthew further includes between the parable and its interpretation an explanation of parables' revelatory purpose, asserting that Jesus spoke in parables to fulfill the prophecy—"I will open my mouth to speak in parables; I will proclaim what has been hidden from the foundation of the world" (Matt. 13:35). These interludes affect our interpretation of the wheat and tares, letting us know that when Jesus tells the story, he wants to focus on the eschatologically cosmic foundation and future of the kingdom as an interpretive approach. They also show that, for parables at the very least, interpretation must be revelation.

For many historical readers of the text, the main concerns are as follows: (1) the presence of evil prompts questions about the goodness of those in charge, questions typically assigned to theodicy, and (2) the presence of evil prompts questions about what we are to do in response. So, Augustine, who in preaching the parable to Christians adapts the parable to his audience's situation, focusing on how it may help to understand the question of evil in the church: "[W]e were wishing, if it might be so, that no evil ones should remain among the good."[3] His charge to the church from the parable was toleration and self-reform: "Let the good tolerate the bad; let the bad change themselves, and imitate the good. Let us all, if it may be so, attain to God; let us all through His mercy escape the evil of this world."[4] Augustine assures the Christians that they *will* be competent for judgment at some point, but only when they arrive at the caliber of the angels. For now, though, they need to watch out against pride, for we are all corruptible. Calvin and Luther both follow Augustine in linking this parable to the church, though Luther preached the wheat and tares against inquisition and the burning of heretics while Calvin refuses as irrelevant to the parable itself any interpretation that denies the church the power of the sword.[5] Though much of the debate surrounding the parable has been about what kinds of tares are under scrutiny—in the individual? in the church?—the application of the parable has largely consisted in suggestions for human responsibility, action, or resistance. Thus have many readers assigned this parable to the question of religious tolerance, perhaps making this passage the "proof passage of religious liberty" as Roland Bainton has asserted, or of patience in enduring hypocrisy in the church or in the world.[6]

Jesus' interpretation of the parable is central to our understanding of his eschatological reading and to our understanding of the parable. He ignores completely the question in the parable that had so intrigued the field workers and—likely—the disciples, then until now. When when Jesus interprets the parable, he redirects readers' focus, re-centering their attention to the primordial, present, and proximate kingdom. He emphasizes eschatological divine judgment. Jesus says,

> The one who sows the good seed is the Son of Man; the field is the world, and the good seed are the children of the kingdom; the weeds are the children of the evil one, and the enemy who sowed them is the

devil; the harvest is the end of the age, and the reapers are angels. Just as the weeds are collected and burned up with fire, so will it be at the end of the age. The Son of Man will send his angels, and they will collect out of his kingdom all causes of sin and all evildoers, and they will throw them into the furnace of fire, where there will be weeping and gnashing of teeth. Then the righteous will shine like the sun in the kingdom of their Father. Let anyone with ears listen! (Matt. 13:37-43)

Jesus offers insight into the relationship between interpretation and the kingdom of God, refocusing hearers on God's interpretive judgment and his purposes for the kingdom, rather than on their own role. Jesus almost mechanically assigns symbols their representative partners. This more lengthy explanation, though, emphasizes the authority of the Son of Man at the end of the ages—Christ's judging authority. The parable's use of parent-child relationships in identifying the tenors of the wheat and tares metaphor—"children of the kingdom" and "children of the evil one" respectively—along with the assertion that the righteous will shine in the kingdom of their Father shows again the authority of the Father and the subordination of the good and bad seed to God's authority.

So the parable of the wheat and tares seems to be about human judgment, but it is really about divine judgment as a good part of the growth of the kingdom (especially in the context of the other parables in the section). It leaves open the question of human judgment of evil in the world. Thus the point of the wheat and tares, especially in the context of its surrounding parables, is to center God's kingdom and God's revelation as the context for judgment and evil in the world. As Klyne Snodgrass writes, "Questions about how we should respond to evil are spawned by the parable, but not addressed. . . . We cannot be tolerant of evil, but the destruction of all evil is not our task. We must stop being evil, and we must stop evil from destroying, but how can we stop evil without becoming evil in the process? That may well be the human question."[7] This parable highlights the mote-and-beam effect in any assignation of evil: as soon as the workers suggest uprooting, they are reminded of their own limitations. It also points us to the necessity of subordinating human judgment to God's authority. What we want to know is what we should do about evil; what we need to know, however, is what God will do about evil. His judgment is a warning for ourselves, and we receive God's invitation to join the kingdom, along with transforming forgiveness and revelation.

If the reader of this book has come to this point with questions of how to judge bad books as the paramount issue, this chapter is going to be a bit of a frustration. Into the persistent questions about bad texts and poor texts and ugly texts and lying texts (and so forth) comes a parable about *readers'* evil judgment? That frustration, however, is essential to the argument, and to this approach to text. For it is certain that bad, poor, ugly, and false texts exist in the world—and probably even that every text is at least partly bad, poor, ugly, and false. But, as this parable illustrates, the moment we get excited about putting on our gardening gloves for a long weeding session of books in our mental or physical libraries, we start uprooting the good with the bad. Our judgments, the parable insists, are fallible and must be subject to God's. Thus this chapter actually considers first God's judgment as reorienting our approach to evil in text, and then how, in our pursuit of judgment and our resistance of it, we may be ourselves opening ourselves up to judgment as we all too often uproot the wheat with the tares.

## God's Judgment

But how does a theology of God's judgment particularly reorient our attention to texts? First, the word is judge. Jesus, the divine word, the word that is with God and is God, is the judge. Jesus, the Trinitarian word, is judge by the mystery of the love of the three in one. And meaning, all meaning, comes from this word, and thus from his judgment. Significance is a function of his love and his judgment. God has given authority to the Son, to the word, for judgment. And the Son speaks in the authority of the Father, submitting to him who loves him and gives him all authority, speaking the words of the Father, and giving the spirit without limit (John 5:27, 3:34-35). The word of God as spoken here is a word of judgment.

The word of Jesus as judge makes the meaning of the cosmos by means of its redemptive judgment. The word of judgment preserves meaning, sustains meaning, and cultivates the meaning of the world through his redemption of the world. And his doing so occurs, as Barth points out, as or because "He the Judge became the judged."[8] The judge who is the word, Jesus, achieves redemption by means of his submission to judgment by the word. The accusation against Jesus, "Jesus, King of the Jews"—stands as the written word under which the word, Jesus, submitted to judgment, and by which he erases or detours the written record against us. Because he stands as one fruitful and righteous, in whom the fullness of the word is made manifest, his submission to judgment can redeem. The judgment of the judge who is judged can fulfill the word wholly and make the word, and the kingdom, fruitful as the vine through the Spirit. And the Spirit will also convict the world about judgment, leading in the renewal of the world through that conviction—leading God's disciples into all truth (John 16:11).

Second, the word of judgment is a word of liberation and becoming. That is to say, God's judgment is about cosmic restoration. God's judgment liberates the cosmos from the constraint and violence and tyranny of the fall, renewing its fruitfulness in the community of the new creation. In the letter to the Romans, the apostle writes that "the creation was subjected to futility, not of its own will but by the will of the one who subjected it, in hope that the creation itself will be set free from its bondage to decay and will obtain the freedom of the glory of the children of God" (Rom. 8:20-21). This freedom comes about through the rescue and renewal of the word of God, which guarantees a future to those who believe—as Jesus says "anyone who hears my word and believes him who sent me has eternal life, and does not come under judgment, but has passed from death to life" (John 5:24).

Third, the word's judgment is a judgment of profound, radical, and utter destruction of evil in concert with the eschatological hope of justice and love in the community of the new creation. The tensions of judgment and eschatological love, transformation, and becoming are juxtaposed significantly in a long passage in the second epistle of Peter. In this section, the idea of the word of God is identified as eschatological—promise-oriented—from the very beginning (vv. 2, 4, 5, 7, 9, and 13)—as an agent of creation and preservation. But the word is also, in this passage, always associated with the necessary judgment

> This is now, beloved, the second letter I am writing to you; in them I am trying to arouse your sincere intention by reminding you that you should remember the words spoken in the past by the holy prophets, and the commandment of the Lord and Savior spoken through your apostles. First of all you must understand this, that in the last days scoffers will come, scoffing and indulging their own lusts and saying, "Where is *the promise* of his coming? For ever since our ancestors died, all things continue as they were from the beginning of creation!" They deliberately ignore this fact, that *by the word of God* heavens existed long ago and an earth was formed out of water and by means of water, through which the world of that time was deluged with water and perished. But *by the same word* the present heavens and earth have been reserved for fire, being kept until the day of judgment and destruction of the godless. But do not ignore this one fact, beloved, that with the Lord one day is like a thousand years, and a thousand years are like one day. The Lord is not slow about *his promise*, as some think of slowness,

but is patient with you, not wanting any to perish, but all to come to repentance. But the day of the Lord will come like a thief, and then the heavens will pass away with a loud noise, and the elements will be dissolved with fire, and the earth and everything that is done on it will be disclosed. Since all these things are to be dissolved in this way, what sort of people ought you to be in leading lives of holiness and godliness, waiting for and hastening the coming of the day of God, because of which the heavens will be set ablaze and dissolved, and the elements will melt with fire? But, in accordance with *his promise*, we wait for new heavens and a new earth, where righteousness is at home [emphasis added]. (2 Pet. 3:1-13)

From the flood to the present, the eschatological vision requires that whatever is evil, whatever is contrary to shalom, is to be utterly destroyed so that the community of the new creation can flourish. The new heaven and new earth referred to here are the renewal of the world, which is not a new creation *ex nihilo*, but rather a re-creation akin to the resurrection of the body—in which the sin nature must be completely destroyed, and the body of death done away with. In this same way, the cosmos must undergo the transformation, resurrection, if you will, that marks the radical continuity and discontinuity between the now and not-yet kingdom of God.[9]

Yet, the purpose of scriptural discourse on judgment is always the delay of finality. That is, prophetic statements of God's judgments are only partly performative—they pass judgment, but do not complete the judgment that they pass. Instead, God's judgments are *transformative*. All biblical discourse surrounding judgment defers judgment's finality because it implicitly appeals for repentance that would turn judgment to mercy. The letter emphasizes its own pleading in self-reference—"this is now, beloved, the second letter I am writing to you" in the first verse. Additionally, the final reference to the promise at the end of the passage emphasizes that the word of God not only creates, sustains, and judges through destruction, but works to bring people to redemption and repentance and holiness. In this passage from Peter, we see that the purpose of words about the word's judgment is invitation.

Jacques Derrida has pointed out in his reading of Revelation, the biblical book most associated with cosmic judgment, that the last word is a word of deferral through invitation—"The Spirit and the Bride say come! And let all who are thirsty come!"[10] Peter's letter, too, ends with a series of invitations to holy living—and holy reading. He writes that the church should "strive to be found by him at peace, without spot or blemish," interpret the delay of the promise as "salvation," and read and interpret rightly, rather than to be "carried away by the error of the lawless" (2 Pet. 3:14-15, 17). Peter and John invite their readers to, as Peter says, "grow in the grace and knowledge of our Lord and Saviour" by means of the word of judgment, that is Christ, and by means of words *about* judgment (2 Pet. 3:18).

So, the word of judgment, Christ, and the word about judgment, the word of Christ, is, as we experience it, a profoundly transformative word. Despite its assurance of the word's obliteration of evil, the word yet points toward redemption and reconciliation. Our time is the time of God's revelation of himself through the word, the judgment of which, as we experience it now is always for the purpose of reconciliation. About the word in hell, his descent into hell, there is not space or time to deal in particular, except perhaps to note 1 Pet. 3:18-20, which seems to indicate that God's word of judgment is a word of warning and reconciliation even for those in hell who lived before the time of Christ:

> For Christ also suffered for sins once for all, the righteous for the unrighteous, in order to bring you to God. He was put to death in the flesh, but made alive in the spirit, in which also he went and made a proclamation to the spirits in prison, who in former times did not obey,

when God waited patiently in the days of Noah, during the building of the ark, in which a few, that is eight persons, were saved through water.

In this plea for reconciliation, for the church to "seek peace and pursue it," the Lord is "against those who do evil," but his word is a proclamation "even to the dead, so that, though they had been judged in the flesh as everyone is judged, they might live in the spirit as God does" (1 Pet. 3:12; 4:6). The word of forgiveness is a word that is always saying, never said—seventy times seven, as Jesus says. This word is perhaps an acknowledgment of the temporal tension and confusion in an eternal God's necessary judgment and the will for redemption. As Barth writes, "the final word is never that of warning, of judgment, of punishment, of a barrier erected, of a grave opened. We cannot speak of it without mentioning all these things. The Yes cannot be heard unless the No is also heard. But the No is said for the sake of the Yes and not for its own sake. In substance, therefore, the first and last word is Yes and not No."[11]

It is essential that we hear and read of the judgment of the Lord and respond to it in terms of belief and reconciliation. The parable of the wheat and tares says as much—there is evil, and God will judge it, and the proper response to the God whose kingdom promise and word seems to delay is to believe the word and to always be being reconciled to him. When we consider what Klyne Snodgrass calls "the human question,"[12] raised by the parable of the wheat and tares, how to encounter or judge evil in the world—or, for us, in the text—without being turned evil, an eschatological perspective assists us, for the now-and-not-yet of all creation is also the state of affairs for our selves and our judgment of texts. Stanley Grenz writes, in *Theology for the Community of God*,

> The emphasis on divine will as the standard of judgment assists us as well in understanding the manner in which believers will be involved in the act of judging (Matt. 19:28; Luke 22:30; 1 Cor. 6:2; Rev. 20:4). We are

those in whom and among whom the Holy Spirit is creating obedience to God's intent to establish community. As a result, our lives bring to light the failure of moral creatures who do not live in accordance with God's desire.[13]

We are enabled in Christ to discern through his revelation and in the power of the Holy Spirit. Yet we are not fully conformed to his likeness, so our judgment yet requires and misses the fullness of God's justice. As the kingdom of Christ expands in the community of the new creation, the church's mode of loving community and meaning-making—which includes judgment—will function as space and time for God's self-revelation toward the kingdom's expansion and God's glory. This culminates in the "renewal of all things" at which time the body of Christ, sanctified and enabled by God, participates in God's just judgment of Israel, and even the heavenly beings (Matt. 19:28).

First Corinthians 6, which deals with Corinthians' taking each other to court, demonstrates Paul's articulation of the idea that eschatology reframes our thinking about our ability to judge. Paul writes,

> When any of you has a grievance against another, do you dare to take it to court before the unrighteous, instead of taking it before the saints? Do you not know that the saints will judge the world? And if the world is to be judged by you, are you incompetent to try trivial cases? Do you not know that we are to judge angels—to say nothing of ordinary matters? If you have ordinary cases, then, do you appoint as judges those who have no standing in the church? I say this to your shame. Can it be that there is no one among you wise enough to decide between one believer and another, but a believer goes to court against a believer—and before unbelievers at that? In fact, to have lawsuits at all with one another is already a defeat for you. Why not rather be wronged? Why not rather be defrauded? But you yourselves wrong and defraud—and believers at that. Do you not know that wrongdoers will not inherit the kingdom of God? Do not be deceived! Fornicators, idolaters, adulterers, male prostitutes, sodomites, thieves, the greedy, drunkards, revilers, robbers—none of these will inherit the kingdom of

God. And this is what some of you used to be. But you were washed, you were sanctified, you were justified in the name of the Lord Jesus Christ and in the Spirit of our God. (1 Cor. 6:1-11)

Paul's seemingly out-of-context reference to judging the angels is actually a reframing of the Corinthians' mundane acts of judgment of disputes in light of the present and coming kingdom of God, to which he refers explicitly at the end of this section. Paul writes that when the Corinthians remember the transformation of the whole world in God's kingdom, they will realize that they should be practicing wise discernment of the kingdom even now before the healing of time when their sanctification will mean they are holy enough even to judge heavenly beings. For the Corinthians, this meant that they needed to be willing to judge more—not to surrender authority to a world that does not follow kingdom values. And yet, Paul asserts, discernment of the kingdom is exactly a call to pursue judgment, but a call rather to refrain from the sorts of sins that would necessitate worldly judgment in the first place and to bear with the sins of others. The kingdom, here in 1 Corinthians as in the parable of the wheat and tares, is one whose God is a God of justice; our sin will not stand in that kingdom. Remembering the kingdom of God is to remember that we are hopeless, sunk in sin without the rescuing hope of the risen and returning Christ, who washes, sanctifies, and justifies us. Paul puts whatever rifts between people that require judgment—the sins and the relationships—under the authority of the kingdom first. Within the church, Paul says, the judgment required is the present-future judgment of God, whose judgment and justification are transformative.

Paul is talking about judging within the context of relationships between people, members of the church, here. Because of that, this passage—and Grenz's passage, for that matter, since he emphasizes judging "moral creatures,"[14] which is clearly an anthropological term for him—does not directly address judging things other than people who are outside of the kingdom of God or not yet under the full authority of the kingdom of God. God's working through the church in the kingdom of God means that whatever the case, followers of Christ should not be looking for judgment of their squabbles outside the framework of submission to the kingdom of God.

## Human Judging in the Kingdom

There have been arguments that human judgments in reading may well serve the kingdom of God, even to denounce evil and discern its invasions. For as in the prophets, the denunciation of injustice is part of the future-oriented, reorienting kingdom of God. The characterization of the evil thing as evil makes space for repentance and the ultimate fulfillment of the promises of peace and justice. Then, like the tares, which become fuel, even evil acts become transformed into what makes the kingdom come. Moltmann has argued that "hope's statements of promise must stand in contradiction to the reality which can at present be experienced. . . . They do not seek to make a mental picture of existing reality, but to lead existing reality towards the promised and hoped-for transformation."[15] And thus also judgment may be eschatological, to serve the kingdom's growth and God's glory.

An example of this view is Milton's *Areopagitica*, which in 1644 argued against the Licensing Order of 1643, a law requiring texts to receive approval before publication. The work is often read as a liberal argument against censorship or in favor of freedom of the press. But for Milton, the point was rather to argue against prejudgment of works, not against judgment. Or, perhaps it argues against inferior judgment: "that the determination of true and false . . . might not be in the hands of the few . . . men commonly without learning and of vulgar judgment."[16] Indeed, *Areopagitica* was not even fully against prejudgment, as the essay at a few moments praises the Areopagus for burning books; Milton's fear seems most directed at the undesirable situation of books being judged singly or by inferior judges. But the key for our interests is that Milton argued against licensure primarily out of a drive to protect an English culture of reading and writing, of sharing opinion and correcting opinion through judgment, in an intellectual culture that could ultimately play a role in God's millennial kingdom.

Milton's *Areopagitica* supports the idea that communal interpretive judgments could have eschatological force. He tells an Orphic parable of truth as having come "into the world with her divine Master, and was a perfect shape most glorious to look on," but then after Christ ascended, the world tore the body of truth and thus it is the job of all Christ's followers to go "up and down, gathering up limb by limb still as they could find [bits of truth]. We have not yet found them all, Lords and Commons, nor ever shall doe, till her Masters second comming; he shall bring together every joynt and member, and shall mould them into an immortall feature of loveliness and perfection."[17] Milton places the situation of licensure and judgment squarely in a theological and political context: "Now once again by all concurrence of signs . . . God is decreeing to begin some new and great period in his church, ev'n to the reforming of Reformation it self; what does he then but reveal Himself to his servants, and as his manner is, first to his English-men."[18] But none of this will work without a learned people making themselves into the City of God;

> a City of refuge, the mansion house of liberty. . . . There be pens and heads there, sitting by their studious lamps, musing, searching, revolving new notions and idea's wherewith to present, as with their homage and their fealty the approaching Reformation: others as fast reading, trying all things, assenting to the force of reason and convincement. . . . What

wants there to such a towardly and pregnant soile, but wise and faithfull labourers, to make a knowing people, a Nation of Prophets, of Sages, and of Worthies. . . . [T]here of necessity will be much arguing, much writing, many opinions.[19]

In this sense, Milton is arguing for freedom to publish, but not against in any way the necessity of judgment; for judgment itself, in freely expressed and defended opinions, will arise out of the weighing and testing of ideas. In fact, this situation will bring about a new reformation—an advance in the heavenly kingdom, which, as Milton continues, is made possible because of the earthly kingdom's national discourse, which makes and builds meaning.

Methinks I see in my mind a noble and puissant Nation rousing herself like a strong man after sleep and shaking her invincible locks: Methinks I see her as an Eagle muing her mighty youth, and kindling her undazl'd eyes at the full midday beam; purging and unscaling her long abused sight at the fountain it self of heav'nly radiance; while the whole noise of timorous and flocking birds, with those also that love the twilight, flutter about, *amaz'd at what she means* [emphasis added].[20]

The growth of meaning that occurs through English publishing and the discourse surrounding it will be a glory to the world. Truth will fight for herself in such a system—and we need not think that we know where God will deal it out: "Neither is God appointed and confin'd, where and out of what place these his chosen shall be first heard to speak."[21]

For Milton, a culture of criticism and ideas builds human virtue, and the judgment of falsity and error is part of the process: "He that can apprehend and consider vice with all her baits and seeming pleasures, and yet abstain, and yet distinguish . . . he is the true warfaring Christian."[22] For Milton, Paul's letter to the Thessalonians, cited in *Areopagitica*, is the key: "Prove all things, hold fast to that which is good" (1 Thess. 5:21). In this example, Milton argues that reading's judgment—particularly the exchange of critique and judgment—an almost Habermasian public sphere, really—is the method by which England, despite a vast intermingled (and unavoidably so) field of truth and error, is strengthened in the truth and participates in God's bringing forth of truth in the world. Thus Milton argues against licensure, since it would be inhibiting the communal expression of the most sound and significant ways of judging.

And we may see the benefits of such a culture of prophetic judgment of texts in the public sphere, where the correction and proliferation of ideas leads to innovation. Stanley Fish has written that Milton's real goal in the essay is not freedom of the press, but advocacy of "the process of endless and proliferating interpretations whose goal is not the clarification of truth, but the making of us into members of her incorporate body so that we can be finally. . . a 'living oracle.'"[23] The interpretation-oracle, like many oracles, has a revelatory and eschatological orientation; as the exalted rhetoric makes plain, it is clearly tied to the development of millennial energy. Fish's reading of Milton's proliferation of interpretations gets at a lovely image of a word made future through reading and community in the kingdom of God. Judgment and counter-judgment, interpretation and correction, create an ongoing and communal space-time for revelation of truth, one not willed solely by any individual, but by God, as God ordains, for God's kingdom.[24]

The problem with Milton's glorious idea is that all human judgment fails, even if a public sphere that necessitates judgment may correct flawed judgment at times. Augustine writes in *The City of God* book 19 that though our judgments be necessary for the public sphere to continue, they inevitably do violence against the innocent, leading us to the prayer of all who are thus tragically limited—well, at least those who are pious: "From my necessities, deliver Thou me."[25] Our judgments fix or halt fruitfulness, in a destructive, corruptive way. And while judgment is necessary for meaning-making—and perhaps, if we believe Milton, allows our participation in the kingdom, our own culpability bends our own judgments rather toward the violence of totality than the cultivation of becoming. In a sense, our judgment creates the reality that it pronounces—for there are implications to our judgments. In engaging texts, our interpretations, in judgment, inevitably fix the text's meaning for use, crafting our idolatrous response to the condition of textual limitation. This occurs even when our judgments explicitly choose *not* reading, as in the fixing of texts' meanings by consigning them to the flames—literally or figuratively. In this sort, the reader anticipates the final transformative judgment of God, with evil results.

## Evil Interpretation

Human sin, according to Augustine, is the will's failure, its turning from the beatific good of a creative God to nothingness.[26] An evil decision is one that willingly refuses becoming, turning from the great story set in motion by God to the blankness beyond even the blank page. It is a willed repudiation of the glorious, love-charged, creative plenitude of the interrelational Trinity. Augustine locates evil in the person primarily, an act of disordered desire born out of some incapacity for truly seeing and desiring the beatific good in which we live and move and have our being.

Edward Farley has described how the morphology of disordered desire works, the trading of an ultimate good for a lesser, the process by which we become ensnared by sin and evil.[27] To Farley, it is humans' response to our fundamentally tragic vulnerability that does it. Awareness of our limitation (what Ricoeur calls our "finite freedom"[28]), vulnerability, and elemental passions leads us to the feelings of discontent and alienation in suffering. Our response to this is to repulse the suffering, to seek instead to manage, diminish, or negate our limitation by whatever means we can, to satisfy our elemental passions with secondary or ordinary goods rather than beatific ones. These goods become idols; and of course, idols' nonsatisfaction of the elemental goods becomes the ultimate irony, as the knife of nothingness twists in us when they fail to help us transcend limitation. For even as they replace beatific, eternal good with the contingent, they "mundanize the eternal horizon" and become the basis not for safety and well-being, but for a reinvigorated sense of vulnerability and unsatisfied passion, which prompts further acts of management, diminishment, or negation—not only affecting our own lives, but also others' lives—in short, acts of evil that cause further suffering for the community.[29] People make their own idolatrous slavery thus, a cycle of futile acts of contingency management that keeps them from moving toward and realizing their ultimate purpose and direction.[30]

To refuse community is to refuse eschatological purpose. Any individual turn to nothingness, the idolatry of the mundane, is a refusal to read and be read by the story. It interrupts community, the effects of which alienate us from meaning and from the communities of the kingdom in which meaning becomes. In this way we become both responsible and not responsible for the victimization in which we participate and suffer.

It is far from clear, however, exactly how to characterize the relationship between evil and texts. There is certainly not a simple way to ask the question, for evil is primarily privative—it is a refusal of becoming. If language itself is constituted by becoming, then there is no language that can characterize evil's nonbecoming. Or, to put it another way, there was never any understanding of evil outside of acts of textual and symbolic meaning-making. For Paul Ricoeur, the reason that Augustine's classical theory of evil does not reach beyond anthropological theodicy to a comprehensible sociological theodicy is that, in fact, reason isn't an appropriate avenue for pursuing knowledge about evil. Ricoeur has amply demonstrated in *The Symbolism of Evil* that the mystery of evil is only accessible in any way to us through the sign, the symbol that inheres within the mythic. We cannot come to an understanding of evil without a position, a story or a myth from which we interpret it, and the discernment and interpretation of myths, too, is the way by which we express belief, understand and respond to evil. He gives preeminence to the Adamic myth, which "does not imply that the other myths are purely and simply abolished; rather, life, or new life is given to them by the privileged myth," and they "begin to speak to us from the place from which the dominant myth addresses us," which "operates through the myth by means of a reminiscence and an expectation."[31] The Adamic myth in reminiscence and expectation stands in for the entirety of the eschatological story, out of which we are able to read all things, even sin. "The Christian," Ricoeur writes, "does not say: I believe in sin, but: I believe in the remission of sins; sin gets its full meaning only retrospectively, from the present instant of justification. . . . It follows that the description of sin and the symbolization of its origin by means of the myth belong to the faith only secondarily and derivatively, as the best counterpart of a gospel of deliverance and hope."[32] If this myth gives place and life to other myths, it offers us an opportunity to receive from texts and stories the opportunity to consider evil as nothingness that will be filled, made and remade by the plentitude of the promise of God. Ricoeur's sensible idea is that because epistemology must inhere in hermeneutics, we are prompted to a sort of thinking action through interpretation of myths and symbols that already exist—for the world is, to a certain extent, remade in its own renewing metaphors.[33]

I would like to briefly consider here two general ways reading inhabits tensions inherent within the eschatological vision of the Adamic myth, the tension of "being destined for the good" and being "inclined toward evil."[34] One is in reading's engagement with multiplicity of meaning. I have been characterizing multiple, developing, becoming readings as the kingdom-come plenitude and futurity granted to language through the resurrection. But might it not as easily be considered a cancerous tumor as a first fruit of the Trinity's love? Rather than blessing, the blossoming of meaning in text may feel like a curse—the proliferation of difference and division basically equivalent to malignancy. If a text can mean anything, if there is no way to assert truth or its ethical import, then it sinks into the abyss of nonmeaning through a supersaturation of meaning-options. Indeed, text's unlimitedness, or minimal limitation, in reading, opens it up to the co-optation of whatever power might seize it and corral it. When Ricoeur considers the corruption of language, its ambiguous dual drive between good and evil, he describes the fragmentation of language—with its attendant fragmentation of humanity—as a part of the evil: "the power of naming all beings, which is the royal prerogative of a being created scarcely inferior to God, is so profoundly altered that we now know it only under the regime of division of idioms and separation of cultures."[35] To the extent that any meaning is concurrently already and not yet in the kingdom of God, its indeterminacy is right and proper, for we are all not yet, and the multiplicity of meaning can create ongoing relationship, through dialogue and even correction. But it also means that, as with Eliot's Prufrock, it is impossible to say just what we mean.

Martin Buber's anthropology of evil suggests that evil is an enslavement to indecision, when the soul gives in to and becomes ensnared by the chaos of possibility. Out of the swirl of primordial chaos, the soul "exchanges an undirected possibility for an undirected reality, in which it does what it wills not to do, what is preposterous to it, the alien, the 'evil.'"[36] Evil, Buber writes, is "lack of direction and that which is done in it and out of it as the grasping, seizing, devouring, compelling, deducing, exploiting, humiliating, torturing, and destroying of what offers itself."[37] The first stage is the soul's choice of indecision; the further stages follow—a hardening into a course of indecision, self-alienation—and alienation from the outside world.[38] Good, Buber says, is the choice of a conversion toward the single right direction for the individual soul, the affirmation of the individual self and its becoming toward "the one taut string, the one stretched beam of direction."[39] Rejecting the "undirected plenitude," the good, by an act of will or even conversion, unifies the soul and, choosing repeatedly, stays the course of wholeness and oneness: [40]

> Again and again, with the surge of its enticements, universal temptation emerges and overcomes the power of the human soul; again and again innate grace arises from out of its depths and promises the utterly incredible: you can become whole and one. But always there are, not left and right, but the vortex of chaos and the spirit hovering above it. Of the two paths, one is a setting out upon no path, pseudo-decision which is indecision, flight into delusion and ultimately into mania; the other is the path, for there is only one.[41]

Buber explicitly separates his anthropology of good and evil from more theoretical engagements, so in a sense we might say he is not addressing the specifics about how language's meaning-making touches on good and evil. Fair enough, but since any assigning of evil to texts bears some relationship to author or reader or society, it is appropriate to consider his anthropology as relevant to how we may fail in reading.

For the case of reading, the problem of multiplicity of meaning turns toward evil when the reader's endless differing defers significance so far as to step back from engagement entirely. Such a posture inhibits love by offering no handhold for it, leaving text and reader—and even author—dangling over the abyss. This is tantamount to simply not reading, preferring not to, refusing the act or responsibility of judgment, perhaps simply setting out possibilities ad infinitum with no possible room for response. This becomes the uninterruptible drone of meanings that become a form of oppression because there is no space for being-in-relation to the text in a larger community. And in an endless deferral and differentiation of meaning, the text and the community of readers cannot speak back.

Yet does not the alternative, what Buber touts as the one path, the decision-making and the same, which resists the vortex, itself fall into the same pitfall of evil? Ricoeur points it out clearly in *The Symbolism of Evil*: "Who can realize himself without excluding not only possibilities, but realities and existences, and, consequently, without destroying?"[42] And Buber himself, in his most famous work, *I and Thou*, acknowledges it as well: true actualization, the becoming of anything in the world, occurs through an entering into relation that requires all other possibility to be "exterminated; none of it may penetrate into the work."[43] If done with one's whole being, entering into relation creates something new; it is a receiving of grace and true life through encounter. But, this relation, the *I-You*, is hampered, temporary, doomed within the language of response. For, the conceptualizing of any thing or person, the decision itself, the interpretation, the experience of things, is inevitably a fixing of them in place. As Buber writes, "Only silence toward the You, the silence of *all* tongues, the taciturn waiting in the unformed, undifferentiated, pre-linguistic word leaves the You free and stands together with it in reserve where the spirit does not manifest itself but is. All response binds the You into the It-world."[44] Language itself is the language of relation, the language that creates, a responsiveness in which relationality is itself conceivable and in which the eternal word resides. Yet it must be in the waiting that the relationship forms—for the making of things, their bounding and essentializing and categorizing, is a making of use rather than relation, and slips us outside the true, real life toward which we are called to become. The violence of interpretation—of metaphysics itself, really—is a commonplace.

Even in our mundane readings, simply because our judgments of good and evil stop meaning-making even as they seek meaning, our takes are inevitably mis-takes, as a short example will illustrate. In a recent semester, I put on the short-answer section of a final examination an excerpt from Countee Cullen's "Heritage" in which the author lays out a vision of a black Jesus and asks forgiveness for his need to create a Jesus to whom he can relate, a soulful, physically attractive Jesus. My class had read the text together and discussed it thoroughly, during which discussion I had shared with the class a reading of which I am fond—Peter K. Powers's understanding of the poem as a musing on the relationship between heritage and sexuality, the pressures of homoerotic desire in relationship to both racial and religious heritages.[45] I had chosen the passage for the final examination precisely because I thought students would be able to neatly produce a close reading in a nice, quantifiably insightful way suitable for the awarding of points. Yet, as with so many final exam questions, such a reading can at times tend to elicit a reproduction of class discussion. One student, however, who'd been absent, perhaps, or never read the text during the term, astonished me. He revived the text by opening up other interpretive possibilities. He wrote,

I do not know for the life of me . . . or the grade [which author or title goes with this passage], but I love it. One minute thought: much like some of the prayers of David when he cries out from grief and hurt rather than rejoicing. Do you ever wonder why we have lost sight of this kind of prayer? Do we think God will find it distasteful? I hope my God would never find my honesty distasteful. Doubt is powerful, and so is anger and fear and hurt; they are the composite of the human condition. When I acknowledge mine, I hope God gives me the strength to then [ask forgiveness like Cullen].[46]

I do not always experience the reopening of a book while grading a final exam, but in that moment, this student's reading reinvigorated a text that I had let harden, showing how even an interpretation I had found innovative and insightful had become an ossification of the text. And in time, even that's student's reading hardened. I found over time spent engaging with his work, that the student tended to see mostly what is useful for doubt in literature; he offered the same reading of *Angels in America* (no doubt correctly in both cases, but also fixedly) in a class the following term. This fixity may not be forever, and no doubt this student's abiding love for Tony Kushner's work in particular will ensure that he revisits the text and refreshes that reading, but this situation parallels a broader situation of the possible ways that readings may, even with the best of intentions, close down texts rather than open them. Even as they can, for a moment, make a text an object of wonder or insight, they inevitably halt—as inexorably as the periods of the sentences that comprise our readings. And in doing so, they fix us and the texts that we engage, perpetrating a violence against both.

### Therapy for Judgment?

Kevin W. Hector's recent work *Theology without Metaphysics* has suggested that our subjection to the violence of metaphysical language, particularly in theology, may be avoided in a therapeutic approach. Hector suggests that we may ground and evaluate God-talk within the intersubjective relationality and trajectory of the normative Spirit of Christ. The Spirit grounds and enables our theologies to participate in truth as they accord with the truths the Spirit affirms—even through differences in time, context, performance, and performers. We then judge the truth of our beliefs by a process of "taking true"—an expression and ownership of one's assessments and "recognition" of the Spirit and the Spirit's presence in previous instantiations of those beliefs.[47] This coincides tidily with a participatory, eschatological framework—and Hector follows the thru-line of his argument by linking the theology without metaphysics to expressive freedom and emancipatory critique set in motion by the normative Spirit of Christ.[48] It is the presence of Christ's Spirit with us that allows us, in Hector's view, to evaluate our judgments within the context of the inter-recognitions of the Spirit within the community of believers.

The presence of God with us as creator and just judge, which Hector labels as the "normative Spirit of Christ," is the key to our being able to intersubjectively negotiate the necessity and impossibility of our judgments.[49] I believe that in reading, this means that we are necessarily reliant on revelation and the power of the Holy Spirit. Luther asserts as much even about Matthew's inclusion of Jesus' interpretation of the parable of the wheat and tares:

> But who could have discovered such an interpretation, seeing that in this parable he calls people the seed and the world the field; although in the parable preceding this one he defines the seed to be the Word of God and the field the people or the hearts of the people. If Christ himself had not here interpreted this parable every one would have imitated his explanation of the preceding parable and considered the seed to be the Word of God, and thus the Saviour's object and understanding of it would have been lost.[50]

By re-centering the Savior's eschatological object for his works and his eschatological judgment and understanding of them—in chapter 1, I cited Athanasius' term for it, the "comprehension of God" that undergirds and sustains all things—we can reorient our sense of human judgment of texts.[51] God's interpretation, though, is not a finalizing interpretation. It is becoming and participatory.

Hector makes an effective claim about how judgments may be enacted in the Spirit without recourse to the violence of metaphysics. His argument ends with a claim that a therapeutic approach to language ends in emancipation and justice. Yet though it seems implicit in his argument, Hector doesn't fully map the route by which judgment of language may move from truth-making to reconciliation—the restoration of community through not only judgment, but also grace. For reconciliation, restoration, within all creation there must and will be. Reconciliation will involve judgment, naturally: Revelation 21, which promises the continuity of human culture in the new Jerusalem, completes the statement with a warning, "But nothing unclean will enter [the new Jerusalem], nor anyone who practices abomination or falsehood, but only those who are written in the Lamb's book of life" (Rev. 21:27). However, as Richard Mouw reminds us in *When the Kings Come Marching In*, God's judgment purifies and repurposes the cultural artifacts of the world that would try to oppose God, such that the glories of culture are transfigured and brought into the kingdom.[52] At bottom, because Christ the judge became judged for us, his judgment must in fact *be* reconciliation: as Barth argues, "God's judgment is executed in the forgiveness of our sins."[53] Hector's vision of a just critique of language warrants a further step that it does not fully take, in which the power of the Spirit enables reconciliation through judgment, in which forgiveness and community mark the interpretation of language. In Christ, reading is not only judging, closing down meanings, but is restoring the meaning-making capacity of text, is reconciling, is forgiving texts.

## Notes

1. Louis Althusser, "From Capital to Marx's Philosophy," in *Reading Capital*, trans. Ben Brewster (London: Verso, 1979), 14.

2. Walter Benjamin, "Theses on the Philosophy of History," in *Illuminations*, trans. Harry Zohn, ed. Hannah Arendt (New York: Schocken, 1969), 256.

3. St. Augustine, *Nicene and Post-Nicene Fathers: First Series* VI, ed. Philip Schaff (Peabody, MA: Hendrickson, 2004), 335.

4. Ibid., 335.

5. John Calvin, *Commentary on a Harmony of the Evangelists, Matthew, Mark, and Luke* II, trans. William Pringle (Edinburgh: The Edinburgh Printing Company, 1845), 122.

6. Roland Bainton, "Religious Liberty and the Parable of the Tares," in *The Collected Papers in Church History* (Boston: Beacon, 1962), 95, quoted in Klyne Snodgrass, *Stories with Intent* (Grand Rapids: Eerdmans, 2008), 654.

7. Snodgrass, *Stories with Intent*, 215.

8. Karl Barth, *Church Dogmatics* IV.1, trans. G. W. Bromiley, ed. G. W. Bromiley and T. F. Torrance (Peabody, MA: Hendrickson, 2010), 532.

9. Stanley J. Grenz, *Theology for the Community of God* (Grand Rapids: Eerdmans, 2000), 646.

10. Jacques Derrida, "Of an Apocalyptic Tone Recently Adopted in Philosophy," *Semeia* 23 (1982): 63–97.

11. Karl Barth, *Church Dogmatics* II.2, trans. G. W. Bromiley, ed. G. W. Bromiley and T. F. Torrance (Peabody, MA: Hendrickson, 2010), 13.

12. Snodgrass, *Stories with Intent*, 215.

13. Grenz, *Theology for the Community of God*, 630.

14. Grenz, *Theology for the Community of God*, 630.

15. Jürgen Moltmann, *Theology of Hope* (Minneapolis: Fortress Press, 1993), 18.

16. John Milton, "A Second Defense of the People of England against an Anonymous Libel," in *The Prose Works of John Milton*, trans. and ed. George Burnett (London: 1809), 391.

17. John Milton, "Areopagitica," in *The Riverside Milton*, 1017–18.

18. Ibid., 1019.

19. Ibid., 1019.

20. Ibid., 1020.

21. Ibid., 1023.

22. Ibid., 1006.

23. Stanley Fish, "Driving from the Letter: Truth and Indeterminacy in Milton's *Areopagitica*," in *Remembering Milton: Essays on the Texts and Traditions*, ed. Mary Nyquist and Margaret W. Ferguson (New York: Methuen, 1988), quoted in Flannagan, 990.

24. Milton's own prophetic phraseology in the *Areopagitica* was nearly without effect in his own time; it is through time that Milton's ideas were made possibly helpful—for, according to one biographer, at the time of the pamphlet he was thought to be a "crackpot" (qtd. in Flannagan 992). He was advocating, in other of his writings, ideas still considered problematic by many Christians, divorce on other grounds than adultery. But *Areopagitica*, too, has had a significant future—an influence on Jefferson's "Bill for Religious Freedom in Virginia." I do not mean to suggest that Milton's text, in supporting American democracy, has entered specifically and providentially therein to its eschatological future of American democracy triumphant. But Milton clearly wrote as if he believed that the sorts of arguments made in his essay—and responses to them—were key to the bringing about of an English national public discourse that would prepare the way for the kingdom of God.

25. St. Augustine, *The City of God* (New York: Modern Library, 2000), 683.

26. St. Augustine, *Augustine: Confessions and Enchiridion* VII, trans. and ed. Albert C. Outler (Philadelphia: Westminster, 1955), chapter 5, chapter 8.

27. Edward Farley, *Good & Evil: Interpreting a Human Condition* (Minneapolis: Fortress Press, 1990), 119–38.

28. Paul Ricoeur, *The Symbolism of Evil* (Boston: Beacon, 1967), 248.

29. Farley, *Good & Evil: Interpreting a Human Condition*, 134.

30. Ibid., 136.

31. Ricoeur, *The Symbolism of Evil*, 309, 6.

32. Ricoeur, *The Symbolism of Evil*, 307.

33. Richard Kearney, "On the Hermeneutics of Evil," in *Reading Ricoeur*, ed. David M. Kaplan (Albany: State University of New York Press, 2008), 71–88.

34. Ibid., 246.

35. Ibid.

36. Martin Buber, *Good and Evil* (New York: Charles Scribner's Sons, 1953), 127.

37. Ibid., 130.

38. Ibid., 134.

39. Ibid., 127.

40. Ibid.

41. Ibid., 127–28.

42. Ricoeur, *The Symbolism of Evil*, 312.

43. Martin Buber, *I and Thou*, trans. Walter Kaufmann (New York: Charles Scribner's Sons, 1970), 60.

44. Ibid., 89.

45. Peter Powers, "'The Singing Man Who Must Be Reckoned With': Private Desire and Public Responsibility in the Poetry of Countee Cullen," *African American Review* 34, no. 4 (2000): 661–78.

46. Jerome Hicks, in an assessment administered by the author, December 2012. Used by permission.

47. Kevin W. Hector, *Theology without Metaphysics* (Cambridge: Cambridge University Press, 2011), 234.

48. Ibid., 266, 284.

49. Ibid., 38.

50. Martin Luther, "The Parable of the Tares Which an Enemy Sowed in the Field," in *The Sermons of Martin Luther* II, trans. and ed. John Nicholas Lenker (Grand Rapids: Baker, 1983), 101.

51. Athanasius, *On the Incarnation* (Crestwood, NY: St. Vladimir's Seminary Press, 2011), 53.

52. Richard Mouw, *When the Kings Come Marching In*, rev. ed. (Grand Rapids: Eerdmans, 2002), 29–30.

53. Barth, *Church Dogmatics II.2*, 752.

# Literary Scrivenings 2:
# The Double Bind of Judgment

The texts in this second section of scrivenings do not refer much to God's judgment. There are judgments aplenty and even angels crashing through bedroom ceilings. But rather than considering God's role in demarcating and eliminating evil, these stories take us rather to what Klyne Snodgrass called "the human question" associated with evil: "We must stop being evil, and we must stop evil from destroying, but how can we stop evil without becoming evil in the process?"[1] Henry James's novella *Daisy Miller* and Tony Kushner's play *Angels in America* engage questions of human judgment, one demonstrating the dangers of judgment, the other the necessity of judgment. For the one who reads for the future of the word, juxtaposing these texts yields a sense of bewilderment about the double bind of human judgment: it is both necessary and corrupt.

## Pushing Daisies:
### Henry James's *Daisy Miller* and Judgment's Injustice

Henry James may seem like an odd inclusion in a set of scrivenings about evil and judgment, especially when in light of his famously scathing denunciation, in "The Art of Fiction," of Walter Besant's call for literature with "a conscious moral purpose."[2] For James, moral fiction, if such a category exists, is grounded in liveliness, interest, and air of reality, rather than a set of taboos or platitudes. A good piece of fiction survives by its possession of these lively qualities of writing, and a bad piece of fiction dies for lack of them. James writes in "The Art of Fiction" that "the bad [novel] is swept with all the daubed canvases and spoiled marble into some unvisited limbo, or infinite rubbish-yard beneath the back-windows of the world, and the good subsists and emits its light and stimulates our desire for perfection."[3] James's dismissal of morality as Besant articulates it does not entirely indicate a lack of interest in the subject—even if he does redefine morality as liveliness. Indeed, his interest in the survival and afterlife of fiction is a broader, more integrated, or rather, more *organic* vision of the moral and of judgment than the strictures of morality to which Besant was referring. James's language of subsistence here makes fiction what he calls "a living thing, all one and continuous, like any other organism," and in his preface to *The Portrait of a Lady*, suggests that "the 'moral' sense of a work of art [depends perfectly] on the amount of felt life concerned in producing it."[4] In a moral text, both the text and the author must be full of living, quality consciousness. Since for James, writing and reading were basically the same act of awareness, this requirement for consciousness extends to the reader, too. If a rich consciousness inheres in the writer, text, and reader, a text can escape limbo for a better afterlife—or perhaps even subsistence.

By these standards of morality, however, *Daisy Miller* might have seemed to James doomed. And he expresses a somewhat guilt-ridden interest in *Daisy Miller*'s life, and future afterlife, maybe even as having consequences for his own. Recollecting his intentions for the title of the work, James wrote: "Flatness indeed, one [reader] must have felt, was the very sum of her story; so that perhaps after all the attached 'A Study' [the subtitle of the work] was meant but as a deprecation . . . to the reader, of any great critical hope of stirring scenes."[5] To him, *Daisy Miller* the book was perhaps as dead as Daisy Miller the character, largely as the result of his failure in writing. But James rewrote the text as a play with a happy ending in 1882, revised the text heavily (90 percent of sentences) for its reissue in 1909, crafting a new introduction to it, and so on. He also revived Daisy's situation in figures such as Ralph Touchett in *Portrait of a Lady* and Milly Theale in *Wings of the Dove*. He was haunted by figures who, like Daisy, died too soon (such as, significantly, a beloved cousin, Minny Temple, who died in 1870): he wrote about his obsession with it in a preface to *Wings of the Dove*, "I can scarce remember the time when the situation [of a character dying young] . . . was not vividly present to me."[6]

James's obsession with the possibility of afterlife within the form and content of his writing led to some singular thoughts about the relationship of consciousness to the afterlife for not only the text, but the person, too. He wrote in a 1910 essay, "Is There a Life after Death?," "But what of those lights that went out in a single gust and those life passions that were nipped in their flower and their promise?" He suggests that afterlife is tied to consciousness within life, and asks, "How *can* there be a personal and differentiated life 'after' . . . for those for whom there has been so little of one before?"[7] James argues in the essay that "the quantity or the quality of our practice of consciousness may have something to say to" the quality of a personal afterlife.[8]

Now, by this view, if Daisy Miller—girl or text—did not have a life or afterlife, if her grave was just a "raw protuberance among the April daisies," it was because James did not do a good enough job at making her lively before she died.[9] And if both making Daisy live and getting an afterlife worth having for himself depend on his own level of felt life and consciousness—as expressed in writing, which also lives or dies by felt life and consciousness, then failing at Daisy Miller would be a weighty failure indeed, one with perhaps eternal consequences. The moral consciousness of literature in James becomes eschatological.

In *Daisy Miller*, American-born Frederick Winterbourne is staying in the little town of Vevey in Switzerland, where he meets an attractive compatriot, Daisy Miller. Daisy, in the course of her European travels begins to incite scandal in the American set abroad by her friendship with an Italian man. Winterbourne, charmed by Daisy, remains unable for much of the story to judge Daisy's essential character as good or bad: Is she an innocent flirt or a dangerous coquette?

James characterizes Winterbourne and other socialites of the story as studious readers—with Daisy as a primary text. At both the beginning and the end of the story, Winterbourne is as his friends say, "studying" in Geneva;[10] where "studying" is a euphemism for pursuing women.[11] Mrs. Walker, a Rome socialite, is "one of those American ladies who, while residing abroad, make a point . . . of studying European society; she had on this occasion collected several specimens of her diversely-born fellow-mortals to serve, as it were, as textbooks."[12] And, in the climax of the text, the narration pictures Winterbourne thinking of Daisy as a "riddle . . . to read."[13]

The nearly mocking use of the language of scientific inquiry and method in the story demonstrates the way the readers in *Daisy Miller* seek to bind their human texts into a static, fixed body of knowledge—judging them as futureless and stereotypical as textbook categories. Winterbourne's social and readerly craft is couched in the language of hypothesis, evidence, observation, and analysis, which, in keeping with his chilly name, freeze the floral heroine as in a cryogenic experiment.

This sort of reading seeks to develop in the social world of American high society abroad a set of rules for interaction—what we might call a grammar for proper usage, since judgment facilitates social use. Winterbourne seeks to find a category in which to read Daisy—one that will help him determine how to behave with her in future. When first confronted with Daisy, he tries to figure out the "formula" that applies to Daisy:

> Miss Daisy Miller looked extremely innocent. Some people had told him that, after all, American girls were exceedingly innocent; and others had told him that, after all, they were not. He was inclined to think Miss Daisy Miller was a flirt—a pretty American flirt. He had never, as yet had any relations with young ladies of this category. He had known, here in Europe, two or three women—persons older than Miss Daisy Miller, and provided, for respectability's sake, with husbands—who were great coquettes—dangerous, terrible women, with whom one's relations were liable to take a serious turn. But this young girl was not a coquette in that sense; she was very unsophisticated; she was only a pretty American flirt. Winterbourne was almost grateful for having found the formula that applied to Miss Daisy Miller . . . he wondered what were the regular conditions and limitations of one's intercourse with a pretty American flirt. It presently became apparent that he was on the way to learn.[14]

This passage repeatedly refers to social categories, such as "flirt" and "coquette," and moral norms that apply to these. The repetition of "after all" in describing what Winterbourne had heard from others about American girls suggests that the judgments from onlookers are definitive and authoritative in establishing behavioral guidelines. On the one hand, if Daisy were judged extremely innocent, this would require strictly delimited conversation and interaction—"regular conditions and limitations" necessary to protect virginity and inexperience. On the other, terms such as "coquette," "dangerous," and "terrible" seem to be constraining labels of another sort, requiring avoidance (or, perhaps, a illicit liaison, if one were willing to take the consequences).

When Winterbourne reads Daisy, though, and puts her in a category explicitly labeled "pretty American flirt," he does so without knowing the substance of the label. The hypothesis requires the proof. His attraction to Daisy allows their continued interaction; it keeps him from closing down his reading and truly judging. The moment when Winterbourne hazards the interpretation that Daisy Miller is a flirt, he does so looking forward to exploring the category through *interaction* ("intercourse") with Daisy. And so the passage continues with a lengthy conversation between the two. Admittedly, Winterbourne wants to find the formula to figure Daisy Miller out once and for all. For a time, however, he is unable to do so; and, because of that, their relationship develops.

Winterbourne's early reading of Daisy, for all its desire to close down, cannot, and in its failed attempts actually crafts a future possibility for her—a romantic future in which he imagines eloping with her. Winterbourne makes a hypothesis about how to understand Daisy; yet unlike the textbook or even the formula, this offers a space for responsiveness between reader and text. James writes, "He was ceasing to be embarrassed, for he had begun to perceive that she was not in the least embarrassed herself," and "she gradually gave him more of the benefit of her glance."[15] When he resists the temptation to categorize Daisy—"it was not, however, what would have been called an immodest glance, for the young girl's eyes were singularly honest and fresh"—the argument and counterargument he presents lead to interaction and further contact: "Before long it became obvious that she was much disposed toward conversation."[16] In this moment of interpretation, what seems clear is the speculative, propositional, and above all relational nature of the assessment. Winterbourne is attempting to engage Daisy, rather than pronouncing his final or terminating judgment. His ideas about her, supported by varying evidentiary behaviors and mannerisms, are arguments that open rather than close the discussion.

The aim in Winterbourne's study is to hit on a final knowledge that he figures would lead to truth and justice. James writes, "[I]t was probable that anything might be expected of her. Winterbourne was impatient to see her again, and he was vexed with himself that, by instinct, he should not appreciate her justly."[17] But Daisy confounds him: "It would . . . simplify matters greatly to be able to treat her as the object of one of those sentiments which are called by romancers 'lawless passions'. . . . But Daisy, on this occasion, continued to present herself as an inscrutable combination of audacity and innocence."[18] In his mind, his inability to determine her position leads him to "not appreciate her justly," but we see that it is only his inability to determine her position that allows him to avoid injustice (what Daisy later calls his letting the other socialites be "unkind" to her).[19]

James's use of the term "justly" reorients his "study" of Daisy Miller along ethical lines. In another key scene Winterbourne is shown with his aunt, Mrs. Costello, who describes Daisy and her family with firm judgment: "They are very dreadful people."[20] Winterbourne responds, "They are very ignorant—very innocent only. Depend upon it they are not bad."[21] Mrs. Costello asserts firmly her intention to remain in the realm of ontology: "They are hopelessly vulgar. . . . whether or no being hopelessly vulgar is being 'bad' is a question for the metaphysicians. They are bad enough to dislike, at any rate; and for this short life that is quite enough."[22] Mrs. Costello's judgment privileges metaphysics over ethics, while her nephew seems to privilege Daisy's physics, so to speak, over both. The language in the above quotation even hints that such ontological judgments deny Daisy the sort of lively future she seeks and Winterbourne seems to want. She can have no future interaction socially with other characters in the story if she is definitively vulgar, only an assignation to a static category. And the irony of the aunt's words—particularly her reference to short life—rings terribly true for poor Daisy, as it is Winterbourne's dislike, his hopeless assigning of Daisy to a category of sexual transgression, that precipitates her death.

At the climax of the story, we see Winterbourne achieve his goal of finalizing his judgment of Daisy—the textbook type of reading that is at least half responsible for Daisy's death. At the key scene, Winterbourne sees Daisy and Mr. Giovanelli at the Coliseum at midnight—alone: "Winterbourne stopped, with a sort of horror; and, it must be added, with a sort of relief. It was as if a sudden illumination had been flashed upon the ambiguity of Daisy's behavior and the riddle had become easy to read. She was a young lady whom a gentleman need no longer be at pains to respect."[23] This illumination is the assigning of Daisy to a textbook category—we can practically superimpose scare quotes on the torturous euphemism "a young lady whom a gentleman need no longer be at pains to respect." His seeking of knowledge has "stopped" and Daisy ossifies. Now that he knows Daisy's position, he can stop reading her, stop the process that had resulted from his "want of instinctive certitude as to how far her eccentricities were generic, national, and how far they were personal."[24] Without certitude, Winterbourne had been able to treat Daisy kindly, to spar with his aunt over Daisy's qualities and denounce Mrs. Walker's cruelty to her. With certitude, his response is "almost brutally" worded: "I believe that it makes very little difference whether you are engaged or not!"[25] But she does not answer, except to give up on her resistance to Roman Fever. After she has become ill with the fever, Daisy asks her mother three times to tell Mr. Winterbourne she never was engaged to Winterbourne's rival, thus demonstrating that she still desired ongoing communication with

Winterbourne. But the desired communication never occurs. When Winterbourne finalizes his interpretation, his despair pushes her to despair.

This scene recurs in James's experience and literature. It echoes his cousin Minnie Temple's comment to James a few days before he last saw her, "If I begin to be indifferent to what happens, I shall go down the hill fast."[26] It reappears in the response of Milly Theale, the heroine of *Wings of the Dove* who turns "her face to the wall"[27] when she discovers her hopes for true love of Densher are impossible. The loss of a future hope for each is death to them.

Winterbourne later confesses to his aunt that he is guilty of an injustice toward Daisy Miller—the high ethical cost of his terminal interpretation. But Henry James felt himself to be implicated, too, alongside Winterbourne, for the nipping of Daisy's life in the bud, for he found, even in the story's success, a spate of foregone conclusions from his audience. Surely a text could not engender the liveliness James wanted for his work if it was so summarily and finally boxed and packaged by critics. A first editor rejected it, a friend guessed, because it inflicted "an outrage upon American girlhood."[28] William Dean Howells seems to have been only able to read the most pedantic of morals in the piece. He writes, "All of poor Daisy's crimes are purely conventional. . . . Who has not met them [Daisy Millers] abroad?" He continues, "[T]here is no question whatever as to the effect of . . . [the] defiance of conventionalities abroad. All the waters of the Mediterranean cannot wash clean the name of a young lady who . . . takes a walk with a fascinating chance acquaintance . . . . an American girl, like Daisy Miller . . . has no more chance of going through Europe unscathed . . . than an idiot millionaire has of amusing himself economically in Wall Street. This lesson is taught in Mr. James's story,—and never was necessary medicine administered in a form more delightful and unobtrusive."[29] Another textbook.

And in the public eye, Daisy became popular, inspiring hats, shaping speech, and coming to embody a certain type of American girl. Another type to pin on a card and collect.

Yet the history of reading *Daisy Miller* has not been so type- or textbook-making as that. Unlike many of James's fictions, *Daisy Miller* has subsisted, not because of controversy, exactly, or fuss, but because a long history of study in particular has reshaped the understanding of Daisy and the novel, shifting focus at times from Daisy to Winterbourne, to scientific and historical contexts for the novel. Through readings, the consciousness surrounding the text has thickened and crafted a future for Daisy—perhaps a forgiveness of her rebellion, perhaps a reconciliation with American postures in the American century. Daisy herself continues to be what she called Winterbourne: a "queer mixture" that remains irreducible.[30] For example: in his 1909 preface, James tells the story of a conversation with friends that harkened back to seeing a few possible Daisy Millers outside a hotel in Venice. James's companion declared that the women at the hotel could never match the allure of the textual Daisy Miller, since she "made any judgment . . . impossible."[31] "Your pretty perversion of [the truth you had in mind]," James's companion had said, "or your unprincipled mystification of our sense of it, does it really too much honor— . . . you have yielded to your incurable prejudice in favor of grace— . . . Those awful young women capering at the hotel-door, *they* are the real little Daisy Millers that were; whereas yours in the tale is such a one as couldn't possibly have been at all."[32] Scholars have scoffed at the thought of James perfectly remembering this conversation enough to represent it accurately years after. But contrary to James's friend, I believe that rather than making Daisy less possible, a resistance to type/finality in judgment makes her more bristly with life—more alive, rather than less. I think James thought so too, for he declared that Daisy

Miller "provided for mere concentration, and on an object scant and superficially vulgar—from which, however, a sufficiently brooding tenderness might eventually extract a shy incongruous charm."[33] The gerund here points to ongoing, faithful, contemplative, and studious kindness of reading: "sufficiently brood*ing* tenderness" can change stereotypes of Daisy's vulgarity into a mysterious charm, the charm that readers still feel when encountering the text.

And the text's ending need not be read as only tragic, either. Winterbourne's return to "studying" after his confession to his aunt has most often been read as a sign of the return to his old, society-bound habits of separating people into categories. It could, though, be a return to the sort of engagement that marked his earlier interactions with Daisy, the study, the ongoing, never settled, brooding tenderness that transforms its object in extracting from it a mysterious charm. He might well imagine another elopement, a future hope, at least. James's own continued studying of the Daisy situation and the Daisy figure in *Wings of the Dove* and *Portrait of a Lady* could be the same hoping that by thickened consciousness, the amount of felt life could be increased, and a negative, fixing judgment could be replaced with interaction and future life.

## We Will Judge Angels:
### *Angels in America* and Judgment's Necessity

Even more explicitly than *Daisy Miller*, Tony Kushner's *Angels in America: A Gay Fantasia on National Themes* centralizes judgments of all kinds—of lives, people, texts, and, ultimately God. The play does not figure people as texts to read as *Daisy Miller: A Study* figures the Americans as textbooks for Mrs. Walker. It does, however, like *Daisy Miller*, show people as cases for judgment—their lives related to "the judge in his or her chambers, weighing evidence, books open."[34] Yet instead of suggesting that judgment unjustly fixes its object and denies it a future, *Angels in America* seems to show the opposite.

The story centers on two couples. Joe and Harper are Mormons who have migrated from Salt Lake to New York where Joe is a head clerk for the chief justice and writes major conservative decisions for him while Harper struggles with Valium addiction and the growing sense that Joe does not love her. Prior and Louis are a gay couple, together for four and a half years. Prior has been diagnosed with AIDS and is beginning to decline; Louis, who cannot handle suffering, abandons him and takes up with Joe instead. The text foregrounds judgment in several ways—Joe's job working for the highest court in the state, his relationship with Roy Cohn (a notoriously corrupt powerbroker under investigation with the threat of disbarment), the various stereotypes under which the various characters judge each other, and, of course the explicitly apocalyptic, ceiling-crashing entrance of angels into the story and the text. In the play, Prior is chosen by an angelic host to be a prophetic messenger of a new, angelic plan for humans in light of God's ostensible abandonment of the cosmos: stasis. *Angels in America* may be about, ultimately, the way that having AIDS in America provides a particular vantage point from which to judge—a sufferer's judgment—both the nation and the nation's God. It reveals, too, I think, the extent to which judgments—textual and otherwise—are necessary for, and perhaps equivalent to forgiveness and revelation. For the purposes of this book, such an idea drives us toward further theological and literary inquiry.

The main figure that Kushner uses to work through ideas about judgment is Louis. The text shows him as always seeking to avoid judgment and guilt—by hiding, by exhaustively defending his positions, and by complicating situations so that they are impossible to judge. He also preemptively assigns himself a vague, overarching guilt so that no one can accuse him, thereby side-stepping reproach. An example of these moves early in the play is when he apologizes to Prior for not introducing Prior to anyone at his grandmother's wake, with an offhand self-deprecation that functions as a justification: he always gets "closety at these family things."[35] When Louis can't avoid feeling guilty about particular sins, such as the fact that he had pretended his grandmother was dead years before she actually died in order to avoid visiting her in her decline, he tries to get others to declare him innocent, as when he talks to a Rabbi about it. But Louis does not want to confess in the sense of taking responsibility for his actions. He seems to have a problem with love and responsibility in the real world, preferring theoretical workarounds to the responsibilities of actual life.

In a scene with Louis and Prior in bed, the play allows Louis full vent of his hopes that complexity will allow people to avoid judgment—hopes that, in time, the play denies him. Ostensibly explaining what he thinks is a Jewish sense of justice, Louis says,

> It's the judge in his or her chambers, weighing, books open, pondering the evidence, ranging freely over categories: good, evil, innocent, guilty; the judge in the chamber of circumspection, not the judged on the bench with the gavel. The shaping of the law, not its execution . . . that it should be the questions and shape of a life, its total complexity gathered, arranged, and considered, which matters in the end, not some stamp of salvation or damnation which disperses all the complexity in some unsatisfying little decision—the balancing of the scales.[36]

Of course, this sort of thing completely contradicts the Rabbi Louis had consulted earlier: "Catholics believe in forgiveness. Jews believe in Guilt."[37] Also, Prior shoots back that all of Louis's high-falutin' ideas are "reassuringly incomprehensible and useless" in the face of real-world injustice.[38] The subtext of this conversation—the real subject of it—is whether or not Louis can justify abandoning Prior in the time of his disease's most distasteful and burdensome aspects. And it's obvious the answer is no: the situation seems utterly, pristinely clear, absolutely easy to judge. Indeed, Kushner emphasizes the ease of the judgment in the Rabbi's incredulity at Louis's behavior—"Why would a person do such a thing?"[39] Who abandons a dying lover or grandma in the time of need? In the face of Louis's resistance to actual judgment through theoretical mumbo jumbo (Louis, in one memorable obfuscation, says that "justice is an immensity, a confusing vastness . . . God"), Prior brings judgment back to the inescapability of the body and the world.[40] Prior cites evidence of his physical illness—new lesions, blood in his stool—as evidence of his mortality, but Louis tries to deny the fact by remaining in what the audience easily sees is an avoidance of reality.

Kushner returns to the courtroom motif in the scene where Louis announces that he is leaving Prior; this moment emphasizes both Louis's resistance to being judged and the folly of resistance. Louis actually says "I won't be judged by you." In Prior's wounded and angry response, he sets up an imaginary court complete with all the standard rhetoric: "Bang bang bang. The court will come to order," "Has the jury reached a verdict?," and "We have reached a verdict, your honor."[41] The case to be judged is whether or not Louis can be blamed for his walking out. Louis insists that "[t]his isn't a crime, just—the inevitable consequences of people who run out of—whose limitations . . ."[42] Prior declares that Louis's "heart is deficient" and "his love is worth nothing."[43] The audience sides unequivocally with Prior.

Louis's defense is to accept and acknowledge his own pervasive and theoretically vast guilt to avoid actual responsibility for what he is doing to another human being, yet Kushner exposes the poverty of this type of preemptive—and largely theoretical—self-judgment in

Louis's pseudo-confession. For, he theorizes his move to abandon Prior in the second person rather than the first: "You can love someone and fail them. You can love someone and not be able to . . ."[44] This grammar of guilt acceptance actually transforms a confession into an accusation of the other by means of a hazy theory. But Prior unmasks this and brings the discussion down to the real world: "You *can* theoretically, yes. A person can, maybe an editorial 'you' can love, Louis, but not *you*, specifically you."[45]

Louis makes this same move with Belize, the play's purest soul, when he admits that he is a racist in order to deflect the power of Belize's claims against him and his theories. The audience sees this for the ruse it is through Belize's response. "[Y]ou're so guilty, it's like throwing darts at a glob of jello, there's no satisfying hits, just quivering, the darts just blop in and vanish," she says, acknowledging the way the structure of his conversation turns to make condemnation of him impossible.[46] Even the image of the jello here is a soft-bodied, less-physical thing—Louis's avoidance of embodiment and the responsibility that it carries. Louis attaches to bigger images and theories of guilt to distance himself from actual bodies through metaphoric and religious symbolism—"Biblical things, Mark of Cain, Judas Iscariot and his silver and his noose, people who . . . in betraying what they love betray what is truest in themselves."[47] Louis cannot think of the actual consequences or judgment—largely because he has not experienced any. He had pretended his grandmother was dead years before she died, but suffers no repercussions from this in the play, since she is dead. (He still fears the consequences, though, and urges the Rabbi to make sure the corpse does not escape the coffin—to nail it down tight so he can escape another body.). He wants the theoretical consequences, wants to commit to the theory rather than the actual. He looks for what the scriptures say about "someone who abandons someone he loves at a time of great need," denying the obviousness of its wrongness, which the Rabbi's confusion over his question only reinforces.[48]

Kushner goes even further, placing an indictment of Louis's behavior unexpectedly in the mouth of Joe, Louis's newly out lover, a conservative law clerk and protégé of corrupt politician Roy Cohn. When Louis is beginning to back off from his relationship with Joe because of Joe's conservative political commitments and the fierceness of Joe's assertions of love, Joe accuses Louis of the very violence and injustice that all his theories seek to avoid. Joe says, "[Y]ou think the good thing is to be guilty and kind always, but it's not always kind to be gentle and soft, there's a genuine violence softness and weakness visit on people."[49] Joe is wrestling with the ideals of corrupt lawyer and politician Roy Cohn. He tries to preach some of the self-interested ideology that Roy has pushed on him for years—but he still wants Louis to come back to him, and has trouble getting beyond that. But when Joe says, "You ought to think about . . . what you're doing to me. No, I mean. . . . What you need. Think about what you need," he is actually trying to show his own love for Louis by giving up what he wants.[50] When Joe slips in the above speech, telling Louis to think about what he is doing to him, the audience is again reminded of the collateral damage brought by Louis's trying so hard to muddy the waters of guilt and responsibility in order to avoid judgment.

Louis needs judgment and consequences so that he can be forgiven and his victims restored. The play brings him to an acceptance of this need when he comes face to face with Roy Cohn's dead body—a real corpse that cannot be theorized away. Louis, squirming over hospitals and his own cuts and bruises from a fight with Joe, encounters Cohn's death as justice rendered. Looking at Roy Cohn's body, and touching Roy's forehead (a move that visually and theatrically links the two, since Louis at that moment in the play is sporting a mark-of-Cain forehead cut), gives Louis a sense of actuality and consequences. It takes Louis into the concrete world of responsibility for actions—as Belize articulates it, "[Roy] was a terrible person. He died a hard death."[51]

This is the first step, but Louis also needs to view the fruit of just judgment: forgiveness. In the scene, Belize articulates the miraculous heart of forgiveness when she, in the act of stealing Roy's now useless stash of AZT for Prior, forces Louis to say Kaddish over Roy's body. When Louis expresses incredulity that Belize wants him to say Kaddish over such a reprehensible, corrupt person—"I can't believe you'd actually pray for . . ." Belize responds, "Louis, I'd even pray for you."[52] For Belize, the consequences that others have experienced, their own suffering for their own failings, prompt her to love and forgiveness. She says, "A queen can forgive her vanquished foe. It isn't easy, it doesn't count if it's easy, it's the hardest thing. Forgiveness. Which is maybe where love and justice finally meet. Peace at least. Isn't that what the Kaddish asks for? Peace?"[53] Belize emphasizes the key aspect of the Kaddish prayer as the granting of forgiveness—or at least the asking for reconciliation and peace through justice and love.

At the end of the play, when Louis tries to make amends and go back to Prior, we see a working out of the formula outlined by Belize, that where love and justice meet can be forgiveness and a moving into revelatory community. Louis's admission of his guilt is not that much different than previous ones, but his willingness to come back after having messed up is an effort, likely, toward a better loving: "You could . . . respond, you could say something, throw me out or say it's fine, or it's not fine but sure what the hell."[54] If Prior throws Louis out, Prior denies truth and reconciliation by shutting down dialogue and real engagement. If Prior says it is fine, then he denies the actual truth. If Prior says it is not fine but what the hell, there is no justice. Prior's response, however, gives Louis a true sense of the scope of the offense, offers judgment and consequences, and continues in love. He responds that he loves Louis, and that Louis cannot come back to their partnership, "not ever."[55] The terseness of the statement here joining love and consequences indicate a finality that is judgment's trademark. It should be all over for Louis.

Yet their relationship does not end. Kushner shows ongoing healing and restoration through Prior's judgment of Louis's behavior in the Bethesda scene where Belize, Prior, Louis, and Hannah (Joe's mother) are talking together around the statue of the Bethesda angel fountain in Central Park.[56] The scene includes the story of the healing fountain: "If anyone who was suffering, in the body or the spirit, walked through the waters of the fountain of Bethesda, they would be healed, washed clean of pain."[57] Their conversation shows the extent to which justice—the truth and its right consequences—plus love equals forgiveness. Louis makes progress through his experience of true judgment. In the Bethesda conversation, he even quotes his grandmother, whom he earlier betrayed, bringing her words into the ongoing community that hopes for healing.[58] What Kushner offers us here is the sense that there is truth and reconciliation—not amnesty, but ongoing relationship, growth, and healing for both of Louis and Prior, the blessing of more life in any case. Louis is not utterly different, but he has exchanged abstract theory and an abhorrence of politics for the sense that "only in politics does the miraculous occur."[59] Or, he has begun to learn from his grandmother, who would always say, "Go know."[60] Prior keeps the relationship going without the romance, refusing to repay abandonment for abandonment.

So it seems that in *Angels in America* interpretive judgment is an avenue toward healing and relationship. Yet the role of text itself in the play may call that thesis into question. For texts and books have a literal and cosmic presence in the text. God is a "male flaming Hebrew letter," who, in creating people and time created desire and change, which are the source, in the angels' view, of all pain, death, and destruction.[61] And that "male flaming Hebrew letter" has apparently abandoned the cosmos. In God's absence, the angels have compiled a book, a message, which they give to Prior as a latter-day Jonah: the book of stasis. The angels believe that since God's creation has unleashed the forces of time and change and death and destruction, stasis and separation may be the way back from the precipice toward humans' drive in their propensity to move and intermingle in the desire and change of life. The "new law" of the angels, which they explain to Prior, is as follows.

> Forsake the Open Road:
> Neither Mix Nor Intermarry: Let Deep Roots Grow:
> If you do not MINGLE you will Cease to Progress:
> Seek Not to Fathom the World
> and its Delicate Particle Logic:
> You cannot Understand, You can only Destroy,
> You do not Advance, You only Trample.
> Poor blind Children, abandoned on the Earth,
> Groping terrified, misguided, over
> Fields of Slaughter, over bodies of the Slain:
> HOBBLE YOURSELVES!
> There is No Zion Save Where You Are![62]

The book of the future, the prophecy of the angels, is a prophecy that will slow down and stop the supposed progress of the world, as progress is the source of all pain and destruction. Creation and desire and its attendant disasters will then cease. Rather than *having* or *creating* a future in the kingdom of God, in *Angels in America*, text functions to manage the crisis by refusing the future. Even Louis, who wants to refuse judgment as a way to refuse the future, sees his refusal to judge as associated with text: we should look at judges as people with "books open."[63] When the angels offer Prior the book of stasis, text seems to function as anti-prophecy rather than prophecy. The open book seems then to be a static place, where no judgment can bring anyone forgiveness, but where hurt and time themselves stop. The play reveals a sort of anti-textual, and therefore anti-stasis, posture when Prior refuses the book, wrestles with the angel, and demands a blessing. Instead of wanting the book, "the Tome of Immobility" and the end of desire, Prior demands the blessing of "more life."[64]

Of course, the idea of demanding more life, and even the scene in which Prior demands it, are themselves the forwarding of stories that advance a qualified messianism that belies the apparent anti-textual posture. In the play, Prior wrestles with the angel in order to return the book of immobility, which is an allusion to Genesis 32—except the angel gets the hurt thigh instead of Jacob. And though Prior seems to suggest that a refusal to wait is a refusal to believe that God will come back, Prior's fury at God's leaving does not actually suggest the absence of hope that it might seem to. Prior's fury at God is utterly relational, and he advises the angels to prosecute God rather than simply stop believing: "He isn't coming back. And even if He did . . . If He ever did come back, if He ever *dared* to show His face, or his Glyph or whatever in the Garden again . . . if after all this destruction, if after all the terrible days of this terrible century He returned to see . . . how much suffering His abandonment had created, if all He has to offer is death, you should *sue* the bastard. That's my only contribution to all this Theology. Sue the bastard for walking out."[65] Prior is unable, even in an angry, would-be denial of God, to keep away from the thought that God will come again. His anger is so close, after all, to love. He wrestles with an angel and wrestles with God, making his own future a future of the text.[66]

Another textual future that appears in the play is in the recitation of the Kaddish, a traditional Jewish prayer form that is prayed in synagogue and for the dead, uttered in full in the play. The scene is critically important and sets up the framework of the major movement toward hope in the play—that justice plus love equals forgiveness. The play actually uses a *deus ex machina* of sorts to emphasize the importance of the act and the words themselves, as Ethel Rosenberg's ghost appears to Louis and helps him say Kaddish by repeating after her in a very funny scene.[67] A translation of the prayer is this:

> Magnified and sanctified be His great name in the world which He created according to His will. And may He establish His kingdom during your life and during your days, and during the life of all the House of Israel, speedily and in the near future, and say, Amen.
> Response: May His great name be blessed forever and ever. Blessed, praised and glorified, exalted, extolled and honored, adored and lauded be the Name of the Holy One, blessed be He, beyond all blessings and hymns, praises and songs that are uttered in the world, and say, Amen. May there be abundant peace from heaven and life for us and for all Israel, and say Amen. May He who makes peace in the heavens, make peace for us and for all Israel, and say, Amen.[68]

Rather than focusing on the sins or accomplishments of the dead, the Kaddish in fact situates a life by making preeminent God's messianic kingdom on earth; the prayer is primarily one of praise and blessing for the coming kingdom of God.[69] The quotation of the whole, along with the play's apocalyptic energies, makes the overall work eschatological in scope. It focuses attention first of all on divine justice, since the Kaddish is "understood as an acknowledgment of divine justice; by reciting this magnificent hymn of praise, the bereaved proclaim, that in spite of his loss, he will not rebel against God but will lead the congregation in singing his praise."[70]

The prayer insists on the larger community or collectivity—one larger than the dead person him- or herself. For the Kaddish is never to be recited alone, a fact demonstrated in the very form and content of the work. The "and for all Israel" and the repeated collective injunction "and say, Amen" emphasize the call-and-response that joins the community together in the praying of the prayer. In the play, Kushner pictures the community of Roy Cohn with his dead victims (e.g., Ethel Rosenberg) and living enemies (e.g., Louis). The voices of the dead and the living together establish peace through the testimony of the person's victims by placing a person's life story within the larger purposes of the kingdom of God. (We may argue that Roy Cohn's dead body is in no position to be in community here—and he certainly wants no real community—he goes straight to hell, where, in Kushner's "optional" scene, he begins working up a defense strategy for God Almighty.) And in the touching of the dead body—the concreteness and actuality of it—and the praying of the prayer, aided by the ghost of Ethel Rosenberg, Louis finds the beginning of change. Belize says "Thank you Louis you did fine," and in a move that both bombastically takes credit and relinquishes credit-taking completely, Louis counters "That was fucking miraculous!"[71]

Yet even in this advancing of the future of the text, the Kaddish stands, as it were, also under judgment in a play where God is absent and, according to the narrative backstory, has been absent since the 1906 earthquake in San Francisco. Louis says the prayer with a tissue on his head instead of a yarmulke. He says the prayer as a secular Jew who has not had a bar-mitzvah, thinking that the prayer, which is really in Aramaic, is in Hebrew. The majority of the audience wouldn't understand a word of the prayer, either. It's as if this very situation of reading highlights and judges what Joseph Heinemann has pointed out—that the Kaddish actually has no address to God in the second person.[72] The miracle community that joins together to make the prayer meaningful in the community of the dead and living is framed by the scenes of Prior's judgment of God and the angels.

The play ends with a textual future in the Bethesda epilogue, which, though it does not explicitly mention written text, makes the messianic kingdom's arrival, the Millennium, a future of the story of the angel of Bethesda from the second temple period. In the scene, while Prior narrates, Louis tells the story of the angel, Belize tells of its healing effects, and the character Hannah, who has been changed and healed herself through a relationship of care and service to Prior, points to the future of that story—its non-ending ending: "When the Millennium comes . . . [t]he fountain of Bethesda will flow again. . . . We will all bathe ourselves clean."[73] The epilogue of the play shows a community of hope that rests on the foundation of the largest story—of good creation and its promises: "You are fabulous creatures, each and every one. And I bless you: *More Life*. The Great Work Begins."[74] In this way, the glyph of the creator himself, or perhaps Prior as the stand-in for the absent creator, moves toward the millennial community of healing and renewal. Kushner is never short on unflinching critique of what he views as God's abandonment of humanity, of God's execution of the divine plan for the universe. But that is just what makes Kushner's vision of judgment so interesting: it is so consistent with his understanding of judgment as absolutely necessary for true love and peace. He seems, after all, to want to forgive God by judging him—making "the bastard pay" by requiring him to do what he had planned to do from the beginning: expand blessing and peace to heal and restore after a century of loss. Until God steps in, Prior will do the blessing, and Louis will pray the Kaddish. The judgment leads to eschatological hope—the hope in the story of Bethesda and creation—persists, even so. It is an angry messianism, though.

## The Double Bind

These two scrivenings seem to offer contrary visions of how judgment ought to relate to text. Henry James's *Daisy Miller* suggests that judgment of people—and, by metaphor, texts—fixes them, halting their becoming, and, in fact, terminating their liveliness by cutting them off from genuine relationships because of repressive social norms. Tony Kushner's *Angels in America* suggests, seemingly contrarily, that the suspension of judgment—the tome of immobility—is what halts the growth and becoming of love, and that prevents relationships and responsibility within social groups. The tension between these two ideas—that judgment is absolutely necessary to the development of love and community and that at the same time judgment is a fixation fraught with violence toward the other—takes us to a central paradox of scripture: we may not judge, but we must. It is also a paradox of meaning-making via textuality—that any interpretation forwards and halts a literary text's meaning-making simultaneously. Each reading is a fixing in place and a furthering.

In the tension between the two, in the Spirit of God, where reading is concurrently judgment and resistance of judgment, we find ourselves judging and being always judged by our judgment of texts. The call-and-response of reading is fraught with possibility and danger; it is a double-bind that pushes us forward by the grace of the promise into action always already compromised by our failure in kingdom love. We need what Belize informs us is the prayer of the Kaddish, namely, the peace granted by the coming Messiah in what Hannah calls the Millennium. We need the reconciliation of the future of the word—the judge and justifier, author and finisher of the word. We need to learn how to forgive texts.

## Notes

1. Klyne Snodgrass, *Stories with Intent* (Grand Rapids: Eerdmans, 2008), 215.

2. Henry James, "The Art of Fiction," *Essays on Literature* (New York: Library Classics of the United States, 1984), 53.

3. Ibid., 49.

4. Henry James, *The Art of the Novel*, ed. R. P. Blackmur (New York: Charles Scribner's Sons, 1934), 54, 45.

5. Ibid., 268–69.

6. Ibid., 288.

7. Henry James, "Is There Life after Death?," in *In After Days* (New York: Harper & Brothers, 1910), 215, 201.

8. Ibid., 201.

9. Henry James, *Daisy Miller* (London: Penguin, 2007), 63.

10. Ibid., 4.

11. Ibid., 64.

12. Ibid., 47.

13. Ibid., 60.

14. Ibid., 12.

15. Ibid., 8.

16. Ibid.

17. Ibid., 19.

18. Ibid., 41.

19. Ibid., 58.

20. Ibid., 33.

21. Ibid.

22. Ibid.

23. Ibid., 59–60.

24. Ibid., 56.

25. Ibid., 60, 61.

26. Henry James, *Notes of a Son and Brother* (New York: Charles Scribner's Sons, 1914), 514.

27. Henry James, *The Wings of the Dove: A Norton Critical Edition*, ed. J. Donald Crowley and Richard A. Hocks (New York: W. W. Norton, 2003), 361.

28. James, *The Art of the Novel*, 268.

29. William Dean Howells, *"Daisy Miller,"* *Henry James: The Contemporary Reviews*, ed. Kevin Hayes (Cambridge: Cambridge University Press, 1996), 69–70.

30. James, *Daisy Miller*, 28.

31. James, *The Art of the Novel*, 269.

32. Ibid., 269–70.

33. Ibid., 269.

34. Tony Kushner, *Angels in America* (New York: Theatre Communications Group, 1995), 44.

35. Ibid., 25.

36. Ibid., 44–45.

37. Ibid., 46.

38. Ibid., 45.

39. Ibid., 31

40. Ibid., 45.

41. Ibid., 84–85.

42. Ibid., 84.

43. Ibid., 85.

44. Ibid., 84.

45. Ibid., 84–85.

46. Ibid., 99.

47. Ibid., 105.

48. Ibid., 31.

49. Ibid., 207.

50. Ibid.

51. Ibid., 256.

52. Ibid.

53. Ibid.

54. Ibid., 273.

55. Ibid.

56. Significantly, Bethesda, MD was also the location of Ray Cohn's death.

57. Ibid., 279.

58. In Prior's vision of heaven in the play, Louis's grandmother also offers forgiveness to Louis for his abandonment of her.

59. Ibid., 278.

60. Ibid.

61. Ibid., 175.

62. Ibid., 178–79.

63. Ibid., 44.

64. Ibid., 267.

65. Ibid., 264.

66. Ibid., 269. One of the messages that Prior takes back from Heaven, from Louis's grandmother, is "You should struggle with the Almighty . . . It's the Jewish way."

67. Ibid., 288. Kushner, in his Afterword, thanks Harold Bloom for work from an introduction to Olivier d'Allones's *Musical Variations on Jewish Thought*, which helped him understand the Jewish concept of a blessing as an exhortation to "more life."

68. Hayim Halevy Donin, *To Pray as a Jew* (New York: Basic Books, 2001), 219.

69. Joseph Heinemann, *Literature of the Synagogue* (New Jersey: First Gorgia, 2006), 82.

70. Ibid., 83–84.

71. Kushner, *Angels in America*, 257.

72. Joseph Heinemann, *Literature of the Synagogue* (New Jersey: First Gorgia, 2006), 82.

73. Kushner, *Angels in America*, 279.

74. Ibid., 280.

# 4

---

# Forgiving the Text

In the gospel accounts, John the Baptist's ministry rides the line between the necessity and difficulty of judgment. He is a baptizer known for unflinching denunciations and unhesitating warnings (Matt. 3:7). Yet when confronted with Jesus' request for baptism, John almost refuses to perform it, because he knows of his own need for forgiveness. That double bind, between the rock of inevitable, necessary judgment and the hard place of our incapacity for just execution, is where we too are left in the wilderness as readers for the future of the word. When we encounter texts and read, even as would-be scribes for the kingdom, to cultivate their futures for the kingdom insofar as they reveal the word in the world, we encounter their evil and compromises right alongside their gloriously fruitful meaning. And our acts of reading are acts of judgment—whether we intend them as such or not. In our reading, we need to reject the wrong and embrace the right. Yet we are insufficient, unjust judges, incapable of doing so, and all our judgments highlight our own failures at meaning-making as much as the failures of the texts we judge. Our judgments are at best provisional and incomplete and at worst downright false. We fix texts in our meaning-making, or refuse them meaning altogether.

Faced with this bewildering situation, hermeneutics can step forward as judgment that is also forgiveness and reconciliation, a way of walking in the desert. And John the Baptist will be an especially instructive figure here, as through the betweenness of culpability and necessary judgment, he prepares the way and future of the word through the practice of reconciliation. Whether or not John the Baptist was of the Qumran baptizing sects in the tradition that later became famous for its preservation of the Dead Sea Scrolls, he and his followers were known by their contemporaries as "preservers," those for whom the sign of baptism represented salvation from the coming judgment.[1] John himself, too, can be seen as deeply involved in the crafting and preserving of the future of the word—the word himself, Jesus—so that he would be revealed as Christ. As the Gospel of John puts it, "I came baptizing with water for this reason, that he might be revealed to Israel" (John 1:31). Scholars have agreed that John is a prophetic figure, an eschatological figure, and an initiator of the gospel of Jesus Christ. As Ernst Käsemann has observed, Jesus himself pointed out John's eschatological message and importance in salvation history: "drawing him to his side and . . . presenting him as the initiator of the new aeon."[2] He participates in the gospel that he proclaims.

John also prepares the way of the word in two ways: (1) he bears witness to the word, and (2) he participates in the reconciliation of the repentant through baptism. John bears witness to the word in word with his own body since, like Christ, John manifests the future and fulfillment of text—"This is the one of whom the prophet Isaiah spoke when he said, 'The voice of one crying out in the wilderness: "Prepare the way of the Lord; make his paths straight"'" (Matt. 3:3).

The four gospels, which identify John as the "voice of one crying out in the wilderness," figure his mission as the future of a collage of Old Testament texts: Exod. 23:20, an admonition to heed an angel of the Lord; Mal. 3:1, which refers to a messenger of Yahweh identified later as Elijah; and Isa. 40:3, which introduces God's plan to redeem Israel from exile.[3] John's ministry points always to Jesus the word—whose sandal he is not worthy to untie, who must increase while John decreases. Even his question to Jesus from death row, wondering whether Jesus is the one to come, figures Jesus as the future of the word, and Jesus' response is packed with allusions to the word that he fulfills as the word.

John also participates in the gospel's work of reconciliation—preparing and assisting in the repentance of the penitent—by his work in the desert decrying injustice and hypocrisy, his call for repentance, his baptismal practice, and his own repentance and patient submission to the work of the word in the world. And his ministry, between judgment and repentance for the revelation of the word, is one of reconciliation and forgiveness. As Robert L. Webb writes, John's ministry called for everyone to convert and repent and to "express that repentance by receiving his baptism which symbolically mediated the forgiveness given to the person by God and cleansed the person from the uncleanness caused by his/her sins. By so doing, the person would be prepared for the imminent, eschatological judgment and restoration" of Jesus.[4] Anyone who baptizes is in an odd position: beside and like the one who stands in need of reconciliation and forgiveness, but also involved in the work of the one who may truly impute forgiveness to the needy one. The baptizer may even be the victim of the offenses committed by offender, but nevertheless must prepare the way for the reconciliation and present the offender to the true reconciler. Reading is a like reconciliation.

### The Reconciliation of the Word

The last chapter offered a few ways of thinking about how reading may turn toward the privation of evil, namely the fixing-in-place of meaning and the refusal of meaning. This chapter shows how reading's judgment may itself be a forgiving response to offense that emerges out of the experience of the reader with the text. Engaging the confession of the text, reading can be forgiveness.

Words, after all, call out for conversion and reconciliation. The futurity of even the individual word, its hum into the love and becoming of the Trinity, seems halted by the limitation of its present, which rests on the false bottom of a hidden, unaccountable history.[5] Thus the now of any word is a confession of approximation upon approximation, imprecision built on imprecision. The brokenness of the community of meaning-making is evident from within the confession of the word. The sentence, with all its constituents and co-conspirators, is under a sentence. The insufficiency of any word, phrase, clause, or sentence is its provisional end, as the period fixes it. Even from within the question mark or the semicolon, the period periodizes. And the period of the sentence is the always broken—and always breaking—offending gesture. It highlights the alienation of the reader by highlighting improper distinction in time and space. And thus every sentence, every word in its futurity, is a call from within its brokenness for a future; language too groans for the reconciliation, for the reading of the word.

The confession of the text—its groan for reconciliation—may be heard through attention to its deconstruction. As a text's meaning-making ability depends upon binary opposition, a text is groaning under its own self-contradiction; we see the aporia in which the remedy for the text—the becoming of textual meaning toward the kingdom—may also be felt as the poison of incoherence. At the same time that our words are words within the word of God, made to become in meaning-making toward the glory of the Trinity, they are also fashioned in the violence of substitution, the supplement to speech which is the mad, infinite, "linguistic permutation of substitutes, of substitutes for substitutes" which, for Derrida, is the madness of an "unleashed chain . . . not lacking in violence."[6]

But of course, Paul, chained and unchained for the gospel, for whom chains signified thorough opposition—both inhibiting and advancing his spreading of the gospel such that he is an "ambassador in chains" (Eph. 6:20)—reminds us: "the word of God is not chained" (2 Tim. 2:9). Derrida argues that meaning may only inhere in the full presence of the truth within the *logos*—something he feels is impossible because of the patricidal killing of meaning necessary within any act of writing.[7] But the gospel insists that the *logos* is in all things; the word's presence does not abandon, but rather holds up all meaning through the presence of the incarnate one. Instead of patricide as the foundation of the meaning of the word, we have the sacrificial death of the Son—and furthermore, the Son's resurrection, the assurance of an ongoing presence of the word in the word.[8] The presence of Christ, the word, does not abandon the word in text. The word, through the death and resurrection of Christ, reconciles the word to God. As Col. 1:19-20 explains, "For in him all the fullness of God was pleased to dwell, and through him God was pleased to reconcile to himself all things, whether on earth or in heaven, by making peace through the blood of his cross." None of the creation exists outside the reconciling power and peace of the Godhead.

The reconciliation of the creation to itself and to the Lord is the work of the kingdom. But how is it that reading participates in the reconciliation of texts in particular? The production of text and the experience of it are a set of networked relationships, and relationships in a fallen world under grace always evoke a need for reconciliation. In chapter 1, when I considered the relationship of text with all creation, I identified how characteristics that texts share with the created order—particularly becoming-toward-significance and becoming toward the kingdom of God—allow us to treat text as having a future in the kingdom of God. The communal nature of the Trinity, for whom all creation is an overflowing plentitude, an excess of love, is a nature in which the creation—all of it—participates. All created things, including cultural objects made by humans, thus have interrelationship, community, as part of their being and becoming. They are themselves thus subject to and subjects of the brokenness of community that comes from sin. Hence, it should be no surprise, though it is perhaps not a regular way of thinking, that readers who interact with texts as their makers in writing and remakers in reading, should be involved in relationships of gift-exchange with texts through reading and thus should have occasion to reconcile with text.

The gift has played an important role in ethical literary criticism, as exemplified by the work of Wayne C. Booth, which explains how texts may be treated within webs of community by considering the text as in a manner coincident with the gift of an implied author.[9] Since readers imagine authors as part of what they do during the act of reading, the implied author, or work, in Booth's view presents a reader with legitimate claims of responsible engagement and interaction by offering a gift to a reader. Booth presents the ethical claim of the text, or implied author, as an invitation to conversation, to company, and to friendship, asserting that "to decline the gambit, to remain passive in the face of the author's strongest passions and deepest convictions is surely condescending, insulting, and finally irresponsible."[10] The creation of relationship, "the company we keep," is for Booth an act of judgment, a balance between openness to implied-author-others and willingness to close oneself off from those that will potentially harm us. He calls it "a pluralism with limits"—limits contingent on context.[11] Booth gives a number of criteria for this judgment, but the basic metaphor is this: "[W]e arrive at our sense of value in narratives in precisely the way we arrive at our sense of value in persons," and we decide together how the narratives we meet measure up.[12] This communal evaluation is one that takes place internally, as we compare our experiences to others we have had, and externally as we compare our experiences to those that others have had. Booth argues that by taking on characters' roles, opening ourselves to various invitations presented by works, we may grow into an ethical criticism—a judgment of works that negotiates between caring for self and caring for the other of the text. In treating books as friends, Booth hopes, as I do, to go beyond the simple utility of books; he suggests books ought not be simply "business associates, teammates in professional sports, partners in a marriage of convenience," but rather simply "friendly company itself" good just for "the living in friendship."[13] For Booth, judgment, the appraisal of the characters of particular books as potential friends, is a trying-on of roles that a particular work will allow me to play as it shapes my becoming.[14] Ethical criticism is judgment that emerges from experiencing a work as fully as possible, and then frankly deciding whether the sorts of patterns and roles it offers are ones in I wish to continue.

Yet Booth holds back from what might be considered an eschatological goal, and he does so explicitly: "The Christian ideal of universal love escapes us here as it escapes Aristotle; literary criticism cannot build itself on the hope for a world of saints. On the contrary: we know that we must learn—and we can now hope that we *can* learn—to distinguish those 'others' who will nurture from those who may, deliberately or accidentally, destroy or cripple."[15] "My problem," Booth sums up, "is to winnow, from among myriad narrative advisers, those whose seductive plot suggestions are acts of genuine friendship."[16] The need for a fully developed ethical criticism is the negotiation, for Booth, between appropriate self-care and altruism—with the goal of friendship. Booth calls the desired process *coduction*, a conversational judgment of texts with and against other texts in the reader's experience.[17] The metaphor here, of sifting and winnowing, harkens back, perhaps, to the agricultural metaphors of the parable of wheat and tares. Booth imagines the task of dividing wheat and tares as the necessary task of all earnest readers, implying that for some texts, the harvest is already there, and their ends, good and bad, have been reached.[18]

Booth is not making a fully rendered argument here; thus his refusal of Christian universal love is confusing. It seems as if what he is arguing against in Christianity is not just the turn-the-other-cheek ethic, but a sort of bland acceptance—a minority universalist opinion that many would consider heretical. In a more broadly accepted Christian theological anthropology, human judgment of texts would be admittedly and inevitably broken; it would be understood that the Christian ideal of universal love *does* of course escape *us*. Not only our limits, but also our failures keep us from reading as we should.[19] It does not, however, escape God. In fact, the argument of this book is that literary criticism *must* be built on the hope for a world of saints—a world made anew, of interrelational plentitude and shalom, through the redeeming love of Christ. Reading in the future of the word could be a sign, a portent, and, at times, a mechanism of that kingdom. Textual meaning itself is built on love bringing about a world redeemed, a world in which we may hope for the proliferation of peace beyond our broken beginnings.

And Booth himself, in the appendix that closes out his book, actually makes it seem as if he is closer to the universal love position than he would have earlier stated. He cryptically closes *The Company We Keep: An Ethics of Fiction* with an "anonymous" "warning" against deeming books utterly without meaning or value in the world.[20] He frankly declares that "there are hardly any . . . stories" that "have to be called [irredeemably] bad" because they present "no glimpse of some possible path leading upward from the eternally predetermined flux of sub-atomic particles."[21] In a voice very similar to that which has characterized the main body of the text throughout its five hundred pages up to this point, "anonymous" is able to assert meaning's dependence on Christ, even if Wayne C. Booth cannot: "The very effort to get a story told, like the reader's effort to take a story in, is itself a proof that we dwell in the domain of symbol-exchange, an inherently 'elevated' domain by comparison with that of the brute bumps and surges of the merely physical; it baptizes us into the kingdom of the Word."[22] The existence of words in a world that can be conceived as such depends on the word. It is no small thing to make even the most hesitant of gestures in the direction of a larger kingdom—and Booth's "coduction" offers, in this way, the first hesitant steps toward an eschatology of reading.

No text or person escapes the transformative judgment of God (universal does not equal universalist) in the world of the not yet, but our own postures of judgment must be marked by forgiveness and reconciliation. Booth would say that a flexible relationship as we interact with texts, avoiding the oversimple salvation or damnation, allows us to think through a middle way. I would mark out that relationship rather in terms of a theology of reconciliation and forgiveness, allowing it to more fully engage the Trinitarian sustenance and foundation, in which the only possibility for love or forgiveness exists in the love and forgiveness of the Trinity.

The reconciliation of any part of the world to the Godhead and to the rest of creation is the restoration of that created thing to the relationship of gift-giving that characterizes shalom. Forgiveness as I am thinking of it here is not the erasure of fault from within the text at the level of textuality itself, which would be tricky outside of revision and reissue, something that is, incidentally, more and more possible. Nor is it an overlooking of the more conventional sorts of failures and offenses we might ascribe to an implied author and the author's ill-formed progeny. Forgiveness of the text is a crossing of the text's offenses, both the fundamental and the incidental. It is a re-signing of the sign of them under the sign of the cross; it is evidenced by perseverance in reading.[23] Forgiveness is a reading that submits to the judgment with which it judges, all the while moving toward what we have been pursuing under a different name; we have called reading a form of hope, but its new name in Christ is love.

When Paul Ricoeur describes forgiveness between people in his momentous epilogue to *Memory, History, Forgetting,* "Difficult Forgiveness," he suggests that in order to forgive, we must above all unbind the agent—or rather the agency of the agent—from the possibilities and negative capacities emerging out of the faulty action. "Under the sign of forgiveness," Ricoeur writes,

> the guilty person is to be considered capable of something other than his offenses and his faults. He is held to be restored to his capacity for acting, and action restored to its capacity for continuing. This capacity is signaled in the small acts of consideration in which we recognized the *incognito* of forgiveness played out on the public stage. And, finally, this restored capacity is enlisted by promising as it projects action toward the future. The formula for this liberating word, reduced to the bareness of its utterance, would be: you are better than your actions.[24]

The action of forgiving here is mental first, an act of consideration, defining, recognizing, and seeking from within the guilty person a restoration of normality and gift exchange in which the depth of fault and the height of forgiveness may be leveled from within relationship.

In describing the process of forgiveness, Ricoeur uses a textual metaphor that, symbolically read, "gives rise to thought" about how to make forgiveness something not just workable between two people,[25] but within the God-author-text-reader-context complex that characterizes the text. Ricoeur writes that the "intimate dissociation [of the agency of the agent from the growing evil of the act] signifies that the capacity of commitment belonging to the moral subject is not exhausted by its various *inscriptions* in the affairs of the world."[26] The use of the word "inscriptions" suggests at least a family resemblance between the textual and the more broadly conceivable sorts of acts ascribable to an agent. Ricoeur compares and connects our actions, in their temporal ability to set other actions in motion, to textual inscriptions, that is, to moments of writing from within particular contexts that may themselves have some influence on states of affairs. So, his wording here suggests that our actions and their futures are like texts and their futures. When we forgive people, Ricoeur says, we participate in an act of sign-making and significance-giving—of *interpretation*—that allows the actions of a person to be considered regenerated, that allows their inscriptions to be read as not-definitive, for their text-acts to be liberated from the death sentence of the sentence.

Between texts and readers, as between people, such a reading must be miraculous, to overcome the sentence through the sentence itself. Insofar as we read within the word of God, within the Spirit of Christ, the text is both judged by the Spirit within us, brought under the reconciliation of the cross, and, in the fullness of Christ's kingdom, transformed in the "all things new" flowering by that same Spirit (Rev. 21:5). Thus in the very normal act of interpreting texts in their God-author-text-reader-context matrices, our persistence in reading offers them forgiveness, precisely the normality that Ricoeur defines as forgiveness's *incognito*.[27] As we receive from texts and offer them an asymmetrical interpretive response, they begin a future beyond the inscriptions that characterize them so far, the freezing fixings-in-place and the disengaged dismissal. The offending text in all its history of offense as it has trickled down to us is, if we read it, made new in the reading of it—set anew in the context of making meaning with God. Richard Viledesau, in *Theological Aesthetics*, has written of this eschatological seeing that is made possible through participation in divine forgiveness: "To the extent that we participate in the divine mode of life, we see others neither simply as a function of our selves nor solely in their present condition. By virtue of our graced anticipation of the totality of all things in God . . . we ourselves and all others appear in the light of God."[28] When we think of texts in this light, our own position, being converted by such a grace as God gives us, God's beauty—a beauty that embraces even the cross—motivates our own perception and judgment, which makes all our work with words a tearing down of dividing walls, a making peace through his shed blood, a reconciliation with text and with all the network of relations that every text implicitly represents.

The God–author–text–reader–context matrix that is implied here in the notion of forgiving texts, which this argument compares to a more straightforward person-to-person forgiveness, can be rendered a bit more comprehensible from within John Milbank's conception of medieval structures of forgiveness. As Milbank has described it in *Being Reconciled: Ontology and Pardon*, in medieval societies, "the aim of forgiveness was not a lone, self-righteous will to exonerate (without regard to the circumstances or the repentance of the other), but rather charity, which the Middle Ages regarded less as a performance than as a *state* of fraternal, friendly, and harmonious coexistence. . . . Reconciliation, where the bond of love is an exchange of infinite love."[29] The economy of gift relies on asymmetrical reciprocity, which does not make distinctions between "the free active subject and the inert object."[30] As Milbank puts it, "for these societies, a thing exchanged is not a commodity, but a gift; and it is not *alienated* from the giver but expresses his personality, so that the giver is *in* the gift, he *goes with* the gift. Precisely for this reason a return on the gift is always due to the giver, unlike our modern 'free gift.'"[31] This jointure of gift and giver allows us to at least begin to think about how the implied author of a text may be calling for reconciliation and exchange from within the text. For we conceive of text as gift, not merely from implied author to implied reader but also from the divine author, under whose authorship all authors author. This divine giver is given—self-giving—within the word. The "harmonious coexistence" proceeds from the infinite love of the infinite God. Thus forgiveness's restoration of gift exchange participates in and extends the infinite love of the Trinity through the giving and receiving of the text. As with Milbank's analysis of interpersonal forgiveness, in text only God's incarnation allows for any accessible victim to be empowered to forgive, for victims of all textual violence are either lost to time because of their victimization or else divinely unassailable. In Christ's incarnation, and in the Spirit of Christ with us, Christ may represent both the lost victim, assaulted by the false word of accusation, and the authority that can, in fact, forgive. For in text, the word as victim and the word as judge face together and forgive the fault of the word.

The presence of the spirit of Christ, then, the word in which all our words are formed and in which we read, makes it possible for us to forgive the text. The Spirit has the authority to enforce the judgment of the written code and guides us into it so that our reading may offer a just sense of the gift that is offered within the text. The Spirit in our reading offers us the surety of God's judgment as well as the warning and conviction of our own sin and righteousness and judgment. The Spirit with us leads us into all truth, toward God's eschatological purposes of the cosmos. Yet, at the same time, the spirit of Christ, the one who was crucified, has, by submitting to the written code and its judgment, written it over again, a text made new in the future of the resurrection.

Jonathan Tran, in the traditions of Paul Ricoeur and Stanley Hauerwas, has written about how God's forgiveness and restoration of the world within salvation history changes the way we understand our own narratives. He writes that "we tell our stories within the story of God's self-giving forgiveness," for God's forgiveness *is* in fact a renarration, a putting of our stories within God's story: and "when God forgives, he re-narrates our stories . . . for restoration" with an eschatological goal in mind.[32] Tran is particularly trying to deal with the problems of cultural memory and theology surrounding the Vietnam War; to do so he figures the past as a person walking around with us, and our forgiveness of the past as the forgiveness of a person, accomplished likewise through our own small, regular acts of renarration. When we forgive as Christ would have us do, Tran writes, we, while not being able to approach the omniscience of God as to the larger story, put the past as a story into the versions of the stories that we can renarrate. That is, we put the story of the past within the sacraments of the liturgy. When we repeat the sacraments, we reorient the memory of trauma by placing it into the eternal—as made present in the Eucharist. Tran writes that the "church's continual re-enactment of Christ's presence in the sacraments displays again and again God's lordship over time."[33] When we receive the Eucharist, an opportunity to participate in the church's remembrance, we invite the revelation of God, who shows himself in the sacraments: "the one who is both past and present meaning of time shows himself."[34] Thus the sacrament is God's revelation of the healing of time, a revelation of the full story; our participation in the sacrament is the placing of our stories by grace, by the Spirit of the word within our words and acts, into the eternal story.

And in the reading of text, as the text is a past or a thing we experience again and again as memory, we have likewise the opportunity to place the text into the larger story. Reading as forgiveness in the sacramental sense described above allows us to think through how the eternal healing of time is manifest in the reading of any object—however poorly or commercially made. For moments become sacramental as God reveals through them. Reading is transformed by sacrament, as all of life is transformed by sacrament, into the remembering of salvation history, an experiencing of God in the present, and presaging the *parousia*. In reading, we have the fullness of time.

Forgiveness of the text restores to it response-ability, both in preserving its presence and its relation of its incapacities, and also in preserving for it a future, a role or status as a site of giving and receiving. Bringing it away from fixedness, forgiveness refuses or reverses textual arrest; it receives the text's gifts in a context of already-received grace. When we forgive a text, we put it into gift relation with us again, that we, in reading, may give to it ongoing life as it gives to us its textual and aesthetic gifts.

## Postures of Forgiveness

Forgiving a text allows it to participate in the community of the fellowship of the creator and the creation—in a way that is present to our consciousness and that opens our hands to receipt of the revelation of the word—to bearing witness. But with the text from which we have received (or taken) offense, forgiveness seems more confusing or painful in actuality than theory. And while this project has always sought to define what happens when we read rather than being particularly prescriptive about how we ought to do so, an exploration of forgiving reading postures might be helpful. I'm not sure anyone goes after a text in order to be offended by it and then to pursue forgiveness of it, though, for some, the idea that a book is dangerous or bad in some ways makes it more exciting. Even if a person were to read text on purpose because it is dangerous or offensive, usually such a move is rather to see what all the fuss is about than to seek one's own offense. Even masochism is about pleasure. Sometimes, reading a text that others have been offended by is often to prove one's own inoculation against offense, or one's own strength of will, or unbreachable defenses.

Robert C. Roberts has described practices of the virtue of "forgivingness," which, while not the same as reconciliation, may offer insight into how reading may restore to a text its ability to give, its future. The virtue of forgivingness is characterized by a personal "sensitivity to . . . anger-reducing considerations" regarding the offender: "1) the repentance of the offender; 2) excuses for the offender; 3) suffering of the offender; 4) moral commonality with the offender; and 5) relationship to the offender."[35] Roberts's description is about personal emotional disposition that lends itself to forgiveness, namely people's interest in construing their own concerns such that their anger at offense may be diminished. He is not arguing about the possibility of actual forgiveness, nor the height of forgiveness and the depth of fault, as Ricoeur does, but rather the moments of interaction or thinking that tend a person toward forgiveness. As such, these five characteristics may be instructive as we think about what practices of emotional regulation may facilitate our restoration of normality's *incognito* of forgiveness, the pattern of gift exchange with text.

A text's repentance, perhaps, is not an exceptionally clear place to begin, for it is often largely on the level of language's very languageness that it repents—its structure and function, its saying, is always a confession of its insufficiency, as discussed above. Textual repentance or confession, is of course related to a larger problem in the understanding of forgiveness, whether forgiveness may be offered unilaterally. I am trying to skate between the idea that forgiveness requires contrition or repentance, and the idea that it may be granted by suggesting that in a textual sense, every text is always already a confession of its own errors. The confession, perhaps, may seem void of contrition in some cases, though Derrida's vision of a babbling, incoherent, Plato that closes out his observation of *Phaedrus*'s deconstruction in "Plato's Pharmacy," seems at least sorry. The essay ends with the thought of Plato, as imagined by Derrida, which merges in with bits of the text under discussion:

> In the stammering buzz of voices, as some philological sequence or other floats by, one can sort of make this out, but it is hard to hear: *logos* beds itself . . . *pharmakon* means *coup* . . ." that *pharmakon* will have meant: that which pertains to an attack of demoniac possession or is used as a curative *against* such an attack." . . . One ought to distinguish, between two repetitions. —But they repeat each other, still; they substitute for each other. . . . —Nonsense: they don't replace each other, since they are added. . . . One still has to take note of this. And to finish that Second Letter: ". . . Consider these facts and take care lest you sometime come to *repent* of having now unwisely published your views. . . . It is impossible for what is written not to be disclosed. That is why I have never written anything about these things" (emphasis added).[36]

Even Plato, who seems not to want to confess, always already does. And his writing is his own confession, a disclosure, so if repentance is required, a text has always already confessed. Reading, then, becomes a hearing of confession, and an offering of access to another Father for sanctification.

The reader who hears the confession of the text is, in reading, observing its deconstruction, as Derrida does for Plato's *Phaedrus*. This reading is to mark a text's fault and to name the text's naming of its own fault. It is to see the text's coming apart, and to treat its offense as renderable, understandable, or at least mitigable, as in Jesus' formulation, "Father, forgive them, for they know not what they do" (Luke 23:34).[37] With texts, to excuse is to minimize anger at the offenses of the text through explanation of the offenses—it is to give reasons that a text may be at fault. Such imagination will seek the boundaries of the fault and its genealogy of the fault, limning its cracks, which will move a reader toward understanding and potentially reduce the intensity of the emotional response.

The suffering of texts is the suffering perhaps of the implied or actual author—possible ignominy, loss, disappearance, destruction of the text in its offenses and insufficiencies. Recognition or awareness of the suffering—posthumous or otherwise—of the implied author may of course be created from the interaction between text and implied or actual reader. The movement of compassion will condescend from the height of forgiveness to the depth of the fault, and imaginatively feel with the implied author. Compassion for the suffering of the text, of the implied author, is another note in the key of the always dissatisfaction of the not yet. It is a mourning for the meanwhile victory of death.

These postures may seem themselves offensively condescending toward text, especially considering the limited knowledge that a reader—even an expert reader—brings to any text. It must be noted, of course, once again, that the judgments implied in the postures described here are of course subject to what Barbara Herrnstein Smith calls both "contingencies of value" as well as the error and insufficiency of the reader.[38] And this is where the posture of humility, of "moral commonality with the offender," as Roberts puts it, comes in.[39] In considering the offense of the offending text, it makes sense to consider the burdens and difficulties of language as well as the reader's own culpability in interpreting and deploying language. As always with judgment, the mote-and-beam effect is operative here, and the awareness of that operation offers the possibility for the reader to offer as much emotional willingness to normalize relations with the text as possible. For forgiveness—especially of texts—is also an act of love that depends on one's own need for forgiveness. As Richard Viladesau has written, "'religious conversion' or life in God's Spirit allows us to love our fellow creatures in excess of their beauty—that is, of their appeal to 'natural' eros. . . . By means of the divine life in us and (at least as a potentiality) in every other, we are motivated to love others in their limitations, their need, and even their sinfulness."[40] We are able to forgive a text, to read a text in a sense because the moments and acts of reading are themselves our John-the-Baptist moments, our welcome to the sinner in the name of the word of God who has crossed over our own faults and canceled the written code against us.

Roberts' last posture, the desirable maintenance of relationship as a reason for an attitude of forgivingness in the fact of the offensive text, is of course directly related itself to the ultimate aim of forgiveness. If forgiveness proper or reconciliation is the restoration of relationship, then the already-present relationship or the desirability of relationship is one factor that would assist a would-be forgiver in anger mitigation. This may be the motivation, after all, for working imaginatively toward understanding. Two examples, one domestic and one scholarly, may illustrate this. Last year, I read aloud several of Frances Hodgson Burnett's children's books to my daughter and son. It had been many years since I had read the works I had treasured in childhood, and I was deeply disturbed by the treatment of Indians in the texts, a portrayal that had only remained in memory as an oddly negative set of images of unbearably hot weather and poor growing soil on the subcontinent. The ideological commitments of the works—what seemed like some mixture of Christian Science and theosophy—seemed newly visible and newly suspect. I was also surprised and somewhat nonplussed by some of the writing: how *long* and occasionally tiresome (for the children and the throat) some sections of description were! My childhood relationship to the texts was such that I did not *want* to stop reading them because of these offenses or foreclose the opportunity for my children to share in a part of my growing up. I had a motivation to try and maintain the relationship and the reading despite what had turned from pleasure to offense in my experience. Through a process of education, research with the kids, and some selective omission of the horrible illustrations of our Internet-purchased, cheap edition, we read the texts in a manner that I think ended up more attentive than my own childhood reads. My children felt the magic, I think, but in a posture of regular, thoughtful consideration of the text in its faults and glories. Another example involves the need I had for relationship to Thomas Pynchon's *Gravity's Rainbow* as an Americanist literary scholar. My professional obligation afforded me determination in the face of the offense I took to one particularly vile scene and to the text's general resistance to the reader. In each of these cases, the prior or imagined relationship I had with the text in fact prompted me to proceed according to a normalizing of relationship. In short, I read them again, better and closer than I had before. In that way, the desire for relationship or a need for relationship conditioned me to search for factors that might mitigate my offense and then allow me to intensify relationship—not without critique perhaps, but with more of the understanding that comes from the proper exchange of equality rather than condescension.

Roberts argues that these five considerations build inside a person the virtue of forgivingness. As I borrow them from analytic philosophy of emotions and move them toward hermeneutics, they can be related to, or perhaps are constituent parts of, the various habitudes of Christian community described by L. Gregory Jones in *Embodying Forgiveness* or Rowan Williams's *Resurrection*. Jones and Williams offer the sacraments as habitual practices that express forgiveness within the plentitude of the eschatological community in real life. Both emphasize the regularity, the embodiment of the love of the community within the ongoing, not finished, eschatological action of forgiveness.

And so, in this work, too, the practice of the reconciliation of the text must move likewise to the applied, habitual reading of texts themselves. The next section of scrivenings and the conclusion that follows look to do just this as they seek to offer to two famously offensive texts a normality of nonreciprocal exchange in reading that is forgiveness's *incognito*. In so doing, the double-bind of judgment and the mote-and-beam effect will, I trust, be visible. But more than the illustration of this particular set of practices or claims, these last readings step again into the wilderness of our reading position in hopes of meeting there the baptism of the word and the future of the word. These readings are a persistence. In reading the word in the word, these readings hope to show a kind of giving and receiving that opens up the text in meaning-making fruitfulness—small glimpses of the not yet within the now, or perhaps small notes of the call of the Spirit of the word who, with the Bride, always says "Come" (Rev. 22:17). For, hearing that voice, the Spirit of the word whose future makes all things new, has been the devoutly desired consummation of this entire book: "Beyond the desert of criticism, we wish to be called again."[41] In any case, whether or not the particular acts of reading function as good fruit or bad—wheat or tares—relative to that call, in opening the books, these readings offer their own invitation to the community of readers who are willing to open them with me.

## Notes

1.  Hartmut Stegemann, *The Library of Qumran: On the Essenes, Qumran, John the Baptist, and Jesus* (Grand Rapids: Eerdmans, 1998), 219.

2.  Ernst Käsemann, *Essays on New Testament Themes* (Naperville, IL: Allenson, 1964), 43.

3.  Daniel S. Dapaah, *The Relationship between John the Baptist and Jesus of Nazareth: A Critical Study* (Lanham, MD: University Press of America, 2005), 43.

4.  Robert L. Webb, *John the Baptizer and Prophet: A Socio-Historical Study*, Journal for the Study of the New Testament Supplement Series 62 (Sheffield: Sheffield Academic Press, 1991), 197.

5.  Here, I'm thinking of Kevin Hector's *Theology without Metaphysics*, of understanding language in a non-correspondentist way through prior usages—the only theoretically limited and mostly unknowable history of past usages of a word that may establish the meaning of a piece of language.

6.  Jacques Derrida, "Plato's Pharmacy," in *Dissemination* (Chicago: University of Chicago Press, 1981), 89.

7.  Ibid., 166.

8.  See chapter 1 for a more thorough discussion.

9.  See also Alan Jacobs, "Love and the Suspicious Spirit," in *Theology of Reading: A Hermeneutics of Love* (Boulder, CO: Westview, 2001), 77–90.

10. Wayne C. Booth, *The Company We Keep: An Ethics of Fiction* (Berkeley: University of California Press, 1988), 135.

11. Ibid., 489.

12. Ibid., 70.

13. Ibid., 173.

14. See also similar ideas in the work of Mark Edmundson in *Why Read?* (New York: Bloomsbury, 2004), or even, by extension, in the work of Paul Ricoeur on metaphor.

15. Booth, *The Company We Keep*, 266.

16. Ibid., 290.

17. Ibid., 72–73.

18. Alan Jacobs, in *Theology of Reading*, 64–66, critiques what he considers Booth's false dichotomy between exclusion of and openness to potential book-friends. Jacobs suggests that in the taking an approach of charity to neighbor (*agape*) rather than the mutual benefit of friendship (*philia*), the tension dissolves. Justice in reading and the love that surpasses justice emerge out of the context of the church rather than out of the contextless individual decision (which doesn't exist anyway) (142–44). Jacobs's discussion here is brief, but his raising of the church as the necessary context in which the discipline of judgment and charity may be fruitfully enacted is one that we would likely somewhat disagree on. See my discussion on the anthropology of the new creation in chapter 2.

19. See also Jacobs, *Theology of Reading*, 66–67, for a discussion of human limitation in reading.

20. Booth, *The Company We Keep*, 501–2.

21. Ibid., 501.

22. Ibid.

23. Here, I use Crystal Downing's wording of "re-signing" from *Changing Signs of Truth: A Christian Introduction to the Semiotics of Communication* (Downers Grove, IL: IVP Academic, 2012).

24. Paul Ricoeur, *Memory, History, Forgetting* (Chicago: University of Chicago Press, 2004), 493.

25. Paul Ricoeur, *The Symbolism of Evil* (Boston: Beacon, 1967), 237.

26. Ricoeur, *Memory, History, Forgetting*, 490.

27. Ibid., 477 and 485.

28. Richard Viledesau, *Theological Aesthetics* (Oxford: Oxford University Press, 1999), 207.

29. John Milbank, *Being Reconciled: Ontology and Pardon* (New York: Routledge, 2003), 47.

30. Ibid., 167.

31. Ibid.

32. Jonathan Tran, *The Vietnam War and the Theologies of Memory* (Malden, MA: Wiley-Blackwell, 2010), 164.

33. Ibid., 192.

34. Ibid., 196.

35. Robert C. Roberts, "Forgivingness," *American Philosophical Quarterly* 32, no. 4 (1995): 293.

36. Derrida, "Plato's Pharmacy," 170.

37. Ibid., 295.

38. Barbara Herrnstein Smith, *Contingencies of Value* (Cambridge, MA: Harvard University Press, 1998), 30.

39. Roberts, "Forgivingness," 293.

40. Viledesau, *Theological Aesthetics*, 207.

41. Ricoeur, *The Symbolism of Evil*, 349.

# Literary Scrivenings 3:
# The Romance of Reconciliation

An unlikely juxtaposition of novels works toward reconciliation and forgiveness in the final scrivenings and the conclusion of this book: Francine Rivers's *Redeeming Love* (1991/1997), a Christian inspirational romance novel that retells the biblical book of Hosea in gold-rush California and Vladimir Nabokov's *Lolita* (1955), the fictional memoir and apologia of a pedophile. Though it seems reasonably assured that these two texts may never elsewhere come into as close proximity as they do in this book, they do have a few things in common. Both novels take up childhood sexual slavery and pedophilia; both push boundaries; both are significantly revised versions of other works; and both cultivate strong intertextual relationships with other works. Even the covers of recent editions share features, from emphasizing partial faces of young females—a move that emphasizes the lips—to choosing florid cursive titles and prominent anniversary-edition labeling. Most importantly, they both deal with questions of forgivability and redemption; they are, at bottom, attempts to reconcile with the strictures and possibilities of art.

*Redeeming Love* is an evangelical inspirational romance, a subcategory of romance genre fiction. It is a particularly successful member of the popular genre: having sold more than a million copies, it has even greater reach than sales numbers demonstrate, since inspirational fiction physically circulates among readers—primarily women—who share it between family members, church members, and friends. The publisher reissued a twentieth-anniversary edition of the text, and it continues to sell well across paper and electronic formats, even getting some high-profile press: in 2012, American Idol winner Jordin Sparks declared in both *Ebony* and *Entertainment Weekly* that *Redeeming Love* is her favorite novel, one that she has read more than ten times.[1] Yet, it remains unabashedly an inspirational romance novel, a member of one of the most maligned of genres.

I have been accustomed to thinking of romance novels as a dismissable genre. This thinking never came from the moral high ground of a mind untainted by them, however; I read Christian inspirational fiction in early adolescence and was familiar with both early and contemporary examples. But it nonetheless seemed to me that in a reading subculture so tied to abstinence before marriage and faithfulness even in unsatisfying marriage, romance novels functioned primarily as a form of soft porn. I suspected the genre of causing dissatisfaction within marriage. I suspected it of presenting as unquestionable ideas about gender and relationships that ought to be questioned, much discussed, and played out in community. But, in the developing of this book's argument, it became clear that even these areas of offense—perhaps *especially* these areas of offense—are the ground from which the future of the word proceeds in making community through the reconciliation of the word.

The author of *Redeeming Love*, Francine Rivers, has published more than twenty novels, including two *New York Times* bestsellers in the last five years; her book *The Last Sin Eater* was made into a film. She has received numerous awards and has been inducted into the Romance Writers Hall of Fame. *Redeeming Love* is only one of several of her books to have sold more than a million copies—and more than one has been rereleased in an anniversary special edition. Yet Rivers seems to have a conflicted relationship with the romance novels that have made her so successful. Her body of work is starkly divided in two: books from before her conversion (1976–85), when she wrote what she calls "steamy historical romances,"[2] and books from after, when she felt called to become a Christian writer, "to present a story that is all about Jesus. The Lord is the foundation, the structure, and Scripture has everything to do with the creation and development of the characters in the story. . . . If you remove Jesus and Biblical principles from the novel, it collapses."[3] Though Rivers was clearly on her way to a very successful writing career even before her work changed—she won several awards even early on in her career, including a RITA, her website indicates that she has let her earlier books go out of print and that they "are not recommended."[4] Rivers describes in an interview how her conversion changed things: "I had been a writer in the general market for a number of years. . . . After becoming a Christian, I couldn't write for about three years. I thought, 'Why? What's going on here? My life is supposed to be getting better, and it's getting worse.' But I wasn't looking to God."[5] Romance novels, Rivers decided, were something at least potentially toxic. She described her writing of romances as something that took her away from community and relationships, especially her family, and as, she says, "my escape from the world and hard times. It was one area of my life where I believed (mistakenly) that I had complete control. I could create characters and stories to suit me."[6] Rivers wrote secular romance novels and "read them voraciously" as a way to manage her burdens and relational problems.[7] When Rivers converted, she writes, she knew God "wanted no other gods in my life—not my family, not my writing"—hence three years of writer's block.[8]

Rivers limits her pubic critique of the romance novel genre to her way of using it—the real problem was the idolatrous way she sought escape and personal control through romance novels. But the book on which she pivots her entire career, *Redeeming Love*, demonstrates that personal issues with romance as idol had far-reaching implications for her theory and practice of writing romance. Her testimony gives hints of what the book fleshes out much more thoroughly: she needed to reconcile with romance. She says, "So those three years I studied the Bible and soon it didn't matter to me if I ever wrote again. Then we came to Hosea and I could just hear God saying, 'This is the love story I want you to write.'"[9] She felt God had given her a new story, and it *was* a romance, but a reconceived one. *Redeeming Love*'s form—especially its use of the most widely recognized and studied conventions of western historical romance novels of that period—show it to be a reading and a reconciliation with the form. And perhaps, too, a reading and reconciliation with God. For *Redeeming Love* may be the author's statement of faith, but it is also most evidently a working out of salvation, with plenty of fear and trembling. Rivers has stated frankly that her fiction moves out of impasses and questions in her own faith journey: "Almost every story I have written since becoming a Christian has come from a question that regards a struggle in my own faith walk. The plot centers around the different ways that question can be answered by 'the world'—but the quest is to find God's answer."[10] Her express hope is that in the broader scene of Christian writing, writers would explore the hard issues and questions. Her own record of publication demonstrates her commitment to that hope—early on in the boom of Christian publishing at the end of the twentieth century, she was dealing with rape, abortion, sex slavery, and euthanasia.

Given how central a self-conscious sense of the kingdom of God and a relationship to Christ is to the reports from both readers and writers about how they engage with the genre, it seems at least reasonable to consider it seriously, to see if some sort of détente might be possible, to see if we might read even for the future of the inspirational romance and reconcile with it. And, given how works much less expressly religious have offered us ways of working out other ideas about the future of the word in literature, it is possible that even as little-considered a genre—or work—as this may also offer resources for theorizing about the future of the word.[11]

This book has focused on the future of the word, particularly on how reading functions to cultivate the future of texts in the kingdom of God. The last chapter argued that a reader's position relative to the future of the text, given the double bind of judgment and fallenness, must be a kind of reconciliation. To think through the problems and possibilities of how the future of the work might and must be cultivated for reconciliation, the case of *Redeeming Love* is particularly interesting. For Francine Rivers already considers her work a future of the word of God. Some of her post-conversion oeuvre, such as her series exploring the lives of five forebears to Christ, functions self-consciously as an almost midrashic future of the biblical text. All of her novels, even those less immediately tied to the biblical story, proceed very much intentionally on the foundation of the word of God in a way not inconsistent with the theology set forth in chapter 1. Her comments above demonstrate that she operates on the premise that all her words are words within the word of God: "The Lord is the foundation, the structure, and Scripture has everything to do with the creation and development of the characters in the story."[12] She is concerned to make that theology as explicit as possible in the text: in a work such as *Atonement Child*, for instance, which is set in the present day, she names the protagonist Dynah to link the young woman dealing with a rape and unplanned pregnancy to the Genesis-figure Dinah. Rivers views her work, too, as a revelation, or at least a sign, of the word: when describing the goal of her fiction, she writes, "I want to whet the appetite for the real thing: the Bible and a personal relationship with Jesus. I try to weave Scripture throughout the story so people receive the Word and see what it might mean in their lives—how the Lord is present and real and passionately interested in each of us."[13] Rivers gives aspiring authors the advice that they, too, should learn the craft of writing from "the MASTER (daily reading of scripture)."[14]

Her book is, admittedly, an odd future of the text. The novel retells a portion of Hosea—from the first chapters of the biblical book, where God calls Hosea to start a relationship that will become a metaphor for the relationship between God and Israel. Rivers creates the future of that story in a tale of Michael Hosea, a nineteenth-century American, the southern-born son of a slaveholder who has escaped from his family's unjust ownership of people into a career in farming in gold-rush California. He is delivering a load of vegetables to a merchant in the ramshackle gold-town of Pair-a-Dice when God speaks to him, telling him to marry a woman that turns out to be the most beautiful and highly-sought-after prostitute in the town's brothel. Angel had been sold into sexual slavery as a child, worked as a prostitute in various American landscapes, and has suffered forced abortions that have rendered her unable to have children. She has been hardened by the abandonment of her father and by having to witness and survive the suffering and death of everyone she has cared for—most painfully her mother. The novel chronicles Michael's persistent pursuit of Angel under the guidance of the express voice of God (the novel prints God's voice in bold italics and the voice of Satan or an internal enemy in bold). Though Angel flatly turns down Hosea's proposals of marriage, he returns to rescue her from the brothel where she has been severely beaten. He marries her—she is barely conscious during the ceremony—to take her away from the town to his small farm. Angel's confusion about her growing affection for Michael, emerging out of a years-long hatred for men, leads her to run away, but he comes after her time and again, patiently wooing her with the caring help of a neighboring family. When she abandons him for the last time—this time out of love, believing that he would do better to marry another, since she can never bear him children—he lets her go, patiently waiting for her to make the choice to come back. She runs to the city, recaptured by the man who had first turned her into a childhood sex slave, but is miraculously rescued by an upstanding citizen who enters the brothel on divine instructions. Angel converts to belief in God, and begins new work of rescuing other women from prostitution by offering them job training for other careers. After several years, she returns to Michael, finding forgiveness, a happy ending, and the miraculous conception of children. In the text, not only is the book a retelling of Hosea—a future for that biblical book, but the main character, Michael Hosea, also is explicitly modeled on Christ, the "lover of my soul," according to Rivers.[15]

*Redeeming Love* was the author's first attempt to write in Christ. In its composition and publication history as well as content, the book shows what might be described as a sort of "becoming" toward the kingdom. Written after Rivers's conversion, the novel was published by Fanfare in 1991. Rivers's description of the writing process is a confession that accords with even the bold idea that all our words are in Christ: "I felt God's presence throughout the months of work, as though He were telling me His story through thousands of Scriptures as well as explaining the inner heart-ache and quest of each [of] 'my' characters."[16] After selling 120,000 copies or so, *Redeeming Love* (the apparently unredeemed version) went out of print and Rivers sought to get the rights to the text back. She revised it and published it again in 1997 through a Christian publishing house, Multnomah, at least in part on the advice of an editor. In that version, the text became much less explicit about sex and much more explicit about religion. In the redeemed *Redeeming Love*, sex, which is a large part of a story about a prostitute, with both abuse and pleasure present, is described in abstract or distantly metaphoric terms. In addition, several aspects of the text were adjusted to fall within the house style boundaries of the publisher—including the removal of terms such as "whore" (replaced with the euphemistic "soiled dove"). Rivers believes that the adjustments have made it "easier" for some readers to read.[17] So, in addition to the creation of redemptive biblical futures through the writing of romantic western pasts, the publication history demonstrates how Rivers's most important and favorite work, what she calls her "statement of faith" is, in her vision, redeemed.

## Reconciling the Ways of God to Women

The chapters of *Redeeming Love* open with tiny epigraphs from literary and biblical sources—and all these literary references point to the ambitious undertaking of *Redeeming Love*: more than just a statement of faith, it is a statement of faithful poetics. And the first chapter's epigraph, some lines from Keats, points toward the novel's aim.

> But strength alone though of the Muses born
> Is like a fallen angel: trees uptorn,
> Darkness, and worms, and shrouds, and sepulchres
> Delight it; for it feeds upon the burrs,
> And thorns of life; forgetting the great end
> Of poesy, that it should be a friend
> To sooth the cares, and lift the thoughts of man.[18]

On first glance, readers hit on the "fallen angel" as a reference to the main character of the novel, Angel. The word "poesy" is not as commonly remembered to mean "poetry" in present-day English, and so the passage then seems to be more about a person who relies on her or his own strength and thus becomes a fallen angel, feeding on the detritus of life.

Yet the epigraph interacts in multiple ways with the text to show the novel's larger project. The lines come from the poem "Sleep and Poetry," in which a young Keats begs for ten years to immerse himself in poetry's various glories to develop his craft. The poem is famous for its denunciation of poetic forebears and contemporaries that would misuse the poetic subjects afforded them:

> . . . yet in truth we've had
> Strange thunders from the potency of song;
> Mingled indeed with what is sweet and strong,
> From majesty: but in clear truth the themes
> Are ugly clubs, the Poets Polyphemes
> Disturbing the grand sea.[19]

Keats critiques *writing* that beats its audience over the head thematically rather than seeking to embrace the audience. Indeed, the subject of the poem is *not* fallen angels, but rather fallen *writing*. So, far from being useful only for its mention of a fallen angel, this poetic epigraph in *Redeeming Love* announces a far bolder project: the critique of the generic forebears (or perhaps of her self in an earlier version), and the true exploration of the power of a genre.

One example of a formal device that demonstrates the text's ambition to soar above the Aonian mount of its generic forebears is the allusions to Adam and Eve throughout the text, which, along with a series of reversals echo Milton's *Paradise Lost* and *Paradise Regained*. The historical romance setting notwithstanding, the novel opens with a prostitute in a tent town clearly (and ironically) labeled

Pair-a-Dice. The novel follows the sort of paired reversals common in western historical romance novels and also common to *Paradise Regained*,[20] as the last page of the novel makes clear: "Michael had once read to her how God had cast a man and woman out of Paradise. Yet, for all their human faults and failures, God had shown them the way back in."[21] For Angel, the escape from Pair-a-Dice is God's rescue of her and a bringing of her to a state of renewal in a paradisal farm and garden setting. This instance of reversal of the trope—Angel's rescue is a lifting of her rather than a falling, as her grave marker proclaims: "Though fallen low / God raised her up / An Angel" and she is restored—not, perhaps, to innocence, but to healing and renewal.[22] The Keats and Milton allusions solidify Rivers's purposes.

Rivers sets her novel up as a redemption of romance novels—one that does not shy away from critiques of the genre or its uses, but ultimately rescues it by restoring it to possibility—or re-storying it—within a Christian eschatological narrative. On the foundation of Christ, romance novels can, Rivers thinks, allow people to experience God and restored relationships with others. A careful reading of the text shows that the novel aims at multiple instances of response and reconciliation: first, it aims to reconcile a profane genre with a sacred purpose, and second, it aims to reconcile a Christian audience with the romance novel's particularities and possibilities. Through a reconciliation with and perhaps justification of the romance novel genre, the author might also be able to justify the ways of God in Christ to women.

The novel reconceives structural and functional elements of the romance novel—both elements of the larger genre and the specific subgenre of western historical romance novel. To highlight this reconception, I rely on two works: Pamela Regis's *A Natural History of the Romance Novel*, which defines the broader romance novel genre, and the seminal work of Janice Radway, *Reading the Romance*, first published in 1984 and reissued in 1991, which outlines the functional elements of western historical romance. By its pushing of generic norms, *Redeeming Love*, which is clearly a romance novel, allows itself to engage the larger project of not only the consideration of the freedom and betrothal of a heroine to a hero, but also the redemption and relationship of women to Christ.

As Pamela Regis has defined the genre, the romance novel is "a work of prose fiction that tells the story of the courtship and betrothal of one or more heroines."[23] It possesses eight elements that may be endlessly rearranged: "a *definition of society*, always corrupt, that the romance novel will reform; the *meeting* between the heroine and hero; an account of their *attraction* for each other; the *barrier* between them; the *point of ritual death*; the *recognition* that fells the barrier; the *declaration* of heroine and hero that they love each other; and their *betrothal*."[24] In Regis's assessment, the absolute flexibility with which a romance novel may rearrange these elements allows any to become a "governing" or thematic concern in the novel.[25]

It is easy to see how Rivers's use of these elements allows them to develop both the relationship between Angel and Michael as well as the relationship between Angel and God. She does so through a combination of allegory and paired elements within the plot. The *corrupt society* in the story is the brothel town, the mudhole Pair-a-Dice—a loveless, mercantilist town of gold-diggers and whores, each trying to screw each other out of something. The town's name signals its spiritual degradation. The *meeting* between the hero and heroine is divinely ordained: in the 1991 version, Michael's encounter with Angel is spotted with prayer—in the 1997 version, God actually points Angel out to Michael and identifies her as the one. The *attraction* between the couple is the record of an attraction between

Michael and Angel and between God and Angel. Michael's love for Angel is prior to her knowledge or trust in him; it is absolute, complete, unyielding, and utterly redeeming. Angel first believes neither Michael nor God about their love—her first commitment to Michael (the *betrothal*) is a half-conscious "Why not?" that counts for an "I do" in their marriage ceremony. She resists him through much of the novel, feeling her past has disqualified her for love. The *barrier* between them is dual: first, it is Angel's past and the shame related to her sexual slavery, and the corruption that has taken her over; then, as Angel falls in love with her husband, it is Michael himself. He becomes an idol to her, her desire for him standing in the way of her being able to believe in or trust in God. The *point of ritual death* in the novel is, in Regis's explanation, the moment when it seems impossible that the heroine and hero could get together. In *Redeeming Love*, that moment is when Michael decides to accept Angel's decision to leave him—without following her this time. Angel, because she is unable to bear children, feels unworthy of Michael's love, and believes that leaving will allow him to marry Miriam, a neighbor girl. Her inability to accept Michael's unconditional love and acceptance is coincident with her inability to accept or believe in a God that would love unconditionally. Angel goes to San Francisco and is recaptured into the power of the evil Duke, who first made her his prepubescent sex slave. The *recognition* that allows the barriers to fall is Angel's recognition of God's care when she believes, sings a hymn from the brothel stage, and is rescued to a new life by a Christian citizen in the crowd, who not only frees her from Duke's power but also frees two little girls, his most recent victims. When Angel believes in God's love, she can believe in Michael's love, and both barriers between them, her past and her idolatry, fall. And, the *betrothal* takes place in two ways—first in the

1997 version as a formal conversion scene where Angel freely and consciously says "I do" to signify her commitment of her life to Jesus. The novel emphasizes the words' significance: "Words meant for a wedding ceremony."[26] This recognition sets in motion the reconciliations that make a new future for her and Michael, to whom she may return in real love, now that her earlier, barely conscious "Why not?" has been transformed into a truly loving union.

The way that Rivers orients *Redeeming Love* in relation to the twentieth-century romance novel shows the novel's middle way between critique and forgiveness. According to Regis, the twentieth-century romance novel heroine has changed from earlier centuries and is more in control of her life; she already has the things that earlier heroines from eighteenth- and nineteenth-century romance novels sought: an individual identity, freedom, property (or the ability to get it), and the rights to have both work and "companionate marriage."[27] Thus, Regis says, the characteristics of the romance novel alter: when the heroine possesses these rights and possibilities, the hero can return to the novel as a much larger portion of the narrative, and the romance of courtship is largely related to emotion rather than practical, economic, or political position.[28] Rivers's narrative choices here show that she is still working within this tradition. Angel has work and power, and the novel certainly does allow for significant focus on the hero. Yet *Redeeming Love* also denies some aspects of the twentieth-century heroine's characteristic power—indeed calls them into question society-wide. Angel's power in the text—what she comes into the narrative with—is shown to be false, worldly power, and her economic or individual freedom is nothing but slavery. Even Angel's identity is uncertain: born Sarah, she is called Angel, and goes through any number of names in the novel before she can be established, in the love of Jesus and Michael, as Sarah again. And the novel's focus on Michael, the hero, also differing from its twentieth-century counterpart, does not show him altering or going through particular transformations under the power of the heroine or changing in any way, except insofar as he must age and suffer from his sacrificial love for Angel. He is a Christ-figure, after all. In this way, Rivers espouses the idea that any heroine's desire for control and self-procured freedom and power—even sexual power—is a sham in the light of the more real freedom and identity that come in relationship with Jesus' redeeming love.[29] In this way, Rivers is recognizably within romance, but not uncritically so.

In order to craft a work that can reconcile romance novels to Christ, Rivers has to work within and in response to the conventions that form the basis of the genre. Rivers's treatment of the hero and heroine resists the norms of a subgenre of the twentieth-century romance novel—the historical western—by reconceiving masculinity and femininity, a move that not only raises the stakes of the novel in its engagement with gender, but also the theoretical implications for the theological poetics of the romance. She does so by revising the roles of hero and heroine. According to Janice Radway, the ideal western historical romance novel hero's essence is masculinity and strength, sexual virility and experience, with an only latent capacity for tenderness and nurture that the heroine must draw out of him through acts of tenderness and healing.[30] The hero's demeanor is characterized by extreme emotional reserve, and his behavior is initially ambiguous and often threatening or violent toward the heroine or others whom he uses for sexual release.[31] In *Redeeming Love*, that hero role is recognized, critiqued, and revised within the Christ figure of Michael Hosea. The audience recognizes Michael as the hero as multiple characters' remark in internal or external dialogue that he is all man. A conversation between the prostitutes in the brothel emphasizes "all six feet of him. Dark hair. Blue eyes. Broad shoulders. Every inch of him lean and hard. He walks like a soldier." The dialogue suggests he is a stand-out exemplum: "I've had one untried boy after another for the last month," says one of the women. "I'd welcome a man for a change."[32] Yet, though Rivers allows Hosea to be associated with characteristics of the romance novel hero, she does so only to reverse the characteristics of an ideal man: Michael visits a brothel, yes, but to buy a prostitute out of slavery, to marry her with his mother's wedding ring. We find out to our shock, and to Angel's, that Michael is a virgin. The text emphasizes his sexual inexperience more than once, though it does not allow us to think him less manly for it. When Angel taunts him about his masculinity, trying to provoke him to sexual violence, Michael's strength is defined by his resistance to what in many instances of the western historical romance amounts to rape.

In another convergence and divergence from the western romance novel, Rivers reshapes how misunderstanding between the lovers shapes their journey. Unlike the typical hero of the genre, who communicates ambiguously with the heroine, perhaps making her the victim of coldness or violence or even rape out of misunderstood intentions, Michael's communication with Angel is always crystal clear. He announces his unswerving commitment, love, and desire to marry her (usually the end-point of the journey of a romance novel) in their first meeting. He needs to be in tune with Angel about what sex would mean to her in their relationship: "When it means something more to you than work, we'll consummate the marriage."[33] He resists again and again her attempts to seduce him, and finally, only with a lengthy conversation, through which Michael relies on God to help him resist "the depth of [his] physical desire," he finally realizes that in order for Angel to see how different sex can be from the abuse she has experienced, he must show her.[34] In the text, Michael thinks of himself as Adam in the garden, nervous and excited to make love to Eve.

Reconceiving these conventions of western romance novel heroes allows Francine Rivers not just to differentiate between good man and bad, but between the peace and love offered by the world and that offered by God. Rivers takes her allegorical prophet/Jesus figure, Michael, and associates him *not* with the "dangerous men" described by Jayne Ann Krentz, men who are in desperate need of taming by "adventurous women."[35] For Rivers, Michael's interaction with Angel demonstrates that God might not be fully known in the reputation that comes standard issue for those scarred by the judgmental, hypocritical church. Rivers's construction of their relationship also seeks, I think, to suggest conditions under which submission in male-female relationships may be understood by some on other terms than anti-women ones, though whether the book truly achieves its mark on that point is debatable.

Michael, after all, more resembles Radway's vision of the ideal western historical romance hero*ine* than the hero: she is supposed to be virginal, inexperienced, and innocent, but in *Redeeming Love*, Michael fills that bill. And though Angel in *Redeeming Love* is recognizable as a western historical romance novel heroine—she is stand-out beautiful and independent, marked by intelligence and power over men—she, like Michael, inverts many of the key qualities noted by Radway as central to her role's type. Angel is everything else that a romance novel heroine should not be: sexually experienced, indifferent to love, interested in wealth and position, self-conscious, non-nurturing, demanding, and used to controlling men.[36] Yet, we are led to believe, she has aspects of the western historical romance novel heroine that make her at least somewhat conversant with the generic conventions. Even though Angel has sexual experience—she is a victim of pedophilia and sexual slavery, and so embittered that she even has sex with her own father to get back at him for abandoning her mother—she has never experienced sexual desire or pleasure during sex. And even though Angel is rude, cantankerous, self-interested, and so on, she is, Michael knows, only behaving that way because she has not experienced redeeming, transformative love. By asking readers to identify with such a victimized, bitter, and corrupted heroine, and by making her desire for individualistic freedom subordinate to the experience of the love of God, Rivers is risking quite a bit. Janice Radway has written that romance novel readers—at least those she studied—believed that bad romance novels "fail because they ask the reader to identify with a heroine who is hurt, humiliated, and brutalized. At the same time, they evoke fear and worry about female sexuality and hint that a woman's sexual desire might, in fact prove threatening to men."[37] When Rivers asks readers to join and identify with Angel on her journey through this brutal history and its redemption, it is a bold move—she is seeking to unmask sexual and even economic power as illusory in a hypersexualized, individualist culture.[38]

Rivers's readers, the author suggests in *Redeeming Love*, are like Angel: they will not be freed by their own effort, but through their acceptance of the liberating love of God and within the responsibilities of relationships of the community of faith. Thus might Rivers believe that *Redeeming Love* is an empowering romance, but one not predicated on an individualistic freedom, but rather a relational and spiritual freedom in Christ and the church. Angel repeatedly fantasizes about leaving Michael, demanding her rightful wages from her former-madam, and building a Thoreauvian cabin in the woods where she can be alone and free. Yet, Michael unmasks the American individualistic, earn-your-way logic that undergirds Angel's thinking as misguided. When she says, "I want a little cabin in the woods," he responds, "You've already got one." When she says "I want to be free, Michael. Just once in my whole life. *Free!*" he responds, "You are free. You just don't know it yet."[39] As the novel would have it, in surrender to love—both to Michael's love and to God's, Angel finds the freedom she seeks. And, in another scene involving the cabin, Angel finds that it is not by being alone, but by *sharing* their cabin—not just with Michael, but also with a neighboring family in need—that she is able to experience love and community for the first time.

Rivers ensures that readers will juxtapose *Redeeming Love* with other romance novels through her use not only of inversions that reconceive the roles of hero and heroine, but also of a doubling plot—a parallel romance novel within the romance novel against which the first romance plays out. In this way, readers see the way that a redeemed romance—in this case that between Angel and Michael—may in fact perform the work of redeeming a traditional western romance plot. The secondary plot highlights Miriam and Paul: Miriam is the lovely daughter of neighboring settlers, an open, warm, smart, encouraging, virginal, sixteen-year-old foil to Angel, and Paul is Michael's brother-in-law, who has "never been able to stick to anything long" since his wife died.[40] Miriam is already redeemed, and brings her security in the love of Christ to her own legitimate desire for a husband. Paul is wounded and bitter, and centers his bitterness on Angel. He believes that Angel is taking advantage of Michael and that she can never change. When she runs away from Michael, Paul takes her back to Pair-a-Dice, exacting sex from Angel to pay for the ride back, in a rape of mistaken identity: he thinks she is still the whore rather than beloved wife. Paul's bitterness over his wife's death and over Angel's presence in Michael's life causes him to repel Miriam's warm interest and offer of friendship. Miriam is frustrated; she knows that Paul wants her, and that he cannot acknowledge the feelings. Through a series of miscommunications, Angel thinks that Miriam has fallen in love with Michael, while Miriam thinks that Paul cannot get over a misplaced former love for Angel. When Paul finally learns that Miriam loves *him*, he can finally, through spiritual healing (and eventual reconciliation with Angel) show Miriam the real tenderness that he feels but has been too wounded to offer.

Regis would call this part of the novel the reform of the reprobate character, in which Paul, who has never believed in a possibility of change for Angel, is healed and restored in his ability to love.[41] Yet for Rivers, the inclusion of this optional element of the genre highlights the power of specifically Christian redemption in the novel. In a comedic, but telling plot device, Miriam is able to convert Paul's misanthropy and distance into warm affection—the start of his journey toward reconciliation with Angel and God—through a reenactment of *another* biblical book besides Hosea, Ruth. Miriam helps Paul get in touch with his emotions for her by acting out scenes from the book of Ruth, when Ruth presents herself for sex and marriage to Boaz on the threshing floor to gain a kinsman redeemer who will provide for her and her mother-in-law (and, incidentally, keep the ancestral line of Christ moving toward the nativity). Miriam goes to Paul's house in the night and convinces him to marry her by keeping his clothes so he cannot get out of bed until he admits he loves her, at which point, overwhelmed by desire, they plan a hasty wedding. Miriam as heroine of the redeemed romance knows that sex is good, knows that it is more than welcome and wonderful within a marriage relationship, and even pursues it, reworking an understanding of the empowered, twentieth-century heroine within a Christian context. She has a relationship in which her gifts of leadership and wisdom are manifest in the marriage, and in which service to the community and larger body of Christ will even allow the lovers to part for the sake of restoration of the community.

## Reconciling Christians to the Ways of Romance

Getting hold of the 1991 Bantam Fanfare edition of *Redeeming Love* is not easy. The copyright page of the 1997 edition warns: "This is the 'redeemed' version of *Redeeming Love*, published by Bantam Books in 1991. The original edition is no longer available."[42] And in the mess of reprintings, it is sometimes even difficult to be sure that copies purportedly available on the used market or in libraries are in fact the first edition. But reading the original not only showcases the project of reconciling the romance novel to Christ, but also brings into focus the radical project of the 1997 version—to reconcile the Christian reader to the romance novel.

The 1991 *Redeeming Love* clearly keeps one foot in western historical romance novel generic conventions and one foot in inspirational romance novel conventions. Before reading, I predicted the religion in the 1991 novel would be much less explicit, the language somewhat more explicit, and the sex considerably more explicit. Even though those assumptions were warranted, I was still jarred by intentional intermixture of these elements. First, the religion in the trade paperback is not nearly as diminished as expected. While the 1997 *Redeeming Love* puts God's voice in bold italic and the devil's voice in bold, the 1991 version more gently and sporadically italicizes both. God does not point the divine finger at Angel in the 1991 version to say *"This one, beloved"* to Michael Hosea.[43] Nonetheless, the religious elements of the text stand out starkly, in part due to symbolic and allegoric literary connections, but mostly due to their shocking juxtaposition with profanity and sex.

The text boldly pursues a mixture of the inspirational qualities of Christian romance novels and the sexual explicitness associated with its particular brand of historical western romance novels. The text's jointure of sex to religion and even to vulgar speech shows the way that Rivers is trying to allow the redeeming love of Christ to reach far into areas that some nonbelievers assume would be out of bounds. In one example, the first time Michael and Angel have sex, she is trying to block him out of her emotions while he tries to convince her that sex can be more than just male pleasure or using of the female body.

> "You keep shutting me out. I want to be so deep inside you, you can't ignore me. Tirzah, for God's sake, stay with me in this."
>
> "Is it Tirzah now?"
>
> Perspiration beaded on his forehead and the rushing heat grew heavy in his loins. Oh, Jesus, help me. "Stop running from me."[44]

The double entendre of being "deep inside" Angel slams against the sudden and odd inclusion of his use of a biblically symbolic pet name for her—a name that confuses even Angel. Michael draws the name from the location-meaning in Song of Sol. 6:4: "You are beautiful as Tirzah, my love, / comely as Jerusalem, / terrible as an army with banners." Judging from Michael's brief petition at this moment, it seems his relationship with Christ is as present, active, and untroubled by the concurrent intercourse as by morning devotions. Even the inclusion of the cliché of the cry out to God prior to or during orgasm (which again occurs on the following page in the text) reads differently because of the devoted posture with which Michael approaches all of life. The "for God's sake," usually considered mildly blasphemic language, may even be an earnest plea. For Michael's orgasms are prayer-covered throughout the novel; Angel's too. In fact, when Michael looks down as Angel has what the reader believes is her first orgasm, the narrative of his inner thoughts actually marks the occasion with praise: "Oh, to You be the glory, Lord, Lord."[45] And, in another bedroom scene, when they bring each other separately to orgasm through a variety of caresses—ones Angel has imported wholesale from her former life, Michael actually prays afterward, "aloud and with fervent thanksgiving for the pleasures they had taken in one another."[46] Now, quoting from sex scenes in literary criticism is only slightly less awkward than trying to write a decent sex scene in fiction, and it is hardly fair to author or reader. But the juxtaposition of these elements is almost as startling in context as it is out of context. In the larger scope of the original novel, especially when it is read after the redeemed version, the more explicit descriptions of body parts and moments of arousal draw into relief the close-proximity of devotion and sexual intimacy. Angel assumes that sex is bad, something that men seem to need, something never pleasurable for women: "What was his God going to think of this?"[47] At one point in the novel, she tells Michael her misapprehension that God threw Adam and Eve out of Eden because they had sex. Angel believes the two realms are far separated; so do Rivers's implied readers. The text seeks to teach both another way.

*Redeeming Love* invites Christian believers into an experience of Christ's love within and through a quest for answers to questions only expressible in language outside approved evangelical discourse—language that a romance novel, a genre more willing to take its clothes off and talk dirty, could explore.

It seems hard to understand why a novel that was so full of explicit Christian belief even in its unexpurgated version, which sold more than 100,000 copies, would be made so thoroughly unavailable by an author who wrote even the first draft at a prompting from God. The religious content that stood out so starkly within Rivers's redeployment of the western historical romance might have been somewhat bewildering to a secular publisher or audience. There was precedent for the bewilderment: in the 1970s, Janette Oke, a pioneer of western Christian romance novels, had her explicitly Christian romance manuscript turned down by Bantam, the same publisher as brought out Rivers's 1991 *Redeeming Love*.[48] But the lockdown on earlier copies more likely suggests that in the 1990s, when inspirational romance was far more established with a range of Christian-specific publishers, believing readers were used to a set of inspirational-fiction rules for content and language. They would be disturbed by the romantic or dialogic conventions of a western historical romance. For much of what had been religiously "redeemed" about *Redeeming Love*, the entire life of the main character, say, seems to have been redeemed even in the original version. With an allegorical link to Hosea as obvious as this one, it is clear that the redemption has been predestined from the novel's inception—much before the 1997 version. The story cannot exist without its redemptive frame, which seems to be what the author is going for as a Christian writer. The allegorical frame, the redemptive plot, the explicit finding of faith (without the "I do" of the altar call, perhaps, but still with a recognizable morphology of conversion)—all seem to have been present. But the novel's rerelease, with the original's juxtapositions of sex, religion, and crassly realistic language significantly downplayed, found its way to more than ten times the number of readers as the original. In her development of her version of a Christ-based poetics in *Redeeming Love*, Rivers operated on the supposition that not only did a secular audience need to have recognizable elements from western and romance genres to be able to process religious elements generously, but also, a Christian audience needed to be led by the hand to get through crass or sexy bits from romance novels. Here, Rivers found the strictures of Christian publishers of romance novels, which, by the 1990s, were already firmly in place. Rivers and her editor, Karen Ball, went over the text with a fine-tooth comb. Rivers cushioned the redeemed *Redeeming Love* romance novel with even more heavily underlined evangelical shibboleths than the original, and she removed potentially objectionable material.

That seems to have done the trick. But despite the very discernible difference between the sexual tone of the two novels, it is clear that even the 1997 version was quite a risk—a novel seeking to address the hard and emotional issue of a prostitute's full personal recovery and restoration to relationship with husband and God, after all, would need to involve sexual healing to have even a shot at credibility. Portrayals of sex involving metaphors about flight to heaven and opening flowers aside, such a project involves the risky move of opening the pages of inspirational fiction to both exploitative sex scenes and unmistakably pleasurable ones. Early printings of the Multnomah version are framed by editors' warrants of the book's quality and assurances that readers—of appropriate age and maturity, naturally—who granted the book latitude would be spiritually rewarded. Later printings include Francine Rivers's testimony and an apologia for the book in essay form. It is worth pointing out that the editors were not being overcautious in either case. Evangelical readers' mores on this point were strict, particularly in the 1990s, and they still are in many evangelical reading communities. At the evangelical Christian college where I teach, even one of my TAs, who hopes to go on to graduate school in literary studies, was forbidden to read *Redeeming Love* as a voracious adolescent reader because it was too racy. The acknowledgments for the novel say that Rivers's editor was particularly helpful in "redeeming it for the Christian reader."[49] Redemption in this case seems to be an act of writing that makes the value of the text accessible and recognizable to an evangelical reader who might be uncomfortable with either the sexual content of the book or the life history of the protagonist. And any reader that might not be willing to associate with "that kind" of book is confronted then, by the epigraph of the novel, "Let anyone among you who is without sin, be the first to throw a stone at her."[50]

## Forgiving the Romance Novel:
## The Politics and Erotics of Eschatological Reading

When I taught this novel in a seminar on literature and judgment, many students were offended by it—for a number of reasons, especially the novel's treatment of women in the context of its audacious theological message. In particular, the descriptions of bodies seemed to reinforce troublesome versions of femininity and masculinity even as they allowed the eschatological tale to be told. Angel is a version of late-twentieth-century perfection in American beauty—slender, blonde, and blue eyed, facts that the text reinforces *constantly*; she is not just any prostitute, but the most memorable and beautiful prostitute ever. Her victimization seems utterly glamorous, and the abuse she suffers never permanently mars her perfect appearance. When a neighbor woman makes Angel a dress, the text emphasizes that it is too big and will need to be altered down. When Angel, admittedly unwillingly, helps to save a family with a broken-down wagon, the family's littlest girl merges her act of mercy with her blonde beauty and asks, "Angel, mama?"[51]

What troubled the students most was the text's unflinching merger of the theological and sexual content—the way that such a move risked making theologically normative the abnegation of the female under conditions of patriarchal authority and violence. For instance, when Michael goes back into town to bust Angel out of her return to prostitution, she is so overcome with remorse that she goes to bathe in an icy stream, using rocks to scrape off her skin, an image of penitence made ultra-sexual by the text's odd comment that when Michael brings her back into the house, he will not let her bring her clothes with her into the house: "When she bent for her clothing, he pulled her along without them. Half shoving her into the cabin, he slammed the door."[52] Michael throws a blanket at her, and they have a long, difficult discussion in which she reveals her victimization at the hands of a pedophile, all while she is naked. The scene is no doubt theologically symbolic—the nakedness associated with the unveiling of past secrets, which can in no way be hidden from God—Angel being given the coverings by the Christ figure who "ceased thinking of her as Angel—the harlot he loved and who had betrayed him—and saw her instead as the nameless child who had been broken and was still lost."[53] Yet at times, the tenacious, unrelentingly fierce love of Christ represented in Michael edges toward a sort of sexual violence. During another night, when Angel wakes up screaming, Michael decides to show Angel something other than the darkness of her past—the sunrise. Yet the scene begins as a fight, and the text relies on images of violent force to maintain dramatic tension. He "stripped" the quilts off her, and then, after she's pulled them up again, "ripped the bedcovers off," telling her "You can go dressed or naked" and "Get up. Now. You're going whether you like it or not."[54] He does not tell her they are going to see the sunrise—the reader, with Angel, is in the dark. The text has signaled that Michael is trustworthy, but because of that, the scene plays out as supposedly necessary violence at best or emotional manipulation at worst. The first time they have sex, in an emotionally invasive move, Michael forces Angel to say his name and look into his eyes. At the end of the novel, when Angel at last returns to Michael for good, she approaches the house flinging off her clothing piece by piece before she kneels down in front of him in the grass, stark naked, her tears falling on his boots. This is another biblical allusion—a western Mary Magdalene scene—complete with Angel using her hair to wipe the tears away from his boots—except that Michael takes his shirt off to cover her. Symbolically, it works perfectly. Granted, Michael is far more beautiful a specimen of manhood than Christ was purported to be, but obligatory romance-novel beauty aside, even the hero's baring his chest can be tied to Christ's willingness to disrobe on the cross to cover the sins of the world—or, if one prefers, to wash the feet of the disciples (which move Michael has already made earlier in the novel). Yet, the symbolic representation threatens to celebrate the violently procured male control of women's bodies and minds—precisely through its allegorical eschatology.

In reading and researching this novel—both versions—it has become clear that *Redeeming Love* is seriously and legitimately trying something. It is trying to probe out perhaps how the versions and visions of the desiring body—social, sexual, and even political—work in relation to Christianity. These are fascinating questions, played out through the word in the romance novel. The questions are, of course, not without precedent—and more mystics than Francine Rivers have felt themselves compelled to write of the God who in seducing, redeems, and in redeeming, seduces. Julian of Norwich writes, "It is I who teach you to love. It is I who teach you to desire. It is I who am the reward of all true desiring"—something that we tend to conveniently disembody.[55] How does the word made flesh, who dwelt among us, the source and sustainer of both the body of text and the body of sex, arouse our desires—textual, bodily, and spiritual—and in arousing true desire, heal us?

## Reconciling Scholars to Romance

For the most part, scholarly approaches to Christian inspirational fiction have been limited to anthropological literary history or cultural studies.[56] But such fiction might, in the reading, in the discussing, have something to offer theological aesthetics. In that field, discussions of romance novels, if any, would generally fall under theoretical terms such as (bad) *taste, sentimentality,* or *kitsch*—as in the work of Frank Burch Brown, Jeremy S. Begbie, Timothy Gorringe, and John W. de Gruchy.[57] Many of these theorists formulate an approach to theological aesthetics that embraces diversity of approach or preference in works of art—and even allow for popular art. They would not, perhaps, automatically dismiss Rivers's work, but to the extent that inspirational Christian fiction gets discussed in terms of kitsch, they would consider it primarily valuable as a negative exemplar. They raise concerns about works that gloss over dark or discordant aspects of real life, or which, through whatever artistic methods, might allow readers to stagnate in passivity in the face of such discordance. As de Gruchy writes, "The distinction is not between 'fine art' and 'popular art,' but between good art of all kinds and kitsch, that is art which is mediocre and banal. People will always find comfort in kitsch, for that is the whole point of it. But this does not alter the fact that kitsch obfuscates reality."[58] Timothy Gorringe has argued, "Kitsch does make us smile, but it should also make us wary, for it is a training, on a mass scale, in untruth."[59] Jeremy Begbie finds the sentimental fails to tell the truth of the gospel because of a "premature grasp for Easter morning."[60]

*Redeeming Love* does not view itself—and the novel's author does not view herself—as glossing over anything. If anything, Rivers would probably concur with those who critique inspirational fiction for its niceties and push for harder questions. But even so, the conventions of romance novels have tended to be less a repository for thinking about the relationship between art and God, between the word and God, than they might be, in part because of rather wholesale dismissals. It is easy enough to pass over *Redeeming Love* because of its inconveniently dated or overly triumphalist gender politics that tend to make women the possession of men (even comparing them frankly to land, etc.), or even because of its aesthetically ham-fisted messaging system that double underlines—nay, italicizes and bolds—its religious messages to be sure they come through. But doing so would miss the bold risk that the text takes to engage sex and the body within the word and narrative of the kingdom of God's redeeming love. Richard Viledesau, in *Theological Aesthetics*, has written that "'being in love with God' gives us the proleptic anticipation of the beatitude of the eschatological resurrection," the form of our final life in God, which includes the total good of all creation: the final *shalom* of God's kingdom."[61] The merging of sex scenes, vulgar language, and religious language as in the 1991 *Redeeming Love*—and even in the 1997 version—make a case for at least asking the question of the role that desire may play in relationships between people, between readers and texts, or even between readers and God. *Redeeming Love* asks us to consider not only that the need for an erotics of the eschatology of reading is made tangible in a popular romance novel, but also that the future of the word may already be played out in the bodies and brains of its readers who are drawn to the word and to the Lord through its pages.

I suspect that in the early twenty-first century, reading the original, 1991 version of *Redeeming Love* could be a less dangerous prospect for even evangelical readers—and potentially more effective in a hypersexual culture—if only because it does not dance around things that many of my students would acknowledge as present and recognizable in society anyway.[62] The novel retains in its 1991 version all its bold naïveté and willingness to stand as a hybrid text in the world. Would this be a sort of becoming backwards? Perhaps. But given the willingness of the author to let texts become over the development of her own faith journey, it might seem that there is simply more becoming yet to do.

For the linkage of Michael Hosea with Christ causes more trouble in the text than gender trouble as it reaches toward the difficult questions of how the church may engage social and political action. The biblical Hosea's prophecies engage the politics of the time unflinchingly; Michael Hosea, however, seems above all to run away from the available political gambits of the day. The redemption he offers is spiritual, relational, and sexual rather than political or more broadly social. The novel does picture social and economic responses to individual change in several characters: but does so in firmly evangelical terms as a response to individual spiritual experience. When Jonathan Axle, one of the biggest bankers in the city, hears from God, he goes in and rescues Angel and two young girls from the white slaver. He will, in time, raise funds to develop a community house to give housing and job training to former-prostitutes in order to give them options outside of the sex trade. This plot point is strongly in keeping with evangelical work in the abolitionist tradition that has in the present day returned to the forefront of global Christian outreach, exemplified by the work of such ministries as Hagar International or International Justice Mission. And inspirational and sentimental letters have always had a role in such work. But *Redeeming Love* offers us no political or social vision from Michael Hosea except for the interpersonal fellowship of believers, despite the fact that it takes up both political and social questions. Rivers paints Michael's past growing up on a slave plantation in one scene with a gruesome scenario of horrific slave abuse—something straight out of Harriet Beecher Stowe. She shows Michael describing how his father set him to living with slaves for a month in order to try and break him of his compassion for slaves; Uncle Ezra, however, an older slave, leads him to faith. But though Rivers paints Michael as having compassion, she shows him running away from the antebellum South and from a more substantive resistance to slavery as an institution. He actually leaves home after his father gives him "a beautiful, young slave girl of my own to use any way I wanted" because "she was more of a temptation than I could handle."[63] He tells Angel that he never thinks about going back home. But by positioning the narrative's Christ figure as a farmer re-creating the Garden of Eden paradise with his very own renewed Eve in the gold-rush West to escape his father's plantation and its horrors, *Redeeming Love* risks hazarding the idea that Jesus really only cares about getting the white girls out of slavery, not the black girls. And the text's only African American woman is a hypersexualized temptress of the white man. Michael resists raping a slave, and he creates a beautiful life and marriage that heals and rescues a beloved Child of God. But, for the savior of the world—or even for a prophet, really—one hopes for more.

And Michael as Christ also relates problematically to the mostly invisible, ghostly presence of Native Americans in the text. Images of Native Americans are extremely rare in *Redeeming Love*, which ought to be odd in a western historical romance of gold-rush California. In characters' thoughts, images of Native Americans are colored by fear and are articulated in mostly dehumanizing terms. In one notable instance, Michael remembers not putting a marker over his sister's grave because he "hadn't wanted her dug up by Indians or animals."[64] Miriam learns from Indians about building a fire inside a tent in a washtub, but, other than another figure in the text, who had planned to *"convert the heathen Indians,"* there are only a handful of references to Native Americans in the text—images of violence and theft.[65] These views of the characters are consistent with socially available positions under governmental and ecclesial policies during Indian Removal. And the absence of Indians in the narrative in the 1980s and 1990s when Rivers was writing the novel, after the hey-day of the American Indian Movement, is consistent with the erasure and dehumanization that still plague wider American society. It is even consistent with the trends in its closely related genre, the western, in which, as Jane Tompkins has described them: "the Indians I expected did not appear. The ones I saw functioned as props, bits of local color, textural effects. As people they had no existence. Quite often they filled the role of villains, predictably, driving the engine of the plot, threatening the wagon train, the stagecoach, the cavalry detachment—a particularly dangerous form of local wildlife. But there were no Indian characters, no individuals with a personal history and a point of view."[66]

But, the novel unabashedly takes up slavery, both sexual and labor-oriented, in its creation of Michael's past in the South. And slavery, both sexual and labor-oriented, existed in California in 1850—and it most certainly included Native populations. The Pomo, just east of the Yuba on Clear Lake, were plagued by two white settlers who starved, beat, and enslaved the Pomo, sexually abusing girls from the tribe in the late 1840s. When members of the tribe killed two settlers in 1849, the U.S. Cavalry attacked while young men were off hunting in the spring of 1850, killing at least sixty women, children, and older men in what has come to be called the Bloody Lake Massacre. *Redeeming Love*'s explicit engagement of abuse, sexual slavery, and childhood sexual slavery in California in the late 1840s expands the territory of inspirational fiction's engagement with tough social and theological issues. Yet though it at least partially sees the exploitation and abuse inherent in race-related policies of the 1850 moment, the novel leaves African Americans and Native Americans outside of redemption's power, missing opportunities to link the redeemed romance novel's new conception of freedom in Christ with a theology of justice. Indeed, in one telling moment near the end of the novel, a minor character, Susanna, bereaved of her fiancé with whom she was planning to become a missionary to Indians, gives up the plan of missionary engagement, instead taking

Angel's place managing the recovery and training house for former-prostitutes when Angel returns to Michael.

The text stands in a tradition that has sometimes been accused of skirting political and social issues for individual or relational ones, but it may be permissible to offer it a kind of pass: Lynn S. Neal points out that in the evangelical tradition, at the time of her study, "the most powerful type of change comes not through political action or social activity, but rather through religious devotion that inspires individual spiritual change."[67] Under this view, we might see the social action of Angel and Susanna, who run the house for former-prostitutes, as social engagement that emerges directly out of their personal relationship with Christ. But I do not think this can excuse the text, though it does offer a context for understanding where the novel comes from and how it has spoken to readers. Rivers has pointed out in interviews, though, that hard questions are her main—and somewhat unique—area of interest in Christian fiction. She has, especially in crafting Michael's background, raised these particular issues in the story she is telling. And the choice of allegory as vehicle for her story—particularly an allegory of an Old Testament prophet, for whom socio-religious and political issues are always part of the message—also calls her to a higher standard. Given the resources of African American and Native theologies surrounding love, healing, and forgiveness in particular, and the poor (but changing) track record for romance novels in addressing theology and race, *Redeeming Love*'s confession of erasure must also be a call to writers—even to Rivers—to highlight and hear other voices and to support those writers who are doing work at the front of these lines.

I have read this novel as I might any literary text, given my own background and training, by engaging closely with the text's form and production. I have sought to offer the text "small acts of consideration . . . on a public stage" so that it, and perhaps even its author, might find a space for becoming, and in so doing to offer it a "capacity for acting" and a "capacity for continuing."[68] It was a delight to reflect on the full history of its publication and the work's rich play among generic conventions. I found myself growing in respect for the text as I learned, to my shame at my former ignorance, of the rich history of the romance novel and the aesthetic and thematic possibilities of the genre, even through what I consider not insignificant lapses in the political, social, historical, and theological portrayals within *Redeeming Love*. In its reading, the text yielded rich, interesting meanings and created community (between myself and colleagues as I babbled on about it for weeks, and between myself and students as I tested this reading out on them). It also offered theologically relevant ideas and questions about aesthetics and bodies. The particular *method* of reading does not seem to have done the trick: focus groups run by my students for their work or casual conversations in discipleship small groups accomplished similar sorts of small revelations. There are, after all, plenty of angles on the future of the word. Romance novels need not throw us for a loop, any more than any other text. Like us all, *Redeeming Love* is becoming toward the kingdom, through judgments and forgiveness.

## Notes

1. Jordin Sparks, "Thought you knew everything about Jordin Sparks? Think again," *Ebony* 65, no. 1 (2009), http://www.ew.com/ew/article/0,,20619242,00.html. Jordin Sparks, "What I'm Reading," *Entertainment Weekly* 1220/1221 (17 June 2012), 116.

2. Francine Rivers, "Francine Rivers Interview," *TitleTrakk*, 2012, http://www.titletrakk.com/author-interviews/francine-rivers-interview.htm.

3. Francine Rivers, "Writing Tips," *Francine Rivers*, 2010, http://francinerivers.com/about/writing-tips.

4. Francine Rivers, "FAQs," *Francine Rivers*, 2010, http://francinerivers.com/about/faqs.

5. Rivers, "Francine Rivers Interview."

6. Francine Rivers, "A Note from Francine Rivers: Why I Wrote *Redeeming Love*," *Redeeming Love* (Colorado Springs: Multnomah Books, 1997), 465.

7. Ibid.

8. Ibid., 466.

9. Rivers, "Francine Rivers Interview."

10. Rivers, "FAQs."

11. Lynn S. Neal, in *Romancing God: Evangelical Women and Inspirational Fiction* (Chapel Hill: University of North Carolina Press, 2006), and Valerie Weaver-Zercher in *The Thrill of the Chaste* (Baltimore: Johns Hopkins University Press, 2013) have sought to complicate oversimple condemnations of inspirational romance and to account for the publishing boom in romance by focusing ethnographic research on readers. Neal has identified the ways women engage with inspirational romance novels to seek spiritual growth. She writes that scholars need to take romance novels and their readers seriously—not only as "denial of evil or an escape from life" but rather a way to "combat . . . despair with a theology of hope and perseverance" (104). In Neal's field interviews with authors and readers of evangelical romance, both producers and consumers view the texts as spaces for God's work in and among people: "For readers," she writes, "these evangelical romance narratives become a channel through which they can experience the divine" (115). Valerie Weaver-Zercher, focusing on Amish romance novels, uses a similar set of research techniques. She locates the economic success of Amish romance novels more within the strategic approaches of the publishing industry than the readers, but also finds that readers are taught by and even worship through the books in a way comparable to how worshipers engage with religious icons. In addition, the particular setting of the Amish novels serves as well as to assist female evangelical readers in navigating the complex field of gender dynamics, vacillating between conservative and progressive views of femininity. Inspirational romance novels, in these scholars' research, create not only a textually experienced revelation of God, but also significant community, between readers in book groups, congregations, friend networks, and also between readers and authors.

12. Rivers, "Writing Tips."

13. Rivers, "FAQs."

14. Rivers, "Writing Tips."

15. Rivers, "FAQs."

16. Ibid.

17. Rivers, "Francine Rivers Interview."

18. John Keats, "Sleep and Poetry," The Poetical Works of John Keats (London: Macmillan, 1884), 284, ln. 241–47.

19. Ibid., 284, ln. 230–35.

20. Janice A. Radway, *Reading the Romance: Women, Patriarchy, and Popular Literature* (Chapel Hill: University of North Carolina Press, 1991), 150.

21. Francine Rivers, *Redeeming Love* (Colorado Springs: Multnomah Books, 1997), 462.

22. Ibid., 464.

23. Pamela Regis, *A Natural History of the Romance Novel* (Philadelphia: University of Pennsylvania Press, 2003), 22.

24. Ibid., 14.

25. Ibid., 31.

26. Rivers, *Redeeming Love*, 428.

27. Regis, *A Natural History of the Romance Novel*, 57.

28. Ibid., 111.

29. Angel's journey then, is an exploration of issues that Rivers herself experienced and talks about—the idolatrous desire for her identity as writer to offer her the control and freedom that she has realized only comes through Christ. In Rivers's professional website, under the Frequently Asked Questions section (cited above), she repeatedly raises control and freedom as key issues during the process of her conversion. She says about her marriage: "We both had personal issues that brought us close to divorce several times. We wanted our own way and to have control over our own lives. Having control is an illusion. As a child, I'd asked Jesus to be my Savior. What I didn't understand is I needed to surrender my life to Him and allow Him to be LORD of my life as well." She relates this particularly to writing as well: "It was the place I ran to escape, the one area of my life where I thought I was in complete control. (Hardly!) My priorities were all wrong

and needed to be put right. God first, husband and children second (we had three children by then) and third—work."

30. I use Radway's analysis here even though her work is dated and operates from a perspective that was critiqued even in the late 1980s for being limited in scope and unable to escape the condescending frame of reference that had characterized (and continues to characterize) much of the avoidance of and approach to romance novels. Radway's book and its categories are still worth considering here because of her book's particular focus on the historical western romance (however much it mistakes the subgenre for the entire genre), and because Radway's period of study and the primary period of her argument's effect in scholarly and romance-writing culture overlaps significantly with Rivers's time of writing what she calls "steamy historical romances," 1976–85. Radway's reprint edition, which had already begun to affect readers beyond the academy—even writers of romance novels—was published in 1991, the same year the secular mass-market paperback version of *Redeeming Love* was sold. I also find her structural analysis of romance novels in the genre in question particularly useful for outlining points of divergence between Rivers's work as a Christian and the work she had done and read prior to her conversion. Radway's ethnographic research in *Reading the Romance* outlines characteristics of the "ideal" romance novel based on analyses of the romance novels most highly rated as successful and beloved among her sample group—she likewise generates characteristics of the "failed" romance. The ideal romance novel in Radway's view proceeds according to a narrative logic that focuses on the development of a stable and satisfying identity-in-relation. The virginal and innocent heroine opens the novel with a social identity destroyed or in flux, perhaps due to the loss of nurture or the absence of parenting. The heroine's journey in the text develops a stable identity-in-relation by means of interaction with—and eventually the development of a sexual relationship to—an aristocratic male.

31. Through the narrative, the reader is to understand his behaviors as faint signals for deep-seated true and abiding love and is, ultimately, to elicit from his reserve a transformed and transforming declaration of care and commitment that will, upon said commitment, restore to her a cherished, safe space of identity-in-relation. For Radway, this narrative logic suits her readers perfectly—it restores and renews the psyche through a vicarious experience of motherly nurture for women whose primary work at home and in the world is selfless giving. Through the ideal romance, women may reinterpret the behaviors of their patriarchal or otherwise unsatisfyingly

committed and less-than-passionate husbands as signs of demonstrable care that they, upon proper sexual response and interaction, may ultimately elicit from them. The failed romance novel, in Radway's view, seems to threaten too much the unambiguous completion of this journey and development: they do not "provide the reader with the right kind of vicarious emotion. As a result, these romances do not supply a reading experience that replenishes and restores the female reader." This ethnography and interpretation of reader response perhaps establishes Radway's perspective as emerging out of a particular sort of feminism at a particular time, but it juxtaposes fascinatingly with Rivers's vision. See Radway, *Reading the Romance*, 178.

32. Rivers, *Redeeming Love*, 72–73.

33. Ibid., 114.

34. Ibid., 154.

35. Jayne Ann Krentz, *Dangerous Men and Adventurous Women: Romance Writers on the Appeal of the Romance*, ed. Jayne Ann Krentz (Philadelphia: University of Pennsylvania Press, 1992).

36. Radway, *Reading the Romance*, 132.

37. Ibid., 178.

38. The term "hypersexualized" is used in Valerie Weaver-Zercher's *The Thrill of the Chaste* to describe the broader social milieu to which readers of Amish romance novels respond in their purchase, reading, and discussion of Amish fiction. The term is Kenneth Kammeyer's, and it refers to a twenty-first-century culture of pornography and erotica. Yet for readers of fiction aimed particularly at evangelicals, the culture was hypersexual much before the turn of the millennium. We might, however, also think of the term to consider assumptions about the space of the romance novel itself: that it presumes and enacts the centrality of sex as source, sign, and goal of relationship.

39. Rivers, *Redeeming Love*, 198.

40. Ibid., 118.

41. Regis, *A Natural History of the Romance Novel*, 30.

42. Rivers, *Redeeming Love*, 4.

43. Ibid., 53.

44. Francine Rivers, *Redeeming Love* (New York: Bantam Fanfare, 1991), 136.

45. Ibid., 252.

46. Ibid., 285.

47. Ibid., 285.

48. Neal, *Romancing God*, 27.

49. Rivers, *Redeeming Love*, 7.

50. Ibid., 8.

51. Ibid., 234.

52. Ibid., 204.

53. Ibid., 209.

54. Ibid., 136.

55. Quoted in Richard Viladesau, *Theological Aesthetics* (New York: Oxford University Press, 1999), 206.

56. See those discussed above, but also Anita Gandolfo, "A Literature of Their Own," in *Faith and Fiction: Christian Literature in America Today* (Westport, CT: Praeger, 2007): 61–88.

57. For a few examples, see relevant discussions in the following: Jeremy S. Begbie, "Beauty, Sentimentality, and the Arts," in *The Beauty of God: Theology and the Arts* (Downers Grove, IL: IVP Academic, 2007), 45–69; Frank Burch Brown, *Religious Aesthetics* (Princeton: Princeton University Press, 1989), 136–57 and *Good Taste, Bad Taste, & Christian Taste* (New York: Oxford University Press, 2000), 128–59; John de Gruchy, *Christianity, Art and Transformation* (Cambridge: Cambridge University Press, 2001), 74–81; and Timothy Gorringe, "Kitsch and the Task of Theology," *Theology Today* 56, no. 2 (July 1999): 229–34.

58. De Gruchy, *Christianity, Art and Transformation*, 76.

59. Gorringe, "Kitsch and the Task of Theology," 232.

60. Begbie, "Beauty, Sentimentality, and the Arts," 61.

61. Viladesau, *Theological Aesthetics*, 207.

62. Kenneth Kammeyer, *A Hypersexual Society: Sexual Discourse, Erotica, and Pornography in America Today* (New York: Palgrave Macmillan, 2008), referenced in Valerie Weaver-Zercher, *The Thrill of the Chaste* (Baltimore: Johns Hopkins University Press, 2013), 10.

63. Rivers, *Redeeming Love*, 231.

64. Ibid., 117.

65. Ibid., 438, italics original.

66. Jane Tompkins, *West of Everything: The Inner Life of Westerns* (New York: Oxford University Press, 1992), 8.

67. Neal, *Romancing God*, 104.

68. Paul Ricoeur, *Memory, History, Forgetting* (Chicago: University of Chicago Press, 2004), 493.

# Conclusion

This book has argued that texts' meanings are founded on the future of the word of God, on the future of Christ, the word who became flesh. That eschatological future—the glorious plenitude of the community of the new creation—is texts' expansion of meaning within the expanding love of the Trinity for the glory of God. God grants us participation in the future of the word through our participation in Christ, in whom we live and move and have our being. In reading, we cultivate and keep texts for their futures in the kingdom of God. In the time of the not yet, of course, our reading is fraught with sin as our reading's necessary but dangerous judgments trouble textual futures. We curtail the future of texts by presumptive judgment of textual evils or glories; we abandon texts in limbo in our refusals to draw out their meanings. This double bind of judgment, however, is reconciled in the word, in reading that seeks forgiveness in the dissatisfied hope of the *Come, Lord Jesus*. When we persevere in reading through judgment, not abandoning the text, but seeking it out further in its pasts, presents, and futures, we are offering forgiveness—the restoration of relationship between text and reader as God reconciles all things to himself. We reconcile with texts when we receive from them—or receive through them; when we hold them to be, to paraphrase Ricoeur, restored to a capacity for acting.[1] We reconcile with texts when we give to them—or give through them, the meaning of the word, which is forgiveness. Thus through failures, the texts' and our own, the *Come, Lord Jesus* of Revelation is announced within the openness of text, in which the future of the word is made manifest.

The process that I have described through this book is clearly illustrated by—and would be neatly tied up by—a work such as Flannery O'Connor's "Revelation."[2] In that story, a judgmental woman receives a revelation of her own corrupt and fallible judgments, which results in her having a vision of the eschaton. Mrs. Turpin visits a doctor's office with her husband; her thoughts and clichéd small-talk during the wait show how her self-righteous judgments, condemnations, categorizations, and dismissals of everyone in the office fix all those around her with a horrible lack of charity. Mrs. Turpin's world is shaken, however, and her judgments called into question when one of the patients in the waiting room, an ugly and troubled college girl, gets fed up with her platitudes and throws a book at her, calling her a warthog from hell. She returns to her farm, somehow certain that the girl's judgment is a true message and revelation to her. As she contemplates how she could possibly be both a saved woman—a good Christian—and a warthog from hell, she receives a vision of God's different, eschatological judgment. She sees in the sunset sky the saints marching into glory with herself last and all those she judged first. She "lean[s] forward to observe them closer."[3] O'Connor writes the story in free-indirect discourse, which allows the reader to fall into the same net as Mrs. Turpin. Our judgments of Mrs. Turpin's vapid, clichéd thoughts are the same in kind as her judgments of others, but only as we reach the end of the story and see Mrs. Turpin's vision do we realize that she *is* saved. Our judgments (undeniably condemnatory) judge us, and, we realize, the proximate judgments of God will leave us, too, wanting, making her first to our last. We see our own reading within the reading of Mrs. Turpin and O'Connor—in our judgment, we are judged and offered an opportunity to repent for our own lack of charity, receiving ourselves the revelation of God that the text offers to Mrs. Turpin.

This story shows a metaphor, perhaps, of what we may do as we read—allowing our judgments of texts to judge us, persevering in reading as in receiving of a revelation from God, and being aware always of the supreme and surprising judgment of God. Yet texts don't often end with such an explicit vision of the last judgment, the saints marching in with their virtues being "burned away."[4] More often, rather than the "visionary light" in "the "purple streak" across the sky, we encounter the "darkening path" of "descending dusk."[5] O'Connor's text acknowledges the darkening, of course, but insists that the darkness is countered by the singing of the saints in the sky—to which song the fervent listener is privy. But the openness, the *Come, Lord Jesus* of the text, is something that we experience in the haze of the not yet.

As this book comes to a close, I feel compelled to grapple with one more text—a truly hazier one—to acknowledge the not yet within the future of the word: Vladimir Nabokov's 1955 novel *Lolita*. Issues that have crisscrossed these chapters—use, reading, judgment, evil, and the hope of an immortal future—take another turn in both the subject matter of *Lolita* and in the structure of its making. The novel is the infamous fictional memoir and apologia of a middle-aged man of letters, pseudonymed Humbert Humbert, in prison prior to a trial for murder. The novel figures itself as Humbert's trial notes—and the audience as jury to which Humbert will make his defense or confession. In the narrative, HH deceitfully enters into a marriage with Charlotte Haze in order to pursue a relationship with her twelve-year-old daughter Lolita; exploits his wife's death to gain carnal access to Lolita; kidnaps Lolita and sexually abuses her over a number of years; and then kills the (other) pedophile with whom Lolita escapes his clutches. The end of the novel shows the narrator deciding to offer the text not as notes for a trial as he'd supposed, not as a defense or confession, but rather for publication that may immortalize Lolita, his one true love, forever. *Lolita* finds its way onto many of the best-novels lists—of the twentieth century, of the English language, of American literature, and so on, which set up for it a sort of canonical immortality. But it also has a de facto infamous status that joins the top labels. It is, to put it mildly, disturbing, even, as the *New York Times* declared, after fifty years.[6] The history of the novel's reading demonstrates how monstrously the narrator's language has had—and continues to have—the power to enchant and beguile its readers: Robertson Davies famously declared in 1959 that the book is "not the corruption of an innocent child by a cunning adult, but the exploitation of a weak adult by a corrupt child."[7] Even as its literary reputation is assured, the novel remains somewhat implicating, perhaps even corrupting.

The main question of interpretation that has shaped criticism is what *Lolita* is (good) for, a question that rings any number of eschatological bells. The frame of *Lolita* displays this tension; the history of criticism reiterates it. The fictional foreword to the novel, written by an invented psychologist wittily named John Ray, unflinchingly declares, "As a work of art [the book] transcends its expiatory aspects; and still more important to us than scientific significance and literary worth, is the ethical impact the book should have on the serious reader": John Ray describes the objectionable portions of the book, particularly the amorous scenes and fantasies as "strictly functional . . . in the development of a tale tending *unswervingly* toward nothing less than a moral apotheosis" (emphasis added).[8] That word "unswervingly" is important, but for the moment, we will pass it by to observe that Nabokov (as himself) contradicts John Ray in the afterword that closes out the frame, asserting a more aesthetic purpose for the novel: "I am neither a reader nor a writer of didactic fiction, and despite John Ray's assertion, *Lolita* has no moral in tow. For me a work of fiction exists only insofar as it affords me what I shall bluntly call aesthetic bliss, that is a sense of being somehow, somewhere, connected with other states of being where art (curiosity, tenderness, kindness, ecstasy) is the norm."[9] The fictional foreword declares reading *Lolita* is a means to moral revelation; the authorial afterword cries foul. Though it might be easy enough for some to allow Nabokov, as author, to pull interpretive rank on John Ray, it's not quite so simple, since Nabokov's reputation as both a writer and interviewee is tied to trickster tactics and magic-making.

Critical readings that are dominated by the confidently forward foreword insist that the main question of *Lolita* is how or whether it may be used for the betterment of the reader. Colin McGinn is perhaps the most frankly worded of this position. He indicates that literature is part of an education in morality and that reading *Lolita* particularly may function as "an exercise in moral uplift" as the reader encounters both the novel's presentation of subtle evil and its offer of tools in discernment that allow readers to assess and denounce that evil.[10] Yet even readings of *Lolita* that purport to be about aesthetics can't avoid the question of the novel's ethical import.[11] And readings that seek to debunk the novel as ethically revelatory—say by offering Nietzschean, power-driven morality as the more hazy foundation of the morality of the novel, as in Michael Rodgers's work—still can't seem to avoid the question of use: the book, Rodgers says, "is an experience of moral disorientation which leaves us in no confusion about the extent of Humbert's cruelty but in considerable confusion about where that cruelty comes from, how we can account for it, and about what responses we have to it."[12]

In Nabokov's expressed views, the novel is debased when it is simplified to ethics or sociology or politics. There are a few wise souls, he says, who have been sensitive to the text's making and to its rejection of banally oversimple readings, but many more are "lambs" who have a need for a moral or an idea, who wonder why he wrote it or why we have to read it. And Nabokov has no scruples about taking those lambs straight to the slaughter of his formidable intellect: "That my novel does contain various allusions to the physiological urges of a pervert is quite true. But after all we are not children, not illiterate juvenile delinquents, not English public school boys who after a night of homosexual romps have to endure the paradox of reading the Ancients in expurgated versions. It is childish to study a work of fiction in order to gain information about a country or about a social class or about the author."[13] The classic mishandlings of the novel, in Nabokov's view, are those that seek to ferret out of its lewdness the over-under on its chances for moral instruction or the lineaments of its social critiques of America. The forces of his thunderous railings against the ineptitude of those who would pursue such questions seem strong enough to warn off even the most bull-headed ideologues.[14] His novel, he insists, inheres in the complex network of aesthetic nerves that set it out—the "secret points, the subliminal co-ordinates of the novel." He suggests that "these and other scenes will be skimmed over or not noticed, or never even reached" by those who are reading it oversimply.[15] Aesthetic complexity, language's powerful magic and deceit, is what he's after.

The tense divide on issues of purpose evident in *Lolita*'s frame should remind readers of the present work of the introduction's dichotomy between reading as means and reading as end. There, I argued that reading as a means and reading as an end not only collapse into one another, but also point toward a need for an eschatological redemption: reading for the means is insufficiently eschatological, and reading for the end is eschatologically insufficient. Reading's aims in both cases demonstrate the cracking open of the eschatological gap between the now and the not yet. I believe a reading of *Lolita* does something similar—it reaches beyond the moral and aesthetic to what Nabokov calls in an interview the *more*, a more that we see (now) only in loss and haze, and of which traces (only) are visible in writing.[16]

The opening and closing to the narrator's testimony employs the language of life, afterlife, survival, and immortality, associating them with the aesthetic/moral divide in a way almost linked to a sense of personal, though secular, eschatology. The opening refers to seraphs, subsistence of the dead in memory, ghosts, and reincarnation in the course of relating his early childhood.[17] For of course, HH is presumably on trial for his life, and his survival depends on his ability to weave a convincing narrative. At the end of the text, after referring to his writing space as "tombal seclusion," he writes that though he thought to use the writing to "save not my head, but my soul," he will instead make Lolita "live in the minds of later generations" and share the space of "immortality" with her.[18] The text engages the question of a future through the word, through art, though it views that future far more darkly than Christian eschatology, lit only by "lithophanic eternities," not epiphanic ones.[19] The language in *Lolita* fearfully intermixes aesthetics and ethics, which cracks open the gap of a continuation, a future, accessible through language.

The text seems to take up the problem of literary immortality by tying it to the text's ability to concurrently make judgment necessary and impossible. The text, the narrator, and Lolita will live on in aesthetic immortality to the extent that the narrator can keep the reader reading. But one can only keep reading *Lolita* by concurrently judging and not judging at the same time. This is because those that offer an ethical or ideological or political reading of the novel do what Nabokov feels is a childish violence to the text; they miss the "nerves of the novel" and miss the real loss in "pale, pregnant, irretrievable Dolly Schiller dying in Gray Star"—which amounts to not reading.[20] But those that revel in the aesthetic experience, it seems, may themselves, as one critic wrote, "read *Lolita* sprawling limply in your chair, ravished, overcome, nodding scandalized assent," having given up the states toward which aesthetic experience, in Nabokov's view, is supposed to lead us (e.g., kindness, curiosity, tenderness).[21] We miss *Lolita* here, too, as she is magicked away in the enchantment of the narrator's prose. Hence, the text must keep us judging and not-judging by inextricably linking evil and aesthetic bliss—a paradoxical tension.

We see the mixture everywhere in the text. The opening section announces, "You can always count on a murderer for a fancy prose style," a statement that unsettles the one hoping for moral instruction with a hint toward the devious nature of the language, and also unsettles the one hoping for aesthetic apotheosis with a horribly dubious foundation for the art.[22] Everywhere, the most playful, fanciful, and indeed wonderful uses of language become perlocutions of the worst kind. For instance, in the middle of a long discourse "terrorizing" Lolita into secrecy,[23] HH defends himself against her accusations with the following: "I am not a criminal sexual psychopath. . . . *The rapist was Charlie Holmes* [the boy with whom Lolita had sexual intercourse for the first time]; *I am the therapist—a matter of nice spacing in the way of distinction.*"[24] In this surprising wordplay, HH uses a sick joke to justify his own behavior. Further than that, however, the usage embeds the critique of psychology, a major theme in the work, in the very language used to describe it, suggesting that therapy is a nefarious intimacy, both closer than and worse than rape. Such a rhetorical move is by no means a moral in tow; it is an aesthetic undertow. Its magnificent horror pulls us along, still reading.

Through the elaborate haze of the aesthetic construction of the text, and the juxtaposition of standard defense and insistent assertions of malicious intent, the text demonstrates with unmatched power the unteasable blending of beauty and evil within language: "Ladies and gentlemen of the jury. . . . Look at this tangle of thorns."[25] If we look at the tangle of thorns, whether they be Brer Rabbit's briar patch, or the thorns that grow up around Sleeping Beauty's tower, we see language of folktale, fancy, and fantasy. Can we judge the fairy tale? The symbolic resonance of the other tangle of thorns, Jesus' crown, only indicates the potential dangers of thus judging. There are any number of more explicit and elaborate scenes of HH's imaginings, clearly not-real, yet these offer the reader voyeuristic, consumptive violence that arguably demands judgment even as it is a defense against judgment. HH fantasizes about violence toward his wives—he plans to abuse Valeria "very horribly" when he gets her away from her new lover; he plans to murder Charlotte by drowning her in the lake—but cites it among his virtues that he cannot do either. "Oh," HH explains, "I could visualize myself slapping Valeria's breasts out of alignment. . . . And I could see myself, no less clearly, shooting her lover in the underbelly," but then declares of himself and all pedophiles, "Emphatically, no killers are we. Poets never kill."[26] Here, HH's fantasy seems to mitigate his actual violence and abuse by making the worst of his actions only fantasy—and making the act of fancying them the act that saves him from killing. But of course, we know already that HH *is* a murderer. And at the end of the novel, HH even ties that murder to aesthetic production: "Do not pity C. Q. One had to choose between him and H. H. . . . so as to have him make [Lolita] live in the minds of later generations."[27] In HH's view, then, killing Clare Quilty is the pre-requirement of art, since HH doesn't write *Lolita* until he kills.

One way in which the text works on the level of structure to keep the audience reading between impossible and necessary judgment is its use of contingencies as a major plot device—contingencies marked by the motif of the swerve. John Ray sets up the centrality of contingency in the foreword when acknowledging that "had our demented diarist gone, in the fatal summer of 1947, to a competent psychopathologist, there would have been no disaster; but then, neither would there have been this book."[28] Contingency is the swerve that keeps us bending back toward the world of the fairy tale in *Lolita*, but also keeps us from subscribing to a fabular moral. As HH asserts early on, "When I try to analyze my own cravings, motives, actions, and so forth, I surrender to a sort of retrospective imagination which feeds the analytic faculty with boundless alternatives and which causes each visualized route to fork and re-fork without end in the maddeningly-complex prospect of my past."[29] In this world, each swerve might be the branch from a path—where intention is crowded up against contingency, and the deviation, fate, emerges.

In the novel, the swerve is a major motif that represents HH's attempt to scuttle reader fixation on will, responsibility, fate, and judgment. In the opening, mentioned above, John Ray's foreword suggests that the whole story "tend[s] *unswervingly* to nothing less than a moral apotheosis"—but, as with most parts of the foreword, the rest of the text pretty much does the opposite, forming a compendium of swerves. The tale breadcrumbs the swerves, from Charlotte's getting hit by a car in a double swerve to HH's getting caught by police after driving on the wrong side of the road amidst a haze of swerving in the conclusion of the novel. The character Beale, who was driving the car that kills Charlotte, defends his innocence by brandishing an elaborate map that charts his swerves: Charlotte "very clearly and conclusively . . . came into contact with a boldly traced sinuous line representing two consecutive swerves—one which the Beale car made to avoid the Junk dog (dog not shown), and the second, a kind of exaggerated continuation of the first, meant to avert the tragedy."[30] The swerve is something that Beale *means* in response to a contingency, but it is something for which, because of contingency's entrance into the scene, he cannot be held responsible. Even though Beale is wrong that Charlotte was at fault for leaning the wrong way as she slipped, both the narrator and the inquest hold him innocent of Charlotte's death—because of the swerve. As to his own part in Charlotte's death, HH also explains how his own intention met contingency via the swerve, attributing the jointure to the hand of fate, rather than responsibility. He writes,

> I had palpated the very flesh of fate. . . . A brilliant and monstrous mutation had suddenly taken place, and here was the instrument. Within the intricacies of the pattern (hurrying housewife, slippery pavement, a pest of a dog, steep grade, big car, baboon at its wheel) I could distinguish my own vile contribution. Had I not been such a fool—or such an intuitive genius—to preserve that journal, fluids produced by vindictive anger and hot shame would not have blinded Charlotte in her dash to the mailbox. But even had they blinded her, still nothing might have happened, had not precise fate, that synchronizing phantom, mixed within its alembic the car and the dog and the sun and the shade and the wet and the weak and the strong and the stone.[31]

HH wields the haze of contingency and swerve to make difficult the specific assigning of responsibility for Charlotte's death: in HH's retelling, all he did was preserve a journal—an intention, but perhaps a benign one.

The idea of the swerve as it is pictured here bears at minimum a poetic similarity to and at maximum a very close engagement with Lucretius's idea of the *clinamen*, the unpredictable swerve of atoms. In his atomic theory of the universe, *On the Nature of Things*, Lucretius writes, "Though atoms fall straight downward through the void / by their own weight, yet at uncertain times / and at uncertain points, they swerve a bit— / enough that one may say they changed direction."[32] In Lucretius's view, the atomic swerve means that free will is preserved—because the slightest wobble of swerve in atomic trajectory prevents a solely deterministic pathway of atoms (and, by extension) of the composite bodies of atoms—up to the scale of the universe itself. Nabokov's HH uses the swerve's free will as the base upon which contingency acts to produce the hand of "Aubrey McFate."[33] He thus picks out a tenuous path between free will and determination. The map of the accident has the characters' trajectories with their double swerves, and their falls, moving aside from their intentions, and colliding. So that while the paths are drawn as in a history, their movements involve small deviations from intention that for HH are the interruptions of fate. Or perhaps, of Derrida's detour of *différance*, "to resort, consciously or unconsciously, to the temporal and temporalizing mediation of a detour that suspends the accomplishment or fulfillment of 'desire' or 'will,' or carries desire or will out in a way that annuls or tempers their effect."[34] For a literary text to try and work the boundary thus between free will and determinism is difficult, given the text's seeming stasis. HH himself acknowledges as much: "No matter how many times we reopen 'King Lear,' never shall we find the good king banging his tankard in high revelry, all woes forgotten, at a jolly reunion with all three daughters and their lapdogs. . . . Whatever evolution this or that popular character has gone through between the book covers, his fate is fixed in our minds."[35] Lolita, after all, is always already lost; as the text acknowledges on the last page (and in a clue near the first page), the story, as per HH's wishes, won't come to publication until she is dead.

Yet, if a text could produce a continual reading, a connection with "other states of being" through "aesthetic bliss," then Lolita—at least her absence—might "live in the minds of later generations," as HH puts it.[36] An eternal life in literature is a poor consolation prize for dying young, though, or it would be, if Lolita weren't fictional to begin with. Even as fictional, Lolita never has a life or voice in art, because of the machinations and manipulations of HH's deplorable text. We even wonder, as readers, if the last scene in the memoir, which acknowledges the absence and loss of Lolita, isn't just HH conjuring up repentance to move a jury to acquit him. The scene is a memory ostensibly coming to HH during his arrest; he stands on a precipice, hearing a "vapor of blended voices" rise to him from a playground below. He realizes "the hopelessly poignant thing was not Lolita's absence from my side, but the absence of her voice from that concord."[37] Whether this memory is trumped up or not, any immortality for Lolita is unending, mortal silence.

The text's moves to implicate the reader in the double bind of necessary but complicit judgment result in an unhinging liminality. We cannot fail to judge HH—he's a monster—but there is no moral uplift in the denunciation: hardly anyone needs be instructed not to kidnap and rape children for fun. It's not really surprising or interesting or instructive that someone who does kidnap and rape children for fun will likely suffer a fair amount of misery. And, since the text makes us complicit in the erasure of Lolita by the aesthetic fabric of HH's narration—our judgment emerges out of our space of complicity and falls flat. We judge HH's actions, but the text's magic enchants us such that we may barely realize the loss of the real "spoiled artist," Lolita, because of the sleight of hand at work in the construction of HH's art.[38] Our necessary judgment judges us.

Yet, to read Lolita, or rather, to *keep* reading Lolita, is to approach reconciliation between moral meaning and aesthetic bliss—a reconciliation that alone will allow us to truly experience the living loss of Lolita. Concurrent judgment of HH and the aesthetic wonder we feel at the narration may grant us curiosity about Lolita—"pale, pregnant, beloved, irretrievable Dolly Schiller dying in Gray Star."[39] And only by forgiving the text precisely from within its deceitful complexity can we ever see Lolita, anyway. By persisting in the reading of *Lolita*, which is itself our forgiveness meted out through the double bind of the necessary, impossible judgment (which also judges us) we may move toward Lolita's loss. We approach Lolita as asymptotes, meeting her only where aesthetic ecstasy meets infinity.

When point-blank asked in an interview whether or not he believed in God, Nabokov's response linked the production of aesthetic bliss in fiction to the idea of *more:* "To be quite candid—and what I am going to say now is something I never said before, and I hope it provokes a salutary little chill—I know *more* than I can express in words, and the little I can express would not have been expressed, had I not known *more.*"[40] Nabokov is making fun of the interviewer here, of course. But the concept of *more* in connection with the question of belief in God has eschatological potential. Two trigger topics in this statement, *knowing the more* and the *salutary chill*, link the *more* with the language's swerve toward and away from meaning—what this book might call the becoming of the word. Earlier in the interview, Nabokov had described the way art presses up against the *more* thus: "A creative writer must study carefully the works of his rivals, including the Almighty. He must possess the inborn capacity not only of recombining but of re-creating the given world. In order to do this adequately, the author . . . should *know* the given world. . . . Art is never simple . . . at its greatest is fantastically deceitful and complex."[41] The knowing that there is *more* makes it possible to re-create the world through art. That Nabokov lists God as a rival in this project again, though perhaps blasphemous, indicates the scope of the more—its eschatological, or ultimate leanings. And the thrilling swerve of complexity is the only way that the expressible portion of the more can be expressed. Nabokov's hope that his comment would create a "salutary little chill" echoes what he calls, in the essay that follows *Lolita*, "aesthetic bliss, that is a sense of being somehow, somewhere, connected with other states of being where art (curiosity, tenderness, kindness, ecstasy) is the norm."[42] Aesthetic complexity creates the chill, the bliss, the reverberation of response in which the more becomes accessible. [43]

Reading's forgiveness restores nonreciprocal mutual giving, in which readers receive, bestow, and expand meaning-making in the love of the Trinity. By the power of the incarnation, "by right of sovereign victimhood . . . by reason of his enhypostasization by the infinite and innocent *Logos*," the word may speak in the name of all victims, may retrieve even the irretrievable in forgiveness.[44] But in the love of the Trinity, the Spirit of Christ grafts us into participation through reading, by which, in the establishment of mutual giving, we may participate in that reconciliation. But as John Milbank has figured it, the "mutual and unending gift exchange" must be understood as an "absolute faith in the arrival of the divine gift"—it is only within the grace of the word that we may reconcile with the word, or receive revelation as we offer meaning.[45]

Reconciling with *Lolita*, though, we receive as revelation more grief than glory. From within the rich enchantment of language and the glory of its possibilities, we find pernicious deceit and erasure—and our own complicity in it. Our approach to the loss of Lolita, begun through language's complex, implicating bliss, is made ever more galling in the impossibility of her retrieval. So we may long, reading *Lolita*, for the word that will redeem words, for the resurrecting word—for the future of the word within the divine word. We long for what will retrieve, from HH's self-indulgent, "very local palliative of articulate art" the voice of Lolita for the beloved community, imagined in the "vapor of blended voices, majestic and minute, remote and magically near, frank and divinely enigmatic."[46] That longing is the reader fingering the jagged grain of the not yet, the other side of the glimpses we get sometimes of the future of the word as it grows into the community of the new creation. It is the *Come, Lord Jesus* of hope, opening the text again.

Tiffany Eberle Kriner
Advent 2013

## Notes

1. Paul Ricoeur, *Memory, History, Forgetting* (Chicago: University of Chicago Press, 2004), 493.

2. Flannery O'Connor, "Revelation," in *The Complete Stories* (New York: Farrar, Straus & Giroux, 1995), 488–509.

3. Ibid., 508.

4. Ibid., 508.

5. Ibid., 508.

6. Charles McGrath, "50 Years on, 'Lolita' Still Has Power to Unnerve," *New York Times* (September 24, 2005), http://www.nytimes.com/2005/09/24/books/24loli.html?pagewanted=all.

7. Quoted in McGrath, "50 Years on, 'Lolita' Still Has Power to Unnerve."

8. Ibid., 5.

9. Ibid., 314–15.

10. Colin McGinn, "The Meaning and Morality of *Lolita*," *Philosophical Forum* 30 no. 1 (1999): 41. See also McGinn's book, *Ethics, Evil, and Fiction* (New York: Oxford University Press, 1997) for a more extended argument about moral illumination in literature.

11.  See David Andrews, *Aestheticism, Nabokov and Lolita* (Lewiston, NY: Edwin Mellen, 1999).

12.  Michael Rodgers, "Lolita's Nietzschean Morality," *Philosophy and Literature* 35 (2011): 117.

13.  Vladimir Nabokov, *Lolita* (New York: Vintage International, 1997), 316.

14.  But of course they have done nothing of the sort. Not a few major literary critics have made persuasive claims that the text, in inviting a more careful reading, makes moral education for its readers. From Richard Rorty's claim in *Contingency, Irony, and Solidarity* (Cambridge: Cambridge University Press, 1989), 164ff. that the text traps us into realizing our own similarity to HH, to Colin McGinn's assertion in "The Meaning and Morality of *Lolita*" that we understand the wages of sin better from reading a text that so blends the aesthetic and the deplorable, critics have been willing to read John Ray's preface *both* ironically and straight to use the text.

15.  Nabokov, *Lolita*, 316.

16.  Vladimir Nabokov, Interview, *The Playboy Interview: Men of Letters* (Playboy Enterprises, 2013). Kindle edition.

17.  Nabokov, *Lolita*, 9, 10, 11, 15.

18.  Ibid., 308–9

19.  Ibid., 283.

20.  Ibid., 316.

21.  Martin Amis, *The War Against Cliché: Essays and Reviews 1971-2000* (London: Jonathan Cape, 2002), 261.

22.  Nabokov, *Lolita*, 9

23.  Ibid., 151.

24.  Ibid., 150.

25.  Ibid., 9.

26.  Ibid., 87–88.

27.  Ibid., 309.

28.  Ibid., 5.

29.  Ibid., 13.

30.  Ibid., 102.

31.  Ibid., 103.

32. Lucretius, *On the Nature of Things*, trans. Frank O. Copley (New York: Norton, 1977), 34. See also Stephen Greenblatt, *The Swerve* (New York: Norton, 2011).

33. Nabokov, *Lolita*, 52, 56.

34. Jacques Derrida, "Différance" in *Literary Theory: An Anthology*, ed. Julie Rivken and Michael Ryan (Malden, MA: Blackwell, 1998), 389–90.

35. Nabokov, *Lolita*, 265.

36. Ibid., 315, 309.

37. Ibid., 308.

38. When an interviewer once called HH a "spoiled artist," Nabokov responded, "That epithet, in its true, tear-iridized sense, can only apply to my poor little girl." See "Interview with Vladimir Nabokov," in *Vladimir Nabokov's Lolita: A Casebook*, ed. Ellen Pifer (New York: Oxford University Press, 2003), 197.

39. Nabokov, *Lolita*, 316. See also Rorty (cited above) for more on this idea.

40. Nabokov, *The Playboy Interview: Men of Letters*.

41. Ibid.

42. Nabokov, *Lolita*, 314.

43. For Nabokov on reverberation and response in the reader, see *Strong Opinions*, 35.

44. John Milbank, *Being Reconciled: Ontology and Pardon* (New York: Routledge, 2003), 62.

45. Ibid., 154.

46. Nabokov, *Lolita*, 283, 308.

# Afterword

If God has a future for texts and allows readers to participate in those futures, I suspect that participation starts pretty early in the process—from the first scrappy ideas through the long making. And so, I am grateful for the following readers and cultivators of this book, especially for the conversations about it and prayers for it, without which it would have had no future at all. Heartfelt thanks to Beth Felker Jones, Noah Toly, Nicole Mazzarella, Christina Bieber Lake, Miho Nonaka, Caleb Spencer, Erick Sierra, Richard Gibson, Pete Powers, Crystal Downing, Jay Wood, Tim Larsen, Matthew Milliner, Carey Newman, Harold K. Bush, Thomas Gardner, Leland Ryken, Alan Jacobs, Roger Lundin, Edward Blankman, Lisa and Nate Harmon, David Wright, Kim Sasser, Christine Colón, Marissa Sabio, Amy Peeler, Becky Eggimann, Heather Whitney, Jenny McNutt, Shawna Songer Gaines, Aimee Barbeau, Brett Foster, Dan Treier, Jeffrey Galbraith, and Jeffry Davis. The conversations and prayers we shared about this work were crucial to me, and I remain in a state of perpetual wonder and thankfulness as I remember the instances of your generosity. I hope this book does partial justice to the contributions you made. My faults remain, no doubt, but you've helped this word move, I hope, toward its future.

I appreciate the support of the Erasmus Institute at the University of Notre Dame, whose Carey Research Fellowship allowed the first investigations of the topic to emerge in conversation with a group of wonderful scholars: Paulina Ochoa Espejo, Randy Boyagoda, Bryan McGraw, Alan Durston, Stephen D'Evelyn, Bob Sullivan, Dianne Phillips, and the late Sabine MacCormack. Thanks to Trinity Christian College and Messiah College for the opportunity to share early drafts and receive helpful feedback. I'm grateful also to Wheaton College for a sabbatical leave to complete the manuscript, and to the Humanities Colloquium at Wheaton for good discussion when I presented an early chapter to them—especially memorable were comments, notes, snippets, recommendations, and questions from Bruce Ellis Benson, Robert Bishop, Jill Baumgaertner, and Philip Ryken. I'm also grateful to my student research aids over this long process, including Brittaini Maul, Elisabeth Garrison-Clay, Tim Lau, Adam Corbin, Catherine Jones, Jeremy Braunius, and the heroic Geoffrey Hagberg. And thanks so much to my senior seminar from Spring 2013, whose passionate disputations and discussions on *Lolita* and *Redeeming Love* energized me for those sections of the book—especially Madeleine Van Dolah, the most-engaged nodder in the world, who generously read scrivenings for me. The Wheaton College library, particularly Gregory Morrison, David Malone, and Nancy Falciani-White offered ongoing assistance. The Carol Stream Culver's and its wonderful staff led by Amy Adams provided an ideal weekly setting for working out the arguments.

I have appreciated the cheerful, enthusiastic, and seamless efforts from Michael Gibson, Esther Diley, and Lisa Gruenisen at Fortress Press, and copyeditor David Cottingham. God speed your good work on this project and all the others.

Special thanks to my beloved parents, Kathleen Dowd Eberle and Joseph J. Eberle Sr., for prayer, persistent faith, and Grama Camp;

and to my delightful in-law family, Linda and Robert Kriner and Zak and Emily for prayer, support, and Grama Camp help. Thanks to my siblings Kelly Clark, Rebecca Elliott, and Joseph J. Eberle II and their spouses for encouragement and assistance during Grama Camp. Thanks to the Cronk/Matteson family for the writer's retreat on Sacketts Harbor—that camper was the perfect room of one's own to hammer out a chapter. And to Walter and Patti Giles for notes on baptism and Grama Camp support.

Lastly, topmost love and great thanks to the dazzling Fiona and the astounding Beckett whose prayers and encouragement and words of wisdom helped during a project that has almost spanned your young lives; and to my husband Josh for faithful loyalty and kind endurance of shop-talk, especially through the difficult patches in the writing. Now, let's make you a farm.

# Bibliography

Althusser, Louis. "From Capital to Marx's Philosophy." In *Reading Capital.* Translated by Ben Brewster. London: Verso, 1979.

Amis, Martin. *The War Against Cliché: Essays and Reviews 1971-2000.* London: Jonathan Cape, 2002.

Andrews, David. *Aestheticism, Nabokov and Lolita.* Lewiston, NY: Edwin Mellen, 1999.

Anonymous. "Oliver Twist; Or the Parish Boy's Progress. By Boz." *Monthly Review* 1, no. 1 (January 1839).

Arbery, Glenn C. *Why Literature Matters: Permanence and the Politics of Reputation.* Wilmington, DE: ISI Books, 2001.

Athanasius. *Contra Gentes and De Incartione.* Translated by Robert W. Thomson. Oxford: Clarendon, 1971.

_____. *On the Incarnation.* Translated by John Behr. Yonkers, NY: St. Vladimir's Seminary Press, 2011.

Austen, Jane. *Jane Austen's Letters.* Edited by Deirdre Le Faye. New York: Oxford University Press, 1995.

————. *Pride and Prejudice.* London: Penguin, 1972.

Bainton, Roland. "Religious Liberty and the Parable of the Tares." In *The Collected Papers in Church History.* Boston: Beacon, 1962.

Barth, Karl. *Church Dogmatics I.2, The Doctrine of the Word of God.* Translated by G. T. Thomson and Harold Knight. Peabody, MA: Hendrickson, 2010.

————. *Church Dogmatics II.2.* Translated by G. W. Bromiley. Edited by G. W. Bromiley and T. F. Torrance. Peabody, MA: Hendrickson, 2010.

————. *Church Dogmatics IV.1.* Translated by G. W. Bromiley. Edited by G. W. Bromiley and T. F. Torrance. Peabody, MA: Hendrickson, 2010.

————. *The Epistle to the Romans.* Translated by Edwyn C. Hoskyns. Oxford: Oxford University Press, 1933.

Begbie, Jeremy S. "Beauty, Sentimentality, and the Arts." In *The Beauty of God: Theology and the Arts.* Downers Grove, IL: IVP Academic, 2007, 45–69.

Benjamin, Walter. "Theses on the Philosophy of History." In *Illuminations.* Translated by Harry Zohn. Edited by Hannah Arendt. New York: Schocken, 1969.

————. "The Task of the Translator." In *Theories of Translation*. Edited by Rainier Schulte and John Biguenet. Chicago: University of Chicago Press, 1992.

Berkouwer, G. C. *The Return of Christ*. Edited by Marlin J. Van Elderen. Translated by James Van Oosterom. Grand Rapids: Eerdmans, 1972.

Bernstein, Charles. "Artifice of Absorption." In *Artifice and Indeterminacy: An Anthology of New Poetics*. Edited by Christopher Beach. Tuscaloosa: University of Alabama Press, 1998.

Bethune, Brian. "*1Q84*." *Maclean's* 124, no. 45 (2011): 88–89.

Bloom, Harold. *The Anatomy of Influence*. New Haven: Yale University Press, 2011.

————. *How to Read and Why*. New York: Scribner, 2000.

————. *The Western Canon*. New York: Harcourt Brace, 1994.

Booth, Wayne C. *The Company We Keep: An Ethics of Fiction*. Berkeley: University of California Press, 1988.

Boyd, Valerie. *Wrapped in Rainbows*. New York: Scribner, 2003.

Bradley, Arthur. "Derrida's God: Narrating the Theological Turn." *Paragraph* 29, no. 3 (2006): 21–42.

Brito, Manuel. *A Suite of Poetic Voices: Interviews with Contemporary American Poets*. Santa Brigada, Spain: Kadle Books, 1992.

Brodzki, Bella. *Can These Bones Live?: Translation, Survival, and Cultural Memory*. Stanford: Stanford University Press, 2007.

Brown, Frank Burch. *Good Taste, Bad Taste, & Christian Taste*. New York: Oxford University Press, 2000.

————. *Religious Aesthetics*. Princeton: Princeton University Press, 1989.

Bruns, Christina Vischer. *Why Literature Matters: The Value of Literary Reading and What It Means for Teaching*. New York: Continuum, 2011.

Buber, Martin. *Good and Evil*. New York: Charles Scribner's Sons, 1953.

————. *I and Thou*. Translated by Walter Kaufmann. New York: Charles Scribner's Sons, 1970.

O'Callaghan, Paul. *Christ Our Hope: An Introduction to Eschatology*. Washington, DC: Catholic University of America Press, 2011.

Callahan, John F. *In the African-American Grain: Call and Response in Twentieth-Century Black Fiction*, 2nd ed. Middletown, CT: Wesleyan University Press, 1988.

Calvin, John. *Commentary on a Harmony of the Evangelists, Matthew, Mark, and Luke* (II). Translated by William Pringle. Edinburgh: The Edinburgh Printing Company, 1845.

Carr, Nicholas. *The Shallows: What the Internet Is Doing to Our Brains*. New York: W. W. Norton, 2010.

Chrétien, Jean-Louis. *The Call and the Response*. New York: Fordham University Press, 2004.

Cohen, Margaret. *The Sentimental Education of the Novel*. Princeton: Princeton University Press, 1999.

O'Connor, Flannery. "Revelation." In *The Complete Stories*. New York: Farrar, Straus & Giroux, 1995.

Crowe, Brandon D. "Fulfillment in Matthew as Eschatological Reversal." *Westminster Theological Journal* 75 (2013): 111–27.

Dapaah, Daniel S. *The Relationship between John the Baptist and Jesus of Nazareth: A Critical Study*. Lanham, MD: University Press of America, 2005.

Darnton, Robert. *The Case for Books*. New York: PublicAffairs, 2010.

De Gruchy, John. *Christianity, Art and Transformation*. Cambridge: Cambridge University Press, 2001.

Delbanco, Andrew. *College: What It Was, Is, and Should Be*. Princeton: Princeton University Press, 2012.

_____. *Required Reading: Why Our American Classics Matter Now*. New York: Farrar, Straus & Giroux, 1997.

Derrida, Jacques. "Des Tours de Babel." In *Acts of Religion*. Edited by Gil Anidjar. New York: Routledge, 2002.

_____. "Différance." In *Literary Theory: An Anthology*. Edited by Julie Rivken and Michael Ryan. Malden, MA: Blackwell, 1998.

_____. "Of an Apocalyptic Tone Recently Adopted in Philosophy." *Semeia* 23 (1982): 63–97.

_____. "Plato's Pharmacy." In *Dissemination*. Chicago: University of Chicago Press, 1981.

Dickens, Charles. *Oliver Twist: A Norton Critical Edition*. Edited by Fred Kaplan. New York: W. W. Norton, 1993.

_____. "A Preliminary Word." *Household Words* 1, no. 1 (March 30, 1850): 1.

Dickstein, Morris. "Hope Against Hope: Orwell's Posthumous Novel." *The American Scholar* 73, no. 2 (2004).

Donin, Hayim Halevy. *To Pray as a Jew*. New York: Basic Books, 2001.

Downing, Crystal. *Changing Signs of Truth: A Christian Introduction to the Semiotics of Communication*. Downers Grove, IL: IVP Academic, 2012.

Edmundson, Mark. *Why Read?* New York: Bloomsbury, 2004.

Ellul, Jacques. *The Presence of the Kingdom*, 2nd ed. Colorado Springs: Helmers & Howard, 1989.

Farley, Edward. *Good & Evil: Interpreting a Human Condition*. Minneapolis: Fortress Press, 1990.

Felski, Rita. *Uses of Literature*. Oxford: Blackwell, 2008.

Ferrall, Victor E., Jr. *Liberal Arts at the Brink*. Cambridge, MA: Harvard University Press, 2011.

Ferry, David. "Experiencing Translation." Public lecture at Wheaton College, IL, October 1, 2013.

Fiddes, Paul. *The Promised End: Eschatology in Theology and Literature*. Malden, MA: Blackwell, 2000.

Fish, Stanley. "Driving from the Letter: Truth and Indeterminacy in Milton's *Areopagitica*." In *Remembering Milton: Essays on the Texts and Traditions*. Edited by Mary Nyquist and Margaret W. Ferguson. New York: Methuen, 1988.

Flannagan, Roy. *The Riverside Milton*. Edited by Roy Flannagan. Boston: Houghton Mifflin, 1998.

Ford, Richard. "Oliver Twist." *Quarterly Review* 64 (1839): 46–56.

Friedrich, Hugo. "On the Art of Translation." Translated by Ranier Schultze and John Biguenet. In *Theories of Translation*. Edited by Ranier Schultze and John Biguenet. Chicago: University of Chicago Press, 1992.

Gadamer, Hans-Georg. *Truth and Method*, 2nd ed. Translated by Joel Weinsheimer and Donald G. Marshal. New York: Continuum, 1999.

Gandolfo, Anita. "A Literature of Their Own." In *Faith and Fiction: Christian Literature in America Today*. Westport, CT: Praeger, 2007, 61–88.

Gates, Henry Louis, Jr. *The Signifying Monkey: A Theory of African-American Literary Criticism*. New York: Oxford University Press, 1988.

Goossen, Ted. "Haruki Murakami and the Culture of Translation." In *In Translation: Translators on Their Work and What It Means*. Edited by Esther Allen and Susan Bernofsky. New York: Columbia University Press, 2013.

Gorringe, Timothy. "Kitsch and the Task of Theology." *Theology Today* 56, no. 2 (July 1999): 229–34.

Grahame-Smith, Seth. "Books." *Seth Grahame-Smith*.2011. http://sethgrahamesmith.com/.

Grahame-Smith, Seth, and Jane Austen. *Pride and Prejudice and Zombies*. Philadelphia: Quirk Books, 2009.

Greenblatt, Stephen. *The Swerve*. New York: Norton, 2011.

Grenz, Stanley J. *Theology for the Community of God*. Nashville: Broadman & Holman, 1994.

Gunton, Colin. *The Christian Faith: An Introduction to Christian Doctrine*. Malden, MA: Blackwell, 2002.

Harper, Frances Ellen Watkins. "Died of Starvation." In *A Brighter Coming Day: A Frances Ellen Watkins Harper Reader*. Edited by Frances Smith Foster. New York: The Feminist, 1990.

————. "The Dying Christian." In *A Brighter Coming Day: A Frances Ellen Watkins Harper Reader*. Edited by Frances Smith Foster. New York: The Feminist, 1990.

_____. "Iola Leroy." In *A Brighter Coming Day: A Frances Ellen Watkins Harper Reader*. Edited by Frances Smith Foster. New York: The Feminist, 1990.

_____. "A Poem." In *A Brighter Coming Day: A Frances Ellen Watkins Harper Reader*. Edited by Frances Smith Foster. New York: The Feminist, 1990.

_____. "Songs for the People." In *A Brighter Coming Day: A Frances Ellen Watkins Harper Reader*. Edited by Frances Smith Foster. New York: The Feminist, 1990.

Hart, Trevor. "Unexpected Endings: Eucatastrophic Consolations in Literature and Theology." In *Art, Imagination, and Christian Hope*. Edited by Trevor Hart, Gavin Hopps, and Jeremy Begbie. Burlington, VT: Ashgate, 2012.

Hartnett, Kevin. "*1Q84*." *Christian Science Monitor* (November 2, 2011).

Hector, Kevin W. *Theology Without Metaphysics: God, Language, and the Spirit of Recognition*. New York: Cambridge University Press, 2011.

Heinemann, Joseph. *Literature of the Synagogue*. Piscataway, NJ: First Gorgias, 2006.

Hejinian, Lyn. "The Rejection of Closure." In *The Language of Inquiry*. Berkeley: University of California Press, 2000.

Hensher, Philip. "Parallel Lives." *Spectator* (22 October 2011).

Hong, Terry. "*1Q84*." *Library Journal* (September 15, 2011): 69.

Howe, Fanny. *The Wedding Dress: Meditations on Word and Life.* Berkeley: University of California Press, 2003.

Howells, William Dean. "*Daisy Miller.*" In *Henry James: The Contemporary Reviews.* Edited by Kevin Hayes. Cambridge: Cambridge University Press, 1996, 69–70.

Jacobs, Alan. "Love and the Suspicious Spirit." In *The Theology of Reading: A Hermeneutics of Love.* Boulder, CO: Westview, 2001.

_____. *The Pleasures of Reading in an Age of Distraction.* New York: Oxford University Press, 2011.

_____. *A Theology of Reading: The Hermeneutics of Love.* Boulder, CO: Westview, 2001.

James, Henry. "The Art of Fiction." In *Essays on Literature.* New York: Library Classics of the United States, 1984.

_____. *The Art of the Novel.* Edited by R. P. Blackmur. New York: Charles Scribner's Sons, 1934.

_____. *Daisy Miller.* London: Penguin, 2007.

_____. "Is There Life after Death?" In *In After Days.* New York: Harper & Brothers, 1910.

_____. *Notes of a Son and Brother.* New York: Charles Scribner's Sons, 1914.

————. *The Wings of the Dove: A Norton Critical Edition.* Edited by J. Donald Crowley and Richard A. Hocks. New York: W. W. Norton, 2003.

Kamenetz, Anna. *DIY U: Edupunks, Edupreneurs, and the Coming Transformation of Higher Education.* White River Junction, VT: Chelsea Green, 2010.

Kammeyer, Kenneth. *A Hypersexual Society: Sexual Discourse, Erotica, and Pornography in America Today.* New York: Palgrave Macmillan, 2008.

Käsemann, Ernst. *Essays on New Testament Themes.* Naperville, IL: Allenson, 1964.

Kearney, Richard. "On the Hermeneutics of Evil." In *Reading Ricoeur.* Edited by David M. Kaplan. Albany: State University of New York Press, 2008.

Keats, John. "Sleep and Poetry." In *The Poetical Works of John Keats.* London: Macmillan, 1884, 284.

Keeling, Richard P., and Richard H. Hersh. *We're Losing Our Minds: Rethinking American Higher Education.* New York: Palgrave Macmillan, 2012.

Kelts, Roland. "Lost in Translation?" *The New Yorker.* May 9, 2013. http://www.newyorker.com/online/blogs/books/2013/05/lost-in-translation.html.

Kermode, Frank. "John." In *Literary Guide to the Bible.* Edited by Frank Kermode and Robert Alter. Cambridge, MA: Belknap of Harvard University Press, 1987.

Kidd, David Comer, and Emanuele Costano. "Reading Literary Fiction Improves Theory of Mind." *Science* 342, no. 6156 (2013): 377–80.

Kirk, J. R. Daniel. "Conceptualising Fulfilment in Matthew." *Tyndale Bulletin* 59, no. 1 (2008): 77–98.

Kleinknecht, Hermann. "The Logos in the Greek and Hellenistic World." In *Theological Dictionary of the New Testament*, vol. IV. Edited by Gerhard Kittel, Geoffrey William Bromiley, and Gregory Friedrich. Grand Rapids: Eerdmans, 1976.

Knapp, Steven, and Walter Benn Michaels. "Against Theory." In *Against Theory: Literary Studies and the New Pragmatism*. Edited by W. J. T. Mitchell. Chicago: University of Chicago Press, 1982.

Knight, Mark. *An Introduction to Religion and Literature*. New York: Continuum, 2009.

Krentz, Jayne Ann. *Dangerous Men and Adventurous Women: Romance Writers on the Appeal of the Romance*. Edited by Jayne Ann Krentz. Philadelphia: University of Virginia Press, 1992.

Kriner, Tiffany Eberle. "Hopeful Reading." *Christianity & Literature* 61, no. 1 (2011): 101–31.

_____. "Our Turn Now?: Imitation and the Theological Turn in Literary Studies." *Christianity & Literature* 58, no. 2 (2009): 266–72.

Kubota, Yoko. "Surreal Often More Real for Author Haruki Murakami." *Reuters*. Last modified November 25, 2009. http://www.reuters.com/

article/2009/11/25/us-books-author-murakami-idUSTRE5AO11720091125.

Kushner, Tony. *Angels in America*. New York: Theatre Communications Group, 1995.

Lee, Maurice S. "Searching the Archives with Dickens and Hawthorne." *English Literary History* 79 (2012): 747–71.

Levinas, Emmanuel. *Beyond the Verse: Talmudic Readings and Lectures*. Bloomington: Indiana University Press, 1994.

_____. *Otherwise Than Being or Beyond Essence*. Translated by Alphonso Lingis. Pittsburgh: Duquesne University Press, 1998.

_____. *Totality and Infinity*. Translated by Alphonso Lingis. Pittsburgh: Duquesne University Press, 1969.

Levine, Caroline. *The Serious Pleasures of Suspense: Victorian Realism and Narrative Doubt*. Charlottesville: University of Virginia Press, 2003.

Lucretius. *On the Nature of Things*. Translated by Frank O. Copley. New York: Norton, 1977.

Luther, Martin. "The Parable of the Tares Which an Enemy Sowed in the Field." In *The Sermons of Martin Luther* (II). Translated and edited by John Nicholas Lenker. Grand Rapids: Baker, 1983.

Mar, Raymond, and Keith Oatley. "The Function of Fiction Is the Abstraction and Simulation of Social Experience." *Perspectives on Psychological Science* 3, no. 3 (2008): 173–92.

Marcel, Gabriel. "The Encounter with Evil." In *Tragic Wisdom and Beyond: Including Conversations Between Paul Ricoeur and Gabriel Marcel*. Edited by John Wild. Translated by Stephen Jolin and Peter McCormick. Evanston, IL: Northwestern University Press, 1973.

McGinn, Colin. *Ethics, Evil, and Fiction*. New York: Oxford University Press, 1997.

————. "The Meaning and Morality of *Lolita*." *Philosophical Forum* 30, no. 1 (1999): 31–42.

McGrath, Charles. "50 Years on, 'Lolita' Still Has Power to Unnerve." *New York Times*. September 24, 2005. http://www.nytimes.com/2005/09/24/books/24loli.html?pagewanted=all.

McParland, Robert. *Charles Dickens' American Audience*. Lanham, MD: Lexington Books, 2010.

Memmott, Carol. "Q&A with Seth Grahame-Smith, Master of the Mashup." *USA Today*. March 3, 2010. http://usatoday30.usatoday.com/life/books/news/2010-03-04-grahamesmith04_ST_N.htm.

Milbank, John. *Being Reconciled: Ontology and Pardon*. New York: Routledge, 2003.

————. *The Word Made Strange: Theology, Language, Culture*. Oxford: Blackwell, 1997.

————. *Theology and Social Theory: Beyond Secular Reason*. Malden, MA: Blackwell, 2006.

Millner, Michael. *Fever Reading: Affect and Reading Badly in the Early American Public Sphere*. Durham: University of New Hampshire Press, 2012.

Milton, John. "Areopagitica." In *The Riverside Milton*. Edited by Roy Flannagan. Boston: Houghton Mifflin, 1998.

_____. "A Second Defense of the People of England against an Anonymous Libel." In *The Prose Works of John Milton*. Translated and edited by George Burnett. London: 1809.

Moltmann, Jürgen. *The Theology of Hope: On the Ground and the Implications of a Christian Eschatology*. New York: Harper & Row, 1967.

Moore, Marianne. "Poetry." In *The Complete Poems of Marianne Moore*. New York: Macmillan, 1981.

Moretti, Franco. "The Slaughterhouse of Literature." *Modern Language Quarterly* 61, no. 1 (2000): 207.

Mosbergen, Dominique. "George Orwell's '1984' Book Sales Skyrocket in Wake of NSA Surveillance Scandal." *Huffington Post*. Last modified June 12, 2013. http://www.huffingtonpost.com/2013/06/11/orwell-1984-sales_n_3423185.html.

Mouw, Richard. *When the Kings Come Marching In*, rev. ed. Grand Rapids: Eerdmans, 2002.

Murakami, Haruki. *1Q84*. New York: Alfred A. Knopf, 2011.

_____. "As Translator, as Novelist: The Translator's Afterword." In *In Translation: Translators on Their Work and What It Means*. Translated by

Ted Goossen. Edited by Esther Allen and Susan Bernofsky. New York: Columbia University Press, 2013.

_____. "The Novelist in Wartime." *Salon.* Last modified February 20, 2009. http://www.salon.com/2009/02/20/haruki_murakami/.

Nabokov, Vladimir. "Interview with Vladimir Nabokov." In *Vladimir Nabokov's Lolita: A Casebook.* Edited by Ellen Pifer. New York: Oxford University Press, 2003.

_____. *Lolita.* New York: Vintage International, 1997.

_____. *The Playboy Interview: Men of Letters* (Kindle ed.). Playboy Enterprises, 2013.

Neal, Lynn S. *Romancing God: Evangelical Women and Inspirational Fiction.* Chapel Hill: University of North Carolina Press, 2006.

Ngai, Sianne. "Stuplimity: Shock and Boredom in Twentieth-Century Aesthetics." *Postmodern Culture* 10, no. 2 (January 2000).

Nussbaum, Martha Craven. *Not for Profit: Why Democracy Needs the Humanities.* Princeton: Princeton University Press, 2010.

Ong, Walter J. "Maranatha: Death and Life in the Text of the Book." *Journal of the American Academy of Religion* 45, no. 4 (1977): 419–49.

Orwell, George. *1984.* New York: Penguin, 2003.

_____. "Why I Write." In *The George Orwell Reader: Fiction, Essays, and Reportage.* New York: Harcourt Brace, 1956.

Ott, Bill. "*1Q84.*" *Booklist* (September 15, 2011).

Parker, William Riley. *Milton: A Biography*. Oxford: Clarendon, 1966.

Pickstock, Catherine. *After Writing: On the Liturgical Consummation of Philosophy*. Oxford: Blackwell, 1998.

Pieper, Josef. *Faith, Hope, Love*. San Francisco: Ignatius, 1997.

Powers, Peter. "'The Singing Man Who Must Be Reckoned With': Private Desire and Public Responsibility in the Poetry of Countee Cullen." *African American Review* 34, no. 4 (2000): 661–78.

Pullinger, David J. "Putting Librarianship under the Light." *The Christian Librarian* 32 (May 1989): 59–60.

Radway, Janice A. *Reading the Romance: Women, Patriarchy, and Popular Literature*. Chapel Hill: University of North Carolina Press, 1991.

Regis, Pamela. *Natural History of the Romance Novel*. Philadelphia: University of Virginia Press, 2003.

Ricoeur, Paul. *Interpretation Theory: Discourse and the Surplus of Meaning*. Fort Worth: Texas Christian University Press, 1976.

————. *Memory, History, Forgetting*. Chicago: University of Chicago Press, 2004.

————. *The Symbolism of Evil*. Boston: Beacon, 1967.

Riley, Naomi Schaefer. *The Faculty Lounges: And Other Reasons You Won't Get the College Education You Paid For.* Chicago: Ivan R. Dee, 2011.

Rivers, Francine. "FAQs." *Francine Rivers.* 2010. http://francinerivers.com/about/faqs.

———. "Francine Rivers Interview." *TitleTrakk,* 2012. http://www.titletrakk.com/author-interviews/francine-rivers-interview.htm.

———. "A Note From Francine Rivers: Why I Wrote *Redeeming Love.*" In *Redeeming Love.* Colorado Springs: Multnomah Books, 1997.

———. *Redeeming Love.* Colorado Springs: Multnomah, 1997.

———. *Redeeming Love.* New York: Bantam Fanfare, 1991.

———. "Writing Tips." *Francine Rivers.* 2010. http://francinerivers.com/about/writing-tips.

Roberts, Robert C. "Forgivingness." *American Philosophical Quarterly* 32, no. 4 (1995): 289–306.

Roche, Mark William. *Why Choose the Liberal Arts?* South Bend, IN: University of Notre Dame Press, 2010.

———. *Why Literature Matters in the 21st Century.* New Haven: Yale University Press, 2004.

Rodgers, Michael. "Lolita's Nietzschean Morality." *Philosophy and Literature* 35 (2011): 104–20.

Ronning, John L. *The Jewish Targums and John's Logos Theology*. Peabody, MA: Hendrickson, 2010.

Rorty, Richard. *Contingency, Irony, and Solidarity*. Cambridge: Cambridge University Press, 1989.

Sanneh, Lamin. *Translating the Message: The Missionary Impact on Culture*, rev. ed. Maryknoll, NY: Orbis, 2009.

Schleiermacher, Friedrich. "On the Different Methods of Translating." Translated by Waltraud Bartscht. In *Theories of Translation*. Edited by Ranier Schultze and John Biguenet. Chicago: University of Chicago Press, 1992.

Schopenhauer, Arthur. "On Language and Words." Translated by Peter Mollenhauer. In *Theories of Translation*. Edited by Ranier Schultze and John Biguenet. Chicago: University of Chicago Press, 1992.

Schulz, Kathryn. "Murakami's Mega Opus." *New York Times Book Review*. Last modified November 3, 2011. http://www.nytimes.com/2011/11/06/books/review/1q84-by-haruki-murakami-translated-by-jay-rubin-and-philip-gabriel-book-review.html?pagewanted=all.

Schweitzer, Albert. *The Quest of the Historical Jesus: A Critical Study of Its Progress from Reimarus to Wrede*. New York: Macmillan, 1968.

Silko, Leslie Marmon. *Ceremony*. New York: Penguin, 2006.

———. *Yellow Woman and a Beauty of the Spirit*. New York: Simon & Schuster, 1997.

Smith, Barbara Herrnstein. *Contingencies of Value*. Cambridge, MA: Harvard University Press, 1988.

Smith, Gregory A. "A Rationale for Integrating Christian Faith and Librarianship." In *Christian Librarianship*. Edited by Gregory A. Smith. Jefferson, NC: McFarland, 2002.

Snodgrass, Klyne. *Stories with Intent: A Comprehensive Guide to the Parables of Jesus*. Grand Rapids: Eerdmans, 2008.

Sontag, Susan. "Against Interpretation." In *Against Interpretation and Other Essays*. New York: Farrar, Straus & Giroux, 1966.

Sparks, Jordin. "Thought You Knew Everything about Jordin Sparks? Think Again." *Ebony* 65, no. 1 (2009). http://www.ew.com/ew/article/0,,20619242,00.html.

_____. "What I'm Reading." *Entertainment Weekly* 1220/1221 (June 17, 2012): 116.

St. Augustine. *The City of God*. Translated by Marcus Dods. New York: Modern Library, 2000.

_____. *Confessions*. Translated by Henry Chadwick. New York: Oxford University Press, 2008.

_____. *Augustine: Confessions and Enchiridion* (VII). Translated and edited by Albert C. Outler. Philadelphia: Westminster, 1955.

_____. In *Nicene and Post-Nicene Fathers: First Series* (VI). Edited by Philip Schaff. Peabody, MA: Hendrickson, 2004.

_____. *On Christian Doctrine*. Translated by R. P. H. Green. Oxford: Oxford University Press, 1997.

Stegemann, Hartmut. *The Library of Qumran: On the Essenes, Qumran, John the Baptist, and Jesus*. Grand Rapids: Eerdmans, 1998.

Stein, Gertrude. "Poetry and Grammar." In *Lectures in America*. Boston: Beacon, 1967.

_____. "Portraits and Repetitions." In *Lectures in America*. Boston: Beacon, 1967.

_____. *Selected Writings of Gertrude Stein*. New York: Vintage, 1990.

Steiner, George. "The Archives of Eden." In *No Passion Spent*. New Haven: Yale University Press, 1996.

_____. *Real Presences*. Chicago: University of Chicago Press, 1991.

Tanner, Kathryn. *Jesus, Humanity, and the Trinity: A Brief Systematic Theology*. Minneapolis: Fortress Press, 2001.

Todorov, Tzvetan, Lynn Moss, and Bruno Braunrot. "The Notion of Literature." *New Literary History* 38, no. 1 (2007): 1–12.

Todorov, Tzvetan, and John Lyons. "What Is Literature For?" *New Literary History* 38, no. 1 (2007): 13–32.

Tompkins, Jane. *West of Everything: The Inner Life of Westerns*. New York: Oxford University Press, 1992.

Tran, Jonathan. *The Vietnam War and the Theologies of Memory*. Malden, MA: Wiley–Blackwell, 2010.

Trotti, John B. "The Theological Library: In Touch with the Witnesses." In *Christian Librarianship*. Edited by Gregory A. Smith. Jefferson, NC: McFarland, 2002.

Twain, Mark. *Adventures of Huckleberry Finn*. Edited by Thomas Cooley. New York: Norton, 1999.

Uncredited. "*1Q84*." *Publisher's Weekly* (29 August 2011).

Vanhoozer, Kevin. *Biblical Narrative in the Philosophy of Paul Ricoeur*. New York: Cambridge University Press, 1990.

Viladesau, Richard. *Theological Aesthetics*. New York: Oxford University Press, 1999.

Von Balthasar, Hans Urs. *Theo-Drama: The Last Act*. San Francisco: Ignatius, 1988.

Von Humboldt, Wilhelm. "Introduction to His Translation of *Agamemnon*." In *Theories of Translation*. Edited by Ranier Schultze and John Biguenet. Chicago: University of Chicago Press, 1992.

Walker, Alice. *In Search of Our Mother's Gardens*. San Diego: Harcourt Brace Jovanovich, 1983.

Walton, John, and Kim Walton. *The Bible Story Handbook*. Wheaton, IL: Crossway, 2010.

Walton, John. *The NIV Application Commentary: Genesis*. Grand Rapids: Zondervan, 2001.

Weaver-Zercher, Valerie. *The Thrill of the Chaste*. Baltimore: Johns Hopkins University Press, 2013.

Webb, Robert L. *John the Baptizer and Prophet: A Socio-Historical Study* (Journal for the Study of the New Testament Supplement Series 62). Sheffield: Sheffield Academic Press, 1991.

Wellek, René, and Austin Warren. *Theory of Literature*, 3rd ed. New York: Mariner, 1984.

Werner, Craig. *Playing the Changes: From Afro-Modernism to the Jazz Impulse*. Urbana: University of Illinois Press, 1994.

West, Cornel. "Cornel West Explains Why It Bothers Him That Obama Will Be Taking the Oath with MLK's Bible." n.p. YouTube. January 21, 2013. http://youtu.be/96d_CzrfxsM.

Westermann, Claus. *Genesis 1-11*. Minneapolis: Augsburg Press, 1984.

Wolfreys, Julian. *Readings: Acts of Close-Reading in Literary Theory*. Edinburgh: Edinburgh University Press, 2000.

Wood, James. *The Broken Estate: Essays on Literature and Belief*. New York: Picador, 2010.

Woodward, Jon. "Huge Dragonflies." In *Uncanny Valley*. Cleveland: Cleveland State University Poetry Center, 2012.

Wundt, Wilhelm. *Ethics: The Facts of Moral Life*. New York: Cosimo, 2006.

Zizioulas, John. *Being as Communion: Studies in Personhood and the Church.*
Crestwood, NY: St. Vladimir's Seminary Press, 1993.

# Index